EUROPEAN POLITICS

Volume 17 Number 3
July 1994

Special Issue on

THE STATE IN WESTERN EUROPE RETREAT OR REDEFINITION?

Edited by
WOLFGANG C. MÜLLER
and
VINCENT WRIGHT

FRANK CASS · LONDON

Manuscripts, editorial correspondence, books for review and advertisement enquiries should be sent to:

The Administrative Editor, West European Politics,
Frank Cass and Co. Ltd, Newbury House, 890–900 Eastern Avenue,
Newbury Park, Ilford, Essex IG2 7HH, England
Tel: (081) 599 8866 Fax: (081) 599 0984

Before commencing the final draft of their article, prospective contributors are advised to consult the NOTES at the back of the journal.

Authors should retain at least one complete copy of their article; manuscripts are returned only if accompanied by a stamped addressed envelope (or International Reply Coupon). While every care is taken, the publisher cannot accept responsibility for loss of or damage to author's manuscripts.

Annual Subscription: Institutions: £125.00 ($195.00) postage included
Individuals: £38.00 ($60.00) postage included
Single and back issue prices available from the publisher

Published in January, April, July and October by
FRANK CASS AND COMPANY LIMITED
Newbury House, 890–900 Eastern Avenue, Newbury Park, Ilford,
Essex IG2 7HH, England

Contents

Book Reviews

BOOK REVIEWS

Reshaping the State in Western Europe: The Limits to Retreat

WOLFGANG C. MÜLLER
and VINCENT WRIGHT

Throughout Western Europe, it is alleged, 'the state is in retreat'. This volume explores some of the pressures leading to state retreat programmes as well as the nature of those programmes. Focusing exclusively on the functional, rather than the territorial, level it reveals that the reshaping of the state in Western Europe involves different policies across Europe and conflicting tendencies in the impact of the various reform programmes. Whilst the state may be in retreat in some respects, its activity may be increasing in others. And nowhere, not even in Britain, has its key decision-making role been seriously undermined.

Since the mid-1960s there has been a debate in European political science about the problems confronting the nation state. In the early days, the debate was triggered by the inability of West European states to ensure their own defence, by the impact of emergent Europeanisation, by early suspicions of 'overload', by the 'demystification of the state' in some countries as the result of their inability to hold on to their colonies (even if they were perceived as part of the *territoire national*), and by the incapacity of some states to guarantee the loyalty of some of its own citizens whose identities and loyalties were allegedly sub-national in character. Long before the 1990s there were discussions about 'the future of the State'.[1] However, unprecedented economic prosperity and heavily distributional welfare programmes which purchased social peace provided sceptics about state failure with powerful ammunition. Indeed, in retrospect, it can be argued that 'the power of the European nation state reached its highest point at the end of the 1960s, the period 1945–1968 may be considered as that of its (final) achievement: the apogee of a pre-existing process and not the beginning of a new phenomenon.'[2]

The scepticism of many observers was to be shaken with the economic crisis which unfolded after the first oil crisis of 1974, which deepened after the second oil shock of 1979, and which spread, with varying degrees of intensity, to all West European countries in the 1980s. The gentle expansionary incrementalism of the 1950s and 1960s gave way to unpalatable decrementalism in some sectors and to unsatisfied demands in most. 'Stagflation', 'cut-back management', 'resource squeeze', 'fiscal resistance' became commonplace in the language of political and political science discourse. The need to reduce the role of the state became a budget-driven axiom of policymakers.

Coinciding with, and, in part, resultant upon the economic recession were other pressures which moved the debate away from a largely diagnostic one about 'state failure' and 'state overload' to a more prescriptive one geared to analyses about 'state retreat' and 'state withdrawal'. In fact, description often merged with prescription, and need was confused with desire, thus obfuscating the essential issues.

What, apart from the impact of recession, were the major pressures leading to 'state withdrawal'? Broadly speaking, it is possible to identify several interconnected pressures which, combined, squeezed West European states into somewhat convergent policy ambitions which aimed at reducing the role of the state. They are far too familiar to require elaboration, and they are constantly invoked in this volume. They may be summarised as follows:

The ideological pressure. We witness throughout the 1980s a major change in the dominant macro-economic paradigm from Keynesianism to monetarism and neo-liberalism, from *dirigisme* (explicit or gently disguised) to market-driven solutions, from fiscal expansionism to restraint, from mercantilism to free trade.[3] This paradigm shift inevitably involved a radical questioning of the role of the state and of universalistic solutions in many sectors, such as welfare, and an advocacy of policies rooted in individual choice, market-driven competition, targeting and private initiative. The market place was seen as an *inherently* less inefficient and socially unjust system of allocation than the state whose policies were forged by self-interested budget-maximising bureaucrats in league with well entrenched (and often unrepresentative) interests. Explanations for the paradigm shift of the 1980s must be sought not only in budgetary need or in the ideological zeal of governments but was embedded, too, in domestic political and institutional factors, in international market and European Community pressures as well as in rapid technological change – each of these elements interacting with the other in persistent and complex fashion. It was diffused by a host of individuals, think tanks, institutions (often within the state), and international organisations such as the World Bank, the International Monetary Fund (IMF) and the Organization for Economic Co-operation and Development (OECD). The shift took place at a different pace, to a different extent and with different degrees of enthusiasm and commitment across Western Europe. It was also rationalised or legitimised by different discourses: individual freedom and entrepreneurship in the United Kingdom; *'modernisation'* by French Socialist governments; the need to 'prepare for the open market' in Italy, Spain and Portugal. However, whatever the differences, broad convergence in the acceptance of most of the major tenets of the new dominant paradigm was discernible across Western Europe. This question is addressed in particular by the contribution of Müller, but all other contributions also make reference to the ideological factor, for instance of its influence on important policy fields (e.g., social policy).

The political pressure. The new paradigm was propagated by a wide array of individuals and political parties and its translation into policies was facilitated by significant domestic political changes such as the advent of the Thatcher government (whose early 'successes' served as a demonstration effect or model for other governments) in 1979, the traumatic U-turns of the early Mitterrand presidency, the upheavals in Germany in 1989–90, the implosion of the old political order in Italy after 1991, the erosion and then collapse of social democratic hegemony in Sweden. Support for the new paradigm came from the important and increasingly internationalised industrial and financial groups (see below). Of equal importance in analysing the success of the new paradigm are the organisational and intellectual weakness of the 'distributional coalitions'[4] wedded to the previous dominant paradigm, the reshaping of the policy communities and networks with a view to marginalising such groups, and the reorganisation of the state apparatus designed to strengthen the supporters of the new paradigm (often in the Finance Ministries) and weaken its opponents (frequently in industry ministries or ministries devoted to regional aid). Even the policy style changed in some countries such as Britain, as Richardson, in his contribution to this volume, makes clear. It became less accommodating and much more confrontational. Thus, the comfortable and collusive (and often institutionalised) relationships between 'the profligate elites', imbued with social democratic values irrespective of their party affiliations, were gradually and partially dismantled – although with differing degrees of enthusiasm and success. The party political side of this process is analysed in Müller's contribution to this publication. However, 'corporastically-structured' policymaking still prevailed in many sectors of some countries, and even in the United Kingdom key groups have been able to dilute the ambitions of the government.

Changing public perceptions about the role of the state. It is common wisdom now that the public has changed its mind about the proper role of the state. Allegedly the public is now less inclined to receiving state services and more concerned about the costs of these services and the bureaucratic apparatus required for their provision. However, the contribution of Herbert Döring, which looks at the empirical evidence by reanalysing cross-national survey data since the late 1970s, provides a nuanced response to the allegations.

The pressure of the internationalisation of financial and industrial circuits. The financial services revolution, which is studied by Moran in this volume, was unleashed by the USA, gained Japan and the United Kingdom and then spread to Continental Europe. It was, in the words of Moran, 'a series of seismic changes in regulatory structures caused by the combined ambitions of corporate actors and national governments.' It was, as noted below, facilitated by the technological revolution of the 1980s. The internationalisation of financial services has many dimensions and has given rise to immense problems of international or transnational cooperation and regulation. The Bank of Commerce and Credit International (BCCI) scandal – the biggest financial scandal in postwar history – was highly revealing in that respect: a bank with tentacles in many countries, BCCI was able to escape effective supervision, because its regulatory regime was so unclear. Slowly, new international forms of regulation, both formal and informal, are beginning to emerge. More significantly, in terms of state autonomy, it was clear that the Anglo-American model of financial services was likely to become a dominant one, forcing continental European countries to conform.

The internationalisation of industry has been no less significant in reshaping the state. Again, the phenomenon is multi-dimensional, since internationalisation may be evaluated according to the criteria of sales, foreign content, passive portfolio investment, the acquisition of firms or subsidiaries, share-swaps, mergers, joint ventures, licensing deals, supply agreements, etc. By all the standard criteria internationalisation accelerated during the 1980s – 'the frenzied years'. Falling regulatory barriers to overseas investment, diminishing telecommunication and transportation costs, freer and cheaper domestic and international capital markets and the diversification strategies of major financial and industrial actors combined to transform the global economy. Corporate investment across frontiers grew four times faster than world output, and three times faster than world trade between 1983 and 1990, by which date 20 per cent of the world's equity transactions involved foreign investors. Ownership of national industry was radically altered in the process. Even the traditionally reluctant French and Germans have been affected: nearly a third of quoted French shares are now in foreign hands, and across the Rhine major German firms and banks have opened their equity to foreigners. No less significant was the request of Daimler-Benz, one of the flagships of German industry, to seek quotation on the New York Stock Exchange, thus becoming the first German company to do so.

Internationalisation has also involved the growth in the number and size of multinational companies. Figures vary widely: estimates range from 20,000 private transnationally active corporations with 100,000 subsidiaries to 35,000 multinationals controlling some 170,000 affiliates. There is general agreement that the top 100 multinationals control roughly 16 per cent of the world's productive assets, and that about a quarter of those assets are in the hand of the top 300 multinationals. Cross-border raids multiplied in the 1980s and early 1990s: between January 1988 and June 1992 France was Europe's most voracious predator, with 775 deals worth £37 billion, followed by the United Kingdom (982 deals worth £20 billion). The major target of such raids was the United Kingdom (1320 deals worth £85 billion), with France (925 deals worth £23 billion), Germany (901 deals worth £22 billion) and Spain (489 deals valued at £4 billion) trailing behind. Raids on major national companies could provoke major financial and political battles (notably over the Société Générale de Belgique and over Perrier).

One of the major consequences of internationalisation has been the blurring of the national identities of many major companies. And this blurring effect raises some tricky political questions at both the national and European Union level (witness the battles over the permissible level of foreign content). Multinationalisation presents all governments with complex issues. How does one effectively tax these 'stateless firms'? What degree of control can be exercised over their vast internal markets? How to regulate them if regulation is fragmented amongst nation states? How does the nation state prevent its own major firms, intent on multinational diversification strategies from exporting its labour needs to cheaper countries? Whilst the problem of the multinationals can be exaggerated (most 'global firms', on closer examination, tend to buy, produce, employ, distribute, research, raise capital and market in regional clusters around a home base, and have a single nation management), the erosion of national control is undeniable.

The pressure of Europeanisation – both of a formal and of an informal nature.[5] Propelled by various actors – the Commission, the Court, some member states, the major private financial, social and industrial interests – the European Union (EU) has been transformed, and crises in the monetary system should not disguise the remarkable extent of the transformation. Even if we restrict ourselves simply to the impact of formal or institutionalised Europeanisation on the industrial and financial market place the extent to which the Union impinges upon the member states is all too apparent. It is not only a major trade negotiator, but as harmoniser of the Union has dismantled many trade barriers, and as regulator of competition policy it has been involved in preventing price fixing (notably by chemical firms), in liberalising trade (in telecommunications and airlines), in vetting mergers and acquisitions, in slowly opening up public procurement policies (a major instrument of state protectionism for domestic industry), and, often controversially, controlling state aid to both public and private industry. There is also, as Moran in his contribution points out, a decided regulatory creep in the financial services sector – securities, banking and insurance. Moreover, its 'leading constitutional values', which are market protection, price stability, a balanced budget and 'sound public finances' provide the general framework (and often excuse) in which member states now function. As William Wallace has argued, the impact of the Community has been paradoxical: increased market leads to diminished national regulatory activity (with less national differentiation) but Community protection of markets leads to increased regulation.

The regulatory role of the EU is studied in detail by Majone in his contribution to this publication, but it is also underlined by Moran, by Tálos and Falkner and by Richardson. We may expect the regulatory role of Brussels to increase, albeit at a slower rate, in spite of vague promises to respect the principle of subsidiarity, because such a role conforms fully to the logic of the open market. It is not, of course, merely in the financial and industrial sectors that the impact of Europe is being felt. Sensitive areas such as health, education, social welfare, environmental issues have been slowly dragged into the regulatory net of Brussels. The Schengen Agreement, signed first by five, now by eight countries on the European continent, provides for the abolition of internal frontier controls on goods and people, combined with measures for cooperation amongst police, immigration, customs and intelligence services and for common policies on rights of entry and residence. To an extent which is not fully appreciated, the EU is slowly redefining existing political arrangements, altering traditional policy networks, triggering institutional change, reshaping the opportunity structures of members states and their major interests. These interests are now increasingly entangled in relationships at four territorial levels: the international, the European, the national and the local, and for some of those interests it is by no means clear that the national level is the most important.

The technological pressure, the full ramifications of which cannot be underestimated. Several strands of the technological revolution are worth highlighting, since they clearly illustrate how it has contributed to the process of state redefinition. In the first place, states have increasing difficulties in controlling information flows across their national borders. Thus, frustrated Britons will now be able to indulge in soft pornography transmitted by more liberal neighbours. More significantly, the role of foreign television was underlined during the events of 1989–90 in Central and Eastern Europe. Second, technology has played a crucial role in opening up the world's financial markets: liberalisation and technological change have been inextricably entwined. Third, as highlighted by Grande's contribution, technology has transformed some natural national monopolies into sectors susceptible to international and national competition (telecommunications and electricty supply provide good examples), thereby undermining one of the more convincing arguments in favour of public control. Finally, as Wright shows in his contribution, the technological revolution has impacted upon established state hierarchies, organisational structures, working practices and skills, personnel management and service delivery.

Economic crisis, ideological commitment, domestic political change, internationalisation, Europeanisation and technological pressures have fed one another in dynamic and complex fashion. Thus, the economic crisis of the 1970s, like many crises, facilitated reform programmes – 'opening the window for reform'[6] – for governments which were squeezed by other imperatives. The revolution in the financial markets is both an international and European phenomenon in this interconnected maze of factors, disentangling cause and effect is far from easy.

This plethora of reform programmes has clearly had an impact on reshaping the state. But has it involved 'state retreat'?

There is, of course, nothing more difficult than establishing satisfactory criteria for assessing the extent of 'state retreat'. In the first place, it is essential to make a distinction between external 'state retreat' (the erosion of state autonomy in the international and European arenas) which is unquestionable – though difficult to measure (since it varies across countries and sectors) and internal 'state retreat' (the diminution of state authority and activity at the domestic level) which is much more problematic.

In terms of external state retreat, it would appear that, in some respects, state autonomy in Western Europe has been eroded, particularly in some sectors (e.g., agriculture and steel) and control has become more elusive and difficult. However, as a general rule, it would be perfectly plausible to contend that the last 15 years has seen more 'state reshaping' than 'state retreat'. West European states, at both international and European Union level, remain central actors – arguably *the* central actors, even if they are increasingly prisoners of an interlocking network of bargained situations: they are not by-passed or eliminated but rather more constrained. They retain a nodal decision-making position but their action is more indirect, more discreet and more bartered.

In terms of internal state retreat, the picture is a confused one. In the first place, the normal indicators to measure state interventionism (growth of public expenditure, proportion of the GDP consumed by public expenditure, taxation rates, percentage of industry owned by the state) are all problematic. They present aggregate pictures which may give misleading impressions. Thus, the extent of public ownership of industry may provide few clues about the degree of effect *control* exercised. If we move to a more qualitative analysis the picture displays conflicting trends, for it is possible to perceive 'retreat', 'stability' and 'growth' with respect to the role of the state.

State retreat may be seen in the adoption of a wide range of policies: budgetary squeeze; privatization (a multi-dimensional phenomenon); deregulation (which ranges from the removal of controls to the reduction in administrative formalities); marketisation (the introduction of competitive market forces to some sectors to replace bureaucratic systems of allocation); devolution of state authority to non-elected state officials at the territorial level, in public sector industries or in semi-autonomous administrative agencies, or to private agents charged with the implementation of public policy; territorial decentralisation to sub-national 'governments'.

However, we must be prudent in drawing general conclusions about these policies. In the first place, whilst it is clear that some of these programmes aim at the reduction in the *substance* of authority, many are merely concerned with displacing the *focus* or *instrument* of that authority. Is there genuine state reduction if, for example, budgets are now raised or distributed by decentralised or semi-autonomous agents rather than by the central state? Second, the implementation of these policies has been far from complete – even when apparently pursued with zeal: the case of controlling public expenditure best illustrates the limits to the success of radical governments such as those in the United Kingdom. Third, in the pursuit of state reduction, different patterns emerge across Western Europe: for instance, the United Kingdom has been an enthusiastic privatizer but a notorious territorial centraliser, whilst Belgium has been a timid privatizer but a radical decentraliser. Fourth, many apparently radical programmes have built into them safeguards designed to protect state interests (the case of some privatized industries in Britain and France and with many decentralisation programmes). A fifth reason for prudence lies in the time-span involved. Many of the programmes are very recent, and their advantages are 'front loaded' (to borrow a phrase from Richardson's contribution to this publication). The drawbacks become apparent only in the medium to long term, and may have to be remedied by renewed, if reluctant, state intervention. Six, some programmes of state retreat have had the effect of engendering an unintended and unwelcome increase in state activity – although the instrument of that activity might differ. The experience of the privatization of British public utilities illustrate this point admirably: denationalisation has involved the dismantlement of a loose and unsatisfactory form of direct state control and the emergence of a more detailed, effective, if more indirect form of state control through regulatory agencies. Seventh, in adjusting the market-state boundary, for instance, the state has often had to trample on, or marginalise major groups wedded to the status quo.

In short, the general picture of state retreat may mask a partial, nationally differentiated, limited reality with perverse displacement effects and unintended consequences leading to renewed state activity.

Stability in the role of the state may be seen in most sectors. Thus, as Tálos and Falkner make clear in their contribution, there have been cuts in some welfare state benefits and services and some changes in social policies and labour market policies. Yet the 'structural elements' of those sectors remain intact. In education, training and pension provision there has been little or no change in the role of the state. Even in the industrial sector, the state continues to play a key role as owner (in spite of some privatization drives), regulator, trade negotiator, parameter-setter (by its macro-economic, fiscal, exchange rate, competition, labour-market policies). In spite of the reductions, it still showers subsidies of a direct and indirect nature on its firms. Even market-oriented governments, such as Britain and Germany, continue to generate or to tolerate market-distorting protectionist devices to shelter their major industries.

The *increase* in state activity is particularly evident in the regulatory sphere. We have already noted how privatization of public utilities in the United Kingdom had led to a much more detailed, if indirect, form of public intervention. Moran, in his contribution on financial services shows how a largely self-regulated sector has been drawn ever closer into the regulatory net of the state. The pressures of a changing political agenda are also pushing to increased state intervention. New issues, such as mass unemployment, the environment, gender equality, protection of minority rights, immigration, rising crime rates, have required more pro-active states – at domestic, and often at European and international levels. Finally, reductions in state budgets have often involved the dismantlement of universalistic solutions and the adoption of 'targeting' strategies which require a much more intrusive 'means-testing' state.

In disentangling the many threads of the process of state redefinition it is, therefore, important to make distinctions: between external retreat of the state (which has been generally eroded by internationalisation, Europeanisation, multinationalisation and technological change) and internal redefinition which is an infinitely more complex process involving different and even conflicting elements. This complexity is embedded in the conflicting and often paradoxical consequences of the pursuit of multiple and apparently coherent policies. As noted, deregulation in one respect has often generated reregulation in another, whilst market protection has induced increased state activity. It is also possible in some sectors for state 'retreat' in an external sense whilst reinforcing the role of state internally (e.g., in financial services).

Reshaping the West European State has affected the *style* of state intervention, the *form* (in a more indirect, regulatory and enabling direction), the *instruments* (from direct to more semi-autonomous or even private agents of public policy) and even the *substance* of some sectors. However, the extent and pattern differs from state to state – testimony to the enduring importance of the nation states, with their distinctive histories, traditions, constitutions, institutions, opportunity structures and tissues of constraints, policy networks and styles. In retrospect, the 1980s may well be seen, not as the age of state retreat, but of the era which demonstrated the difficulties inherent in the pursuit of such strategies. Hoffmann's contention on the durability of the nation state, made at the outset of the 1980s, appears to be fully justified.[7] Future historians may well point to the fact that the 1980s and early 1990s have involved less a reallocation of authority then a switch from public management back to more traditional modes of state regulation,[8] that the intermeshing of public and private interests has remained intact, and that reshaping the state has been merely part of a constant process of adjusting the borderline between market, state and society. They will almost certainly point to the fact that, in spite of the political and administrative changes in that relationship, the nation state has remained for most of its citizens, a primary source of welfare, order, authority, legitimacy, identity and loyalty.

In attempting to explain the survival of the Western European nation state in spite of (generally exaggerated) crises we perhaps need to look more closely not only at its immense resources but also its infinite capacity for external and internal adaptability. Perhaps the dominant paradigm of the later 1990s may be less critical of the alleged inherent defects of the state and more sensitive to its unshakeable centrality and to its potential.

NOTES

The contributions to this publication were first presented at the conference 'A New Role for the State' in May 1993 in Vienna. The conference was sponsored by the Austrian Ministry of Finance and the Institut für Staats- und Politikwissenschaft of the University of Vienna. We are particularly grateful to Karin Pintér and Dietmar Ecker for their help in organising the conference. One of the contributors to the Vienna conference, Sabino Cassese, was appointed cabinet minister in Italy shortly before the conference. Unfortunately, his new duties did not allow him to participate in the conference and subsequently rework his conference paper for publication.

1. See, e.g., John Cornford (ed.), *The Failure of the State* (London: Croom Helm, 1975).
2. Alan Milward, quoted in William Wallace, 'Rescue or Retreat? The Nation State in Western Europe', unpub. paper, p.9.
3. For a good summary, see Peter Hall, 'The Movement from Keynesianism to Monetarism', in Sven Steinmo *et al.* (eds.), *Structuring Politics: Historical Institutionalism in Comparative Analysis* (Cambridge: CUP, 1992).
4. Mancur Olson, *The Rise and Decline of Nations* (New Have, CT: Yale UP, 1982), pp.43–7.
5. For a discussion of the distinction see William Wallace, *The Transformation of Western Europe* (London: Pinter Publishers, 1990), Ch.4.
6. See John W. Kingdon, *Agendas, Alternatives, and Public Policies* (Boston: Little, Brown, 1984) and John T.S. Keeler, 'Introduction: New Perspectives on Democratic Reform', *Comparative Political Studies* 25/1993, pp.423–32.
7. Stanley Hoffmann, 'Reflections on the Nation State Today', *Journal of Common Market Studies* 30 (Sept.–Dec. 1982), p.22.
8. A point made by Sabino Cassese in his paper to the Vienna meeting.

Public Perceptions of the Proper Role of the State

HERBERT DÖRING

By means of a re-analysis of public opinion surveys between 1973–76 (Political Action), 1985 and 1990 (International Social Survey on the 'Role of Government I + II'), perceptions of government responsibilities are studied over time and across nations. Even if affiliated to government parties, the public, in the short run, does not reinforce prevailing trends uncritically, but in a mood of sophisticated scepticism tends rather to take an anti-cyclical stance. Inspite of a uniform change across all nations from 'interventionist' beliefs to a more 'neo-liberal' creed in the long run, historically endorsed national differences, rooted in inherited attitudes towards the proper role of government still exist.

Any discussion of the retreat and the return of the state, of de-regulation and re-regulation across Western Europe, can be enhanced by the question: how, if at all, has the general public, the popular sovereign of contemporary democracies, reacted to the changing beliefs among academic and political elites about the scope and responsibilities of government? Previously, in the age of social-democratic consensus, social-democratic and christian-democratic/conservative political parties alike supported an expansion of state activities. Meanwhile, eminent academic panels have warned of the dangers of the 'interventionist state' and of an ever increasing 'Inflation législative et réglementaire en Europe'.[1]

How has the public reacted toward this change in approach made by their academic and political elites? Is perhaps the voice of the people even today still nothing more than just the chorus in the old Greek tragedies? Does it merely follow the current happenings of the great political stage like the chorus in Sophocles' *Antigone*, accompanying the specific changes of fate with praise or lamentation?[2] Believing the topic of public perceptions of the role of the state or, for that matter, the government is a pertinent one, this essay sets about rejecting as impertinent a dictum asserted by as eminent a democratic theorist as Schumpeter. In his book *Capitalism, Socialism and Democracy* he stated, poignantly, that the public behaves like a reed swaying in the wind 'incapable of action other than a stampede'.[3] For all his brilliance, Schumpeter for once may be wrong.

Against his pessimism, and the analogy of the consenting chorus, this contribution will attempt to show by means of a re-analysis of a series of cross-national public-opinion surveys between 1973 and 1976 and 1990 two points. First, even if affiliated to government parties, the public does not in the short run uncritically reinforce prevailing trends, but in a sophisticated scepticism rather tends to take an anti-cyclical stance. Second, inspite of a uniform change of public perceptions in the long run from 'interventionist' beliefs to a more 'neo-liberal' creed across all nations studied, there still exist even today historically endorsed national differences rooted in stable attitudes toward the proper role of goverment.

DATA AND METHOD

In particular, four data sets from the comparative social scientists' treasure chest can assist us in resolving the question of whether or not public perceptions are more than the chorus of ancient Greek tragedy. The data sets in question are: 1. the academic opinion poll 'Political Action' surveying eight countries 1973–76; 2. and 3. the 1985 and 1990 academic 'International Social Survey Programme' asking the population in six countries in 1985 and nine in 1990 about their perceptions of the 'Role of Government'; 4. the twice-yearly Eurobarometer interviews carried out by the European Commission's professional staff since the mid-1970s. All these data sets have been stored in openly accessible data archives.[4]

I have looked through the questionnaires of these studies to check for items suitable for my own theoretical interests[5] and have found one dimension in particular, identical in two of the sets and very similar in another. This dimension will be my focus. It deals with the populations' perceptions of the desirable responsibility of the government for economic and socio-political tasks. In precise terms and in identical wording, representative samples of six nations in 1985 and of nine nations in 1990 were asked:

> On the whole, do you think it should be or should not be the government's responsibility to: 1. Provide a job for everyone who wants one; 2. Keep prices under control; 3. Provide health care for the sick; 4. Provide a decent standard of living for the old; 5. Provide industry with the aid it needs to grow; 6. Provide a decent

standard of living for the unemployed; 7. Reduce income differences between the rich and poor?

The standardized answering code ranged from 'definitely should be' over 'probably should be' and 'probably should not be' to 'definitely should not be'. A 'can't choose, don't know' option was also allowed for. The merely fractional amount of respondents choosing this category indicates the question was accepted and understood by those being interviewed.[6] These seven sub-questions open up a dimension of central interest for our analysis of public perceptions of the proper role of the state. In the opinion of respondents in different countries at different points in time, should the government intensify its catering for our every needs in differents walks of life by taking on responsibility? Or should the authorities leave the provision of such services more to private initiative?

These questions are to be found in the two data sets of the 'International Social Survey Programme' (ISSP) of 1985 and 1990. Additionally, although not in precisely the same but only a fairly similar wording, some of those items were asked by the academic survey 'Political Actions' across eight nations between 1973 and 1976.[7] Thus, changing public perceptions may be followed over a period of nearly two decades, from 1973–76 to 1990. As the two modules of ISSP in 1985 and 1990 were specifically devoted to the 'Role of Government', there are quite a few more questions included, opening up additional insights into the perceived role of the state, but for this purpose it appears to be wise to stick to this limited, yet wide-ranging battery of items.[8]

Now, it is well known that public perceptions expressed in response to survey questions may differ widely according to the wording of these questions. Indeed, in an article entitled 'That Which We Call Welfare by any Other Name Would Smell Sweeter', Tom W. Smith demonstrated how, with respect to the US public, the term 'welfare' consistently produced much more negative evalutions than 'the poor'.[9] I would like to tackle this problem head on by just admitting it. Whatever survey question selected for study, it will, to a certain extent, necessarily influence the result. But keeping questions constant does open up reliable insights. Using the same question wording over time across different nations in equivalent translations may keep measurement error at least constant. Thus, both changes over time and nationally specific differences at a given point in time can be studied reliably.

THE WANING OF THE 'INTERVENTIONIST STATE' REVISITED

How have public perceptions about the 'right' amount of government responsibility changed between 1973–76 ('Political Action') and 1990 (ISSP 'Role of Government II')? During the first period under study the then prevailing social-democratic consensus was beginning to fade, and at the time of the 1990 survey conservative governments had been in office in most countries for over a decade. For a first overview only two out of the seven questions above, that is, 'jobs for all' and 'health care for the sick', have been singled out for analysis. This is no arbitrary selection, but is based on a stimulating analysis by Peter Taylor-Gooby. In a forthcoming article he has demonstrated how the above seven items fall into two distinct underlying dimensions in the subtle perception of respondents, of which 'jobs for all' and 'health care' are the two most sensitive issues respectively.[10] In a later section of this article we will replicate and develop further Taylor-Gooby's analysis across all seven items. Here we just update, or rather backdate, his analysis of ISSP 1985 and ISSP 1990 back to Political Action 1973–76, so ensuring a longer time perspective.

In order to allow a quick and yet statistically reliable summary, Figure 1 does not show the usual percentages. Rather than presenting all of the four answering categories mentioned above, which range from 'definitely should be' to 'definitely should not be', just one mean value of perceived government responsibility across all four categories was calculated for each country, for each of the three points over time.[11] The data table below shows all countries with at least two surveys, whereas the figure selects only those countries that had surveys at all three points. Figure 1 and the accompanying data table allow us to check whether or not, and if yes, in which direction, public perceptions have indeed changed. It is, of course, not permissable to calculate a trend with only three points over time. But, as a means of illustration such a rough guide can give us a general impression. In order to facilitate an immediate interpretation, the three points in time are interconnected not by direct lines but by the graphical option 'curve'.

From an inspection of this figure three findings emerge. First, there is nowadays a clear difference, almost a gap, between support for government's responsibility concerning 'jobs for all', namely, an active labour market policy, and the government's catering for 'health care', that is, the provision of basic needs. Whereas in 1973–76 the two fields, 'jobs for all' and 'health care' were almost at the same level close together, there is now a rift in the public perception of these two policy areas.

Second, the steep decline of 'jobs for all' was almost uniform across

FIGURE 1

Perceived Government's Responsibility:
Jobs for all

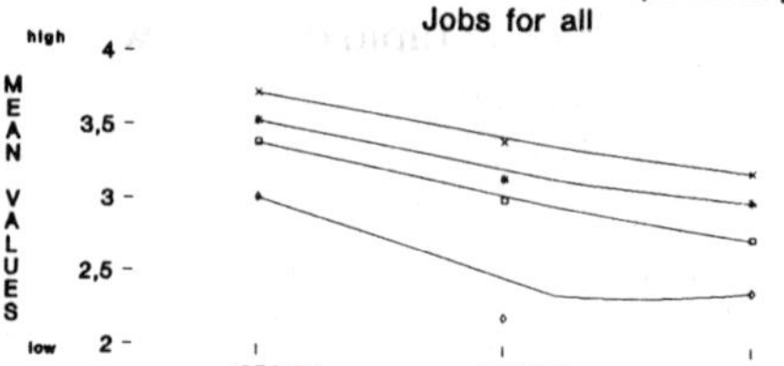

	1973/76	1985/86	1990
AUS		2,55	2,4
A	3,53	3,29	
D	3,53	3,14	2,99
GB	3,38	2,99	2,73
I	3,72	3,39	3,19
USA	3,01	2,19	2,37

Perceived Government's Responsibility:
Health Care

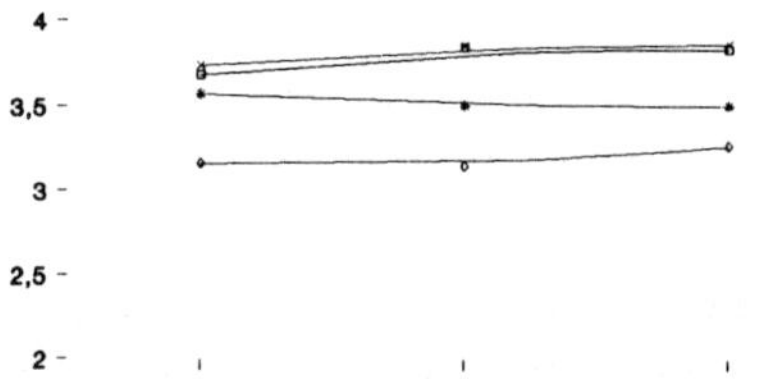

	1973/76	1985/86	1990
AUS		3,52	3,31
A	3,56	3,64	
D	3,57	3,51	3,51
GB	3,68	3,85	3,84
I	3,74	3,86	3,87
USA	3,16	3,15	3,27

Source: Political Action 1973–76, ISSP 1985–85, ISSP 1990

all four nations over the decade and a half with only the USA, having shown the lowest public perception from the outset, witnessing a slight recovery between 1985 and 1990. In the countries not presented in graphic form, but only in the accompanying data table, the change between these two points in time was likewise of a downwards nature.

Third, public support for 'jobs for all' and for 'health care' moved, albeit at different pace, in opposite directions. With the change from social democratic to conservative governments came policies aiming to roll back the responsibility of the state in many areas. Public reaction to these changes was of a diametrically split nature. We observe a steep decline in interventionism but, contrary to the expressed policy intentions of governments, a definite, if not large, rise (with the notable exception of Germany) in public support for the state taking on responsibility in medical care.

These three findings may be interpreted as follows. The readiness of the general public to stand up for social solidarity brought about by active government intervention, has been in rapid decline, whereas the classical liberal tenets of the state's responsibility to safeguard life, liberty and property have remained high. Concerning our theme of whether or not the public is no more than the chorus of a Greek tragedy, the conclusion to be drawn is that there is no such chorus, but two quite different voices expressed by the same popular sovereign at the same time.

In spite of these two (almost) uniform movements, the one up, the other down, relative distances between the nations have hardly shrunk over time. Rather than leading to a convergence, the divergent trend of public perceptions of the responsibility of the government kept steady at cross-national levels of aggregate perceptions. It is to a deeper inspection of these cross-national differences that we now turn before looking into individually coded data for each respondent within each nation.

HISTORICAL DIFFERENCES STILL HOLD STRONG

The International Social Survey 'Role of Government II' of 1990 incorporated four more countries than in 1985 (Hungary, Ireland, Israel and Norway), but omitted Austria. Furthermore, Germany after re-unification is represented by two separate surveys with the same questionnaire, the Western survey being conducted from 12 March to 25 May 1990 and the Eastern survey from 3 to 22 December 1990. Thus altogether nine countries, rather than only the six shown in the preceding figure, may be inspected in Figure 2, which is, however, limited to 1990.

Figure 2 shows for each of the nine nations (with Germany documented by the Eastern and Western survey separately) not only the mean value of perceived government responsibility for providing 'jobs for all' but also the standard deviations. While the mean values show the average public perception per country, the standard deviations allow, as a dispersion around the mean, a first glimpse at the degree of disagreement existent within each nation. This disagreement will be analysed in depth with regard to the individually coded data of all respondents in a later section. Even at this purely aggregate level of Figure 2, a few important distinctions can already be uncovered.

Australia and the USA show the lowest demands. Disagreement is highest in the USA, Great Britain and Ireland. It is tempting to speculate that this clearly visible group of four countries in the lower right field of the chart share a common historical experience of Anglo-American culture extending to Australia. As Tom W. Smith pointed out: 'The contemporary attitudes and policy preferences of the citizenry

FIGURE 2

JOBS FOR ALL – AVERAGE AGREEMENT AND DISAGREEMENT ACROSS 9 NATIONS, 1990

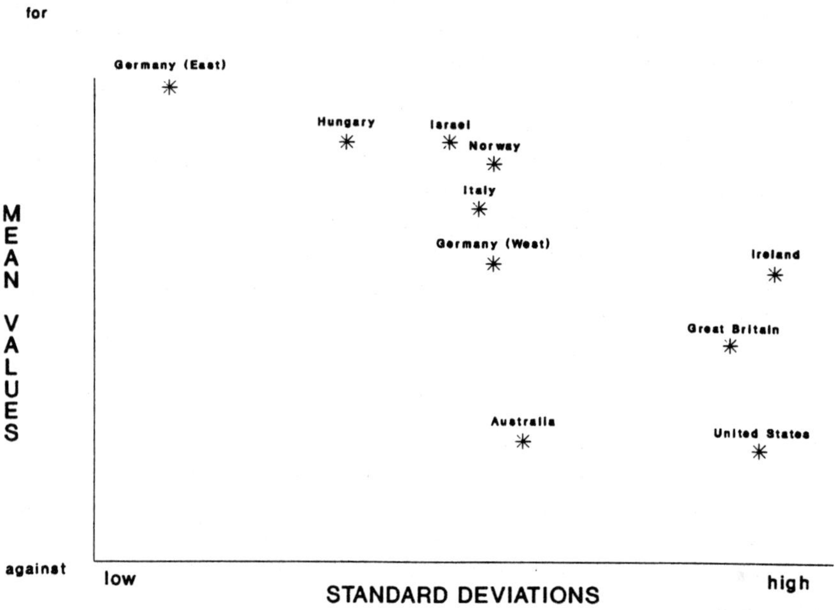

Source: ISSP 1990

in the United States, Austria, Germany, Italy, and the United Kingdom match the differences that exist in the historical development and current implementation of the welfare state. America has generally been less supportive of the principles underlying the welfare state and less eager to expand its scope'.[12] This insight goes back to classical writings as old as the turn of the century when Werner Sombart, in a major work from 1906, tackled the question 'Why is there no socialism in the United States?'.[13]

In a second group of countries mean support for, and disagreement on 'jobs for all' both indicate a favourable attitude to active state intervention. Norway, Italy and Germany, as Continental European states, have had a strong tradition of bureaucratic interventionism. As opposed to this tradition, in an influential book entitled *The State Tradition in Western Europe*, Kenneth Dyson has shown Great Britain to be a non-state oriented society lacking a bureaucratic state tradition.[14] One can add to this that, in contrast to a 'late democracy' like Germany, this pioneer state of modern democracy is a 'late bureaucracy'. As in the USA, a modern professional civil service was not introduced until a rather late stage, after a prolonged spoils-guided system of amateur bureacracy was finally disposed of.

It is, therefore, no accident that even today this difference, anchored in the traditionally stable paradigm of values, is still reflected in the responses of the many thousands to the opinion polls. Historically descriptive theorising and international comparative analysis, operating on the lines of quantitative distribution, can complement each other.[15] Circumstantially it may be assumed that what was possible in the USA as Reaganomics and practised in Britain as Thatcherism, would have been very difficult to realise on the European continent as a result of the diverging structural values historically embedded in these populations.

Finally, the two populations released from the grasps of Stalinist regimes, that is, Hungary and East Germany (the new *Bundesländer* to be precise), give a high priority to 'jobs for all' being the responsibility of any government in spite of their rejection of state socialism. In the contemporary situation of a reunited Germany, one can maintain that the wide discrepancy between the two populations, signalled by the surveys of 1990, show the chances of success for a solidarity pact to be lower than they would have been in the 1970s. As a look back to Figure 1 shows, support for 'jobs for all' was at this time higher in Western Germany.

Up till now only one mean value for each country has been calculated for different points in time. It nows seems apt to prompt the question: Are the differences within a country along the lines of not yet investigated dimensions, such as between trade union members and non-members considerable? If one wishes to study differences within countries, then a simple look at mean values and/or percentages of different levels of agreement per country (the latter not undertaken here since they may be looked up in the codebooks) is no longer sufficient. One has to apply a multivariate analysis of the individually coded data as contained in the data sets.

CONSISTENT PATTERNS OF ATTITUDES

Rather than trying to reinvent the wheel, I would like to start out from work by Peter Taylor-Gooby. In an as yet unpublished paper he ran a factor analysis of perceived government responsibilities for all of the seven items already mentioned above, namely, jobs for all, price stability, health care, pensions, aid to industry, unemployment benefits and redistribution (the latter being phrased as the government's responsibility, or not, to 'reduce income differences between the rich and poor'). This analysis has the advantage of no longer being confined to just two areas of state responsibility, namely health care and jobs as was the case in the graphs. Instead we are able to establish the subtle opinions of all respondents on all seven areas for each country separately.

Taylor-Gooby has shown that in five political systems in 1990 the same variables (apart from jobs and price stability) loaded the same factors as in 1985. Thus the multivariate test proves that answers were not given at random to accidental stimuli posited by interviewers, but were anchored in a set of consistent attitudes. We are not dealing with fickle responses. That jobs and prices, however, should have changed their factor loadings is not surprising. For 'cognitive conflicts' about how to cope with unemployment and inflation arise among political leaders, depending on which economic theory politicians adhere to, and these vicissitudes are easily transmitted to the general public.[16]

In Table 1, I have reworked Taylor-Gooby's factor analyses, but for 1990 only, and limited to four countries: Great Britain, Germany (West), Norway and the USA. Selecting these countries is to follow the 'most dissimilar cases' design, that is, those countries were chosen from the scatter-plot in Figure 2 which displayed the greatest contrasts. (It did not, however, make sense to select Germany (East), showing an even greater contrast, since trade union membership and party affiliations would not be comparable for 1990.) The nature of variables that distinctly load on one factor (printed in bold type) but hardly on the other (printed in normal type) can be used to interpret the content of these latent dimensions. (The statistics programme 'Factor' does calculate coefficients, the so-called factor loadings to be found in the upper part of Table 1.) By means of these coefficients, the programme registers whether a hidden latent dimension lies behind the responses, namely, an opinion that is not directly visible, but of compelling strength.

On one factor the loadings occur almost exclusively for jobs, price stability, aid to industry (in some, if not in all countries), aid for the unemployed and redistribution. As all these aims can only be achieved by an active 'interventionist state', we may justifiably label this factor 'economic intervention'. On the other factor the loadings occur almost exclusively for old-age pensions and health care. I therefore interpret this factor to mean social security for all and not just for needy minorities. The USA that already stood out in marked contrast to all other countries in the aggregate analysis of Figure 2, forming an outlier at the lower right end of the scatter-plot, again exhibits peculiar features in the multivariate analysis of Table 1. For what in other countries is the first

TABLE 1

SMALL IMPACT OF SOCIAL STRUCTURE AND PARTISANSHIP ON ATTITUDES TO THE 'INTERVENTIONIST STATE'

(Four 'most dissimilar' countries, 1990)

Factor analyses (principle components with varimax rotation) of the individually coded, non-grouped responses concerning seven areas of government responsibility:

GREAT BRITAIN

	Factor 1 "economic intervention"	Factor 2 "social security"
Jobs for all	**.78**	.08
Price stability	**.65**	.14
Health care	.08	**.89**
Pensions	.22	**.85**
Aid to industry	.42	.33
Unemployment benefits	**.64**	.25
Redistribution	**.77**	.08
Eigenvalue	2.81	1.16
Variance	40%	17%

GERMANY (WEST)

	Factor 1 "economic intervention"	Factor 2 "social security"
Jobs for all	**.68**	.31
Price stability	**.70**	.22
Health care	.17	**.86**
Pensions	.17	**.85**
Aid to industry	**.72**	-.06
Unemployment benefits	.52	.42
Redistribution	.59	.37
Eigenvalue	3.10	.98
Variance	44%	14%

Regression analyses of the factor scores for "economic intervention" and "social security" on:

GREAT BRITAIN

	b		b	
Income	**-.07**	(.01)	**-.02**	(.02)
Education (years at school)	**-.09**	(.02)	**-.01**	(.01)
TU membership	**.22**	(.08)	**.14**	(.08)
Party preference (coded L - R)	**.15**	(.02)	**.05**	(.02)
Constant	**-2.51**	(.30)	**-.44**	(.16)
R^2 =	**.19**		**.01**	

GERMANY (WEST)

	b		b	
Income	**-.03**	(.01)	**-.01**	(.005)
Education (years at school)	**.06**	(.01)	**.02**	(.007)
TU membership	**.01**	(.01)	**.14**	(.06)
Party preference (coded L - R)	**.03**	(.01)	**.03**	(.01)
Constant	**-1.09**	(.10)	**-.37**	(.14)
R^2 =	**.06**		**.01**	

Unstandardised regression coefficients with standard errors in parentheses

NORWAY

	Factor 1 "economic intervention"	Factor 2 "social security"
Jobs for all	**.75**	.15
Price stability	**.66**	.26
Health care	.18	**.85**
Pensions	.15	**.86**
Aid to industry	**.69**	-.03
Unemployment benefits	**.67**	.23
Redistribution	**.73**	.18
Eigenvalue	3.02	1.14
Variance	43%	16%

USA

	Factor 1 "social security"	Factor 2 "economic intervention"
Jobs for all	.44	**.62**
Price stability	**.62**	.36
Health care	**.84**	.17
Pensions	**.82**	.21
Aid to industry	.55	.36
Unemployment benefits	.35	**.73**
Redistribution	.12	**.84**
Eigenvalue	3.56	.79
Variance	51%	11%

Regression analyses of the factor scores for "economic intervention" and "social security" on:

NORWAY

	b		b	
Income	**-.09**	(.01)	**-.05**	(.05)
Education (years at school)	**-.09**	(.01)	**-.03**	(.03)
TU membership	**.26**	(.06)	**.12**	(.06)
Party preference (coded L - R)	**.16**	(.02)	**.09**	(.02)
Constant	**-2.46**	(.18)	**-.51**	(.10)
R^2 =	**.17**		**.02**	

USA

	b		b	
Income	**-.07**	(.06)	**-.05**	(.008)
Education (years at school)	**-.05**	(.01)	**-.03**	(.01)
TU membership	**-.02**	(-.02)	**.02**	(.02)
Party preference (coded L - R)	**.18**	(.04)	**.17**	(.04)
Constant	**-1.14**	(.20)	**-1.51**	(.19)
R^2 =	**.06**		**.12**	

Unstandardised regression coefficients with standard errors in parentheses

Source: ISSP 1990 – own calculations

factor of 'economic intervention', only shows up in the USA, when prompted, and even then, only, as a very weak second, less important factor.

The factor analyses of Table 1 confirm our major finding in a more subtle way than the aggregate analyses of Figures 1 and 2. There is now a rift in public opinion between state responsibilities perceived in terms of redressing market failures (by intervention) and the general provision of basic needs for everybody such as old-age pensions and health care for the sick. So the question still seems apt: how big are the differences within a country along the lines of not yet investigated dimensions such as between trade union members and non-members? Do citizens affiliated to left-wing parties hold sharply divided opinions in comparison to adherents of right-wing parties? Does a higher level of education correspond with a more liberal opinion of the welfare state or is the opposite true?

SMALL DIVISIONS ON 'INTERVENTIONIST' ATTITUDES

Exploring these pertinent questions, we may carry Taylor-Gooby's analysis a step further by studying the impact of the independent variables of social structure and partisanship for each nation upon the two factor-analytically determined dimensions of 'economic intervention' and 'social security' as dependent variables by means of multiple regression analyses carried out separately for each country. To this intent Table 1 'factor scores' were individually calculated and subsequently regressed on income, education, trade union membership and party preference for each respondent within the four nations.[17] This research design is reported in the lower segments of the four countries in Table 1.

This assessment yielded a clear result. Social structure and partisanship have only a moderately strong, or to put it differently, a rather weak impact upon public perceptions of government responsibilities. There is no element of surprise in the fact that the regression coefficients concerning Factor 2 should be so small, as 'social security' is a 'valence issue' finding almost universal approval. But in respect of Factor 1, the much contested issue of 'economic intervention', it was only in Britain and Norway that both trade union membership and party affiliation showed a moderate effect worth mentioning, as did party affiliation in the USA. As for Germany as good as no, and at best only a minimal socio-structural and party political disagreement amongst the population in relation to the interventionist state was to be found.

Whether the public in a given nation supports or rejects the interventionist state, the overall climate of opinion apparently cuts through all classes, parties and groups with only moderate divergence between them. This may seem unbelievable, but was confirmed by an independent analysis made by the Austrian team of the 'International Social Survey Programme' for Austria in 1985 using a different method.[18] If one adheres to the contention that a national political culture may explain more variance than social structural divisions within each nation, the small R^2s in Table 1 become, for once, a virtue and not a vice.

The rather considerable amount of unexplained variance leaves room to search for other influences such as 'historical accident and the overall ideological climate'.[19] Here, political-cultural differences between nations, hinted at above, are brought back in. Inspection of Figure 1 above led to the observation that differences between countries (with the exception of Germany) remained fairly steady over time in spite of a steep decline in support for 'jobs for all'. As aggregate values, such as national percentages, reduce many a thousand individually coded data to just one average figure for each nation, inferences based on national averages are prone to the ill-famed 'ecological fallacy'. So last but by no means least we should study by means of original individual data the impact of respondents' nationality on their perceptions of the responsibilities of government.

IMPACT OF NATIONALITY STRONGER THAN PARTY AFFILIATION

The crux of the matter lies, of course, in how to measure the impact of national, rather than partisan, affiliations in comparison to each other, as nationality, for the respondents of a national survey, is a nominal constant and not a variable. Social science statistics do, however, supply us with a method to study even non-metric nominal attributes by regression analysis. Let me try and explain this device in non-technical language. Just fancy assembling all those respondents from various countries simultaneously in a single market place or a large open-air field. They will form a representative sample of their respective populations containing higher and lower income people, well-educated and those with only elementary education, trade union members and non-members and those having voted for and/or feeling affiliated to left or right parties. All these attributes are known from the surveys already available. We need only to merge, experimentally, the national samples experimentally into a single multi-national one thus creating a proxy for our open-air field convention.

Now imagine that all these individuals will additionally carry on their backs, or perhaps chests, a clearly visible label signifying their nationality. By calculating and assigning 'proxy' variables standing as scores for their respective national affiliations in this experimentally merged sample, we are in a position to analyse individually the impact of nationality on public perceptions of the proper role of the state.[20] If on this (fictitious) open-air field of our merged sample the question were to be put whether or not it was the government's responsibility to cater for any (or all) of the seven items represented in Table 1, we would then, in this experimental situation, be able to tell whether trade union membership and party affiliations, etc., or whether the national labels carried on their backs would be more indicative in predicting the outcome of the overall answer to the question put.

For the purpose of this essay such an imaginary open-air assembly was created from the cross-national data set of the ISSP 1990 by 'pooling' six national samples into one single, weighted, sample of respondents and by subsequently sticking a label indicating his/her nationalities to each individual's back. Our merged sample (N=10,146) contains 2,398 respondents from Australia, 2,812 from Western Germany, 1,197 from Great Britain, 1,005 from Ireland, 1,517 from Norway and 1,217 from the United States. Rather than continuing with 'factor scores' across all seven items of perceived government responsibilities, let us return, and limit ourselves to, the crucially sensitive, and more perceptible, demand for 'jobs for all' and ask: If we know, on an individually coded basis, whether respondents on our fictitious open-air field are trade union members and/or Australians or Americans etc., which influence will have a stronger impact upon their likely assessment of government's responsibility to 'providing a job for everyone who wants one' (as the precise wording of the questions goes)? The results are reported in Table 2.

The left-hand partial table of Table 2 studies the impact of national affiliations on the perception of the altogether 10,146 respondents.[21] The right-hand partial table analyses separately the impact of standard social structural and partisanship variables for this 'pooled' sample.[22] The results confirm that differences across nations even on the individual basis have more explanatory power than sociological explanations focusing upon standard structural influences. The total variance explained, however, is small in both cases. However, public perceptions of the role of government are, to a certain extent, rooted in cross-national cultural differences, and at any rate more so than in party polarisation. If this is so, and thus to return to our theme of the chorus of Greek tragedy, then the popular sovereign's shifting comments to rapid changes on the great stage of politics constitute not so much ever

TABLE 2

IMPACT OF NATIONALITY ON INDIVIDUAL PERCEPTIONS OF 'JOBS FOR ALL' STRONGER THAN SOCIAL STRUCTURE AND PARTISANSHIP

Regressions (for merged sample of six countries, unweighted N=10146) of support for "jobs for all"

on: nationality ("dummies"):	b	S.E	on: social structure and partisanship:	b	S.E
American	-.61	(.03)	Income	-.03	(.002)
Australian	-.59	(.03)	Education (years at school)	-.05	(.001)
British (Great Britain)	-.26	(.03)	TU membership	.16	(.02)
German (West)	.01	(.01)	Party preference (coded L - R)	.03	(.001)
Norwegian	.33	(.03)	Constant	.97	(.06)
Constant (=Irish)	2.01	(.01)			
R^2 =	.13		R^2 =	.07	
n=	9702		n=	8119	

Pairwise deletion of missing cases. Unstandardised regression coefficients with standard errors in parentheses

Source: ISSP 1990 – own calculations

shifting fickle opinions but a 'critical morality' based on lasting historical experiences.

The objection may come to mind here that the 'chorus of Greek tragedy' motif is, after all, a very short-term phenomonen, and that the three cross-national surveys of 1973–76, 1985 and 1990 studied here, are too long an interval to prove anything about short-term reactions. We must, therefore look for shorter intervals to round up our analysis. In looking for shorter-term fluctuations it always pays to browse through the codebooks of the bi-annual Eurobarometer surveys. They did indeed cover an issue serving as the nearest equivalent to that of an actively interventionist state.

ANTI-CYCLICAL PUBLIC REACTIONS TO FORCEFUL GOVERNMENT POLICIES

In the Eurobarometers of Spring 1979, Autumn 1981 and Autumn 1983, in identical wording, the question was asked: 'We would like to hear your views on some important political issues. Could you tell me whether you agree or disagree with [. . .] the following proposal[s]? : Public ownership of private industry should be expanded (answering code: agree strongly, agree, disagree, disagree strongly). Closer inspec-

FIGURE 3

PUBLIC OPINION ANTI-CYCLICAL TO GOVERNMENT POLICIES IN BRITAIN AND FRANCE, 1979–1983

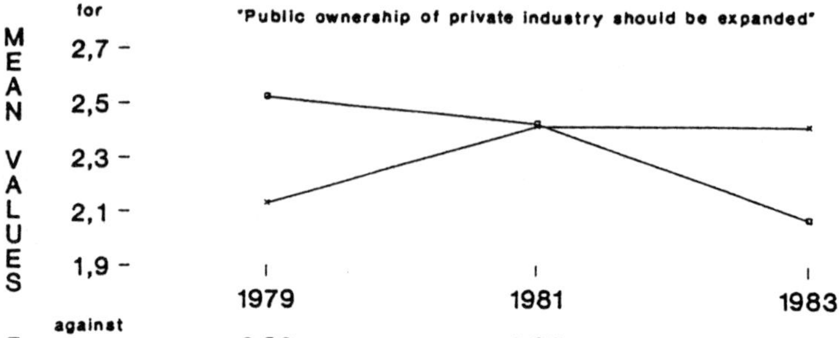

B		2,62	2,08	2,07	-.55
D		2,29	2,26	2,31	+.02
DK		1,83	1,83	1,69	-.14
F	—o—	2,52	2,42	2,07	-.45
GB	—x—	2,13	2,41	2,41	+.28
I		2,21	2,05	2,02	-.19
IRL		2,86	2,72	2,63	-.23
NL		2,11	2,02	1,99	-.12

Eurobarometers 11, 16, 19 (weighted)

Source: Eurobarometers

tion of the answers in Figure 3 (and its accompanying data table) yields a conventional and also a rather unexpected result.

The conventional finding is that concerning the 'collectivist' demand for more industry to be put under state ownership we encounter, as could be expected, a further weakening of the social democratic consensus in most countries. But an interpretation that does not just rely on the manifest message of the data, but interprets their meaning against the context of what real policies, and discussions about them, had taken place between 1979 and 1983 does warrant an unconventional thesis: In the short run the public did not act like a chorus which just reinforces prevailing trends. On the contrary, public opinion took a decisive anti-cyclical stance against any forceful policy changes put forward by governments.

Circumstantial evidence is to be taken from the last column in the data table, where the difference between 1979 and 1983 is calculated.[23] It clearly shows the greatest change was occuring in three countries: France, Belgium and Great Britain. Belgium, where the steepest decline took place, but only between 1979 and 1981, deserves a special case analysis, whose conclusions can only be hinted at here.[24] Apart

TABLE 3

ANTI-CYCLICAL REACTIONS APPLY EQUALLY TO VOTERS OF GOVERNMENT AND OPPOSITION PARTIES

"Public ownership of private industry should be expanded"

Mean Values per party (1= against; 4= in favour)

	Britain				France		
	1979	**1981**	**1983**		**1979**	**1981**	**1983**
Labour	**2.61**	**2.73**	**2.82**	Communists	**3.50**	**3.25**	**2.96**
Conservative	**1.84**	**2.10**	**2.21**	Socialists	**2.84**	**2.76**	**2.54**
Liberal (Alliance)	**2.16**	**2.24**	**2.41**	Gaullists	**1.96**	**1.69**	**1.65**
Other	**2.17**	**2.28**	**2.31**	MRG (Left Radicals)	**2.23**	**2.26**	**1.83**

Source: Eurobarometers 11, 16, 19 – own calculations

from the special Belgian situation, in all countries where there was no change of government policies, just a minor change in support for more 'public ownership of private industry', generally downward, was to be found. But where there was a strong demand for either nationalisation or privatisation by political parties in government, the public, a far cry from the applauding or mourning chorus of Greek tragedy, reacted by expressing opinion precisely to the contrary. This is true in France for nationalisation, which was suggested by the parties of the left and then carried out by the left after gaining power in 1982. Contrary to the project of nationalisation under Mitterrand, opinion moved away more strongly from support for such measures than in most other European countries. In Britain the Thatcher government's forceful move towards privatization coincided ironically with public perceptions that, in contrast to the rest of Europe, shifted to a position of being a little more in favour of public ownership in order to redress the balance.[25]

Further analysis of these data shows that in Britain as well as in France the anti-cyclical reactions equally applied to adherents of both government and opposition parties. As Table 3 shows, in Britain not only respondents affiliated to the Labour Party but also Conservative voters, albeit from a lower level, shifted, in contrast to the actual privatizations, in favour of thinking more favourably about industry under public ownership. In France, as nationalisations were carried out, even the supporters of the Communist and Socialist parties joined in the general decline of support for this contentious policy goal. We may cautiously infer: presumably the public in Western Europe has an initially reserved and sceptical opinion of strategic government policy changes.

This contention of a general anti-cyclical reaction of a sophisticated population against any forceful change of direction by a government may be backed by further circumstantial evidence. The tax protest, foreseen by many as a 'welfare backlash',[26] has not materialised. Once again we witness an anti-cyclical change of opinion and not a strengthening of the trend. Contrary to the financial crisis of the state, in the five political systems covered by Taylor-Gooby the public wished for more state spending, especially on the environment and health.[27] This result is even more impressive in light of the fact the interviewees were told that this would probably mean higher taxes.

CONCLUSIONS

In order to find out how the public reacted to governments' attempts to roll back the state, public opinion surveys of perceived government responsibilities were analysed over three different points in time from 1973–76 to 1990 and across nations for 1990. On the one hand the public behaves pro-cyclically in its support for the roll-back of the state in 'providing a job for everyone who wants one'. On the other hand the public reacts anti-cyclically in terms of reaction to government plans to increase private participation in health care provision.

From these findings it may be inferred interpretatively, going beyond the manifest evidence of the quantitative data, that the readiness of the general public to stand up for social solidarity brought about by active government intervention and redistributive policies has been waning, whereas the classical liberal tenets of the state's responsibility to safeguard life, liberty and property have remained high or even risen in importance. In other words, the public supports, by and large, a change from the 'social-democratic consensus' of an 'interventionist state' to a neo-liberal admittance of market forces, but it stills wants certain basic services to be looked after by the government.

Despite the fact that both trends show up uniformly across nations (with the one-off exception of Germany concerning health care), these movements have not brought about convergence amongst Western democracies. Historically-based contrasts between countries are still evident. Further, multivariate analyses showed public perceptions about the proper role of the state to be more deeply entrenched in cross-national differences of political cultures than in national partisan cleavages and specific national socialstructural differences. The thesis of nationally homogeneous, yet indisputably contrasting opinions on the appropriate role of the state between countries has withstood the tough test of multivariate checking with individually coded data.

In relation to the point of departure of this essay, the 'chorus of the Greek tragedy' analogy was not confirmed but refuted by the facts. The public does not behave in the way the great realist and analyst Schumpeter assumed. It does not follow the ruling trend like a flock of sheep. On the contrary, we even observed in the short run distinctly critical reactions against any forceful government measures among both government supporters and adherents to opposition parties. From this finding it may be inferred that a sceptically reserved public at first adopts an anti-cyclical, contrary opinion. Once policies really work, the historically-based national consensus can be moved in the direction of a new synthesis. Thus politicians should reckon with this contrary public opinion, rather than looking to demoscopic studies for short-term success.

NOTES

1. Charles Debbasch (ed.), *L'inflation législative et réglementaire en Europe* (Paris: Éditions du Centre National de la Recherche Scientifique, 1986).
2. Using the analogy of the chorus of Greek tragedy, I am referring to a debate between two prominent social scientists, Lujo Brentano and Gustav von Schmoller, who quarreled about whether or not social science should be more than just the 'Chorus of Greek Tragedy'. This analogy can, of course, be equally applied to such a mundane field as public perceptions. See Lujo Brentano, *Mein Leben im Kampf um die soziale Entwicklung Deutschlands* (Jena: Diederichs, 1931), p.332: 'Wäre er [. . .] nicht von dem Gedanken geleitet gewesen, daß es Aufgabe der Wissenschaft sei, den öffentlichen Ereignissen lediglich wie der griechische Chor kommentierend zu folgen, unsere Freundschaft wäre nie getrübt worden'.
3. Joseph A. Schumpeter, *Capitalism, Socialism and Democracy* (NY: Harper & Row, 3rd ed., 1950), p.283.
4. *Political Action, An Eight Nation Study 1973–76*. Study No.0765 (Cologne: Zentralarchiv für empirische Sozialforschung). *ISSP=International Social Survey Programme. Role of Government I, 1985*. Study No.1490 (Cologne: Zentralarchiv für empirische Sozialforschung). *International Social Survey Programme. Role of Government II, 1990*. Study No.1950 (Cologne: Zentralarchiv für empirische Sozialforschung). For an overview of the bi-annual Eurobarometer studies see Karlheinz Reif/Ronald Inglehart (eds.), *Eurobarometer: The Dynamics of European Public Opinion, Essays in Honour of Jacques-René Rabier* (London: Macmillan, 1991).
5. It is a relatively easy task to go through the three codebooks of 'Political Action' and 'Role of Government' of the ISSP 1985 and 1990. But rather than coping with the many codebooks of the Eurobarometer surveys, I am indebted to Jürgen Hofrichter for conducting a search in the retrieval system of ZEUS (Zentrum für Europäische Umfragen und Studien), Mannheim on my behalf.
6. See for 1985, variables 101 to 107, and for 1990, variables 49 to 55 in the printed codebooks of ISSP mentioned in note 4.
7. The question wording in 'Political Action' reads as follows: 'Now we would like to

know how you feel about some of the particular issues and problems that people often talk about these days. We would like to know (a) How important these issues and problems are in your view, (b) *How far you feel [the] government has responsibility for them* and (c) how well [the] government is handling these problems. Altogether 12 problems were listed, among which jobs ('seeing to it that everyone who wants a job can have one'), health care ('providing good medical care'), redistribution ('trying to even out differences in wealth between people'), inflation ('fight rising prices') were included.

8. There are many more issues concerning the scope and role of government contained in these rich and still under-utilized survey data that have been stored in public archives. For a book-length exhaustive treatment, see the volume by Ole Borre (ed.), *The Scope of Government*, Vol.3 in the 'Beliefs in Government Series' edited by Max Kaase and Kenneth Newton, forthcoming in 1994. Interestingly the ISSP is to replicate its topical surveys every five years. Therefore the 'Role of Government' may be updated when the 1995 survey becomes available.
9. Tom W. Smith, 'That Which We Call Welfare By Any Other Name Would Smell Sweeter: An Analysis of the Impact of Question Wording on Response Patterns', in *Public Opinion Quarterly* 51/1 (Spring 1987), pp.75–83. For a discussion of these problems see also Robert Y. Shapiro and John T. Young, 'Public Opinion and the Welfare State: The United States in Comparative Perspective', in *Political Science Quarterly* 104/1 (1989), pp.59–89.
10. Peter Taylor-Gooby, 'What Citizens Want from the State: Attitudes to the Role of Government in the International Social Survey, 1985–1990'. Paper (1993), forthcoming in the 'British Social Attitudes' series. See also his 'The Role of the State', in Roger Jowell, Sharon Witherspoon and Lindsay Brook (eds.), *British Social Attitudes: Special International Report* (Aldershot: Gower, 1989), pp.35–58.
11. Rather than showing in detail percentage values for the answering codes ranging from 'definitely should be responsible' over 'probably should be responsible' to 'probably should not be' and 'definitely should not be', Figure 1 calculates from the original data out of those four categories national mean values ('can't choose, don't know' set to zero) for each of the three periods. The coding has been reversed, i. e., a value of 4 does signify a very highly perceived government responsibility per nation and a value of 2 and below a very low one.
12. Tom W. Smith, 'The Polls – A Report: The Welfare State in Cross-National Perspective', in *Public Opinion Quarterly*, Vol.51 (1987), p.406.
13. Werner Sombart, *Warum gibt es in den Vereinigten Staaten keinen Sozialismus?* (Tübingen, 1906).
14. Kenneth Dyson, *The State Tradition in Western Europe. A Study of an Idea and Institution* (Oxford: Robertson, 1980).
15. For a critical discussion see Manfred Kuechler, 'The Utility of Surveys for Cross-National Research', in J.W. Becker, James A. Davis, Peter Ester and Peter P. Mohler (eds.), *Attitudes to Inequality and the Role of Government* (Rijswijk: Social and Cultural Planning Office, 1990). In defence of a combination of historical findings and cross-national quantitative evidence Arend Lijphart, 'The Structure of Inference', in Gabriel A. Almond and Sidney Verba (eds.), *The Civic Culture Revisited* (Boston: Little Brown, 1980).
16. Cf. Fritz W. Scharpf, 'A Game-Theoretical Interpretation of Inflation and Unemployment in Western Europe', in *Journal of Public Policy* 7/3 (1987), pp.227–57.
17. I beg the reader's pardon for using technical language for a moment.
18. See Otto Raubal, 'Erwartungen und Ansprüche an Staat und Regierung', in Max Haller and Kurt Holm (eds.), *Werthaltungen und Lebensformen in Österreich* (München/Wien: Oldenburg Verlag/Verlag für Geschichte und Politik, 1987), table 10.
19. Michael Laver, *Invitation to Politics* (Oxford: Blackwell, 1982), p.123.
20. Since nationality is a category on a nominal scale, it cannot, of course, be treated as 'scores' in regression analysis. A way out is the creation of a set of dummy variables by

treating each category of a nominal variable (such as American, Australian, British, German, Irish or Norwegian) as a separate variable and assigning scores of 0 and 1 for all cases on each of them. The newly created dichotomous variables are called 'dummies' because their scores have no meaning other than standing for a category in the original nominal variable. However, it is necessary to exclude one of the dummies from the regression equation. This excluded category, in Table 2 it is Ireland, becomes a reference category, by which the effects of the other dummies are judged and interpreted.

21. Pairwise deletion of missing cases, even in the analysis of nationalities, where answers may be missing concerning 'jobs for all', reduces the valid cases from 10,146 to 9,702 for the left-hand table.
22. Variables as recoded by the primary collectors of the data in the original data set so as to make left and right party preferences and income in different countries comparable.
23. The entries in each of the three columns do represent again for each nation the mean value of agreement. A coding of 4 signifies 'agree strongly' and of 1 'disagree strongly'.
24. The demands for further nationalisation were pushed by the Walloon Socialist Party. With the ailing steel industries mostly situated in the francophone parts of Belgium the then more prosperous industrial parts of Flanders launched a discussion of preventing Flemish tax-payers' money to be used to bail out flaging Walloon industry by nationalising them. Thus the socio-economic cleavage of the 'interventionist state' overlapped with the regional cleavage. In spite of no nationalisations taking place at all the issue was high on the agenda. (Information courtesy of Lieven De Winter, Louvain-La-Neuve.)
25. Privatization was no doubt popular, though. Having stood at only 33 per cent in 1970, approval had risen to 40 per cent by 1979 (See Ivor Crewe/Donald D. Searing, 'Ideological Change in the British Conservative Party', in *American Political Science Review* 82/2 (1988), pp.361–84, Table 7, p.376. However, as these authors demonstrate from British, and not from cross-national, data many of the basic tenets of Thatcherism became ironically increasingly less popular after 1979.
26. So Harold L. Wilensky, *The Welfare State and Equality. Structural and Ideological Roots of Public Expenditures* (Berkeley/Los Angeles, CA: Univ. of California Press, 1975).
27. Taylor-Gooby (note 10) table 10.

FURTHER READING

J.W. Becker, James A. Davis, Peter Ester, Peter P. Mohler (eds.), *Attitudes to Inequality and the Role of Government* (Rijswijk: Social and Cultural Planning Office, 1990). A collection of essays about the 'International Social Survey' concerning cross-national perceptions of inequality.

Ole Borre (ed.), *The Scope of Government*, Vol.3 of the 'Beliefs in Government' series, edited by Max Kaase and Kenneth Newton; forthcoming. A forthcoming publication by different authors focusing upon all available empirical evidence from many angles.

Roger Jowell, Sharon Witherspoon, Lindsay Brook (eds.), *British Social Attitudes: Special International Report* (Aldershot: Gower 1989), pp.59–86. A collection of essays covering many aspects of the 'International Social Survey Programme'.

Robert Y. Shapiro, John T. Young, 'Public Opinion and the Welfare State: The United States in Comparative Perspective', *Political Science Quarterly* 104/1 (Spring 1989), pp.59–89. Raises important questions about the advantages and pitfalls of measuring attitudes towards state and welfare.

Peter Taylor-Gooby, *Public Opinion, Ideology and State Welfare* (London: RKP, 1985).

Peter Taylor-Gooby, *Social Change, Social Welfare and Social Science* (Hemel Hempstead: Wheatsheaf, 1991).

Political Traditions and the Role of the State

WOLFGANG C. MÜLLER

In the 1970s and early 1980s conservative and Christian democratic parties departed from the 'social democratic consensus' of the 1960s and were converted to economic neo-liberalism. In the 1980s and early 1990s social democrats also shifted considerably towards neo-liberal policy options thereby introducing a new policy convergence with conservative and Christian democratic parties. As a result of these two shifts, the whole political spectrum has shifted to the right compared with the 1960s. Since the major political families advocate a set of similar policies the present situation bears similarities with the 1960s. A new – neo-liberal – consensus has emerged, but it is of limited extent and contains internal tensions. Nevertheless, the policy distance between the major political families in socio-economic questions is smaller now than it was under the 'social democratic consensus' of the 1960s.

In the 1960s and much of the 1970s many observers tended to view the political traditions which had structured the era of mass politics and had provided the basis for bitter fights as exhausted. Daniel Bell has provided the most prominent formulation of this thesis in his book *The End of Ideology* (1960).[1] According to many academics a 'social democratic consensus', as it was labelled later, had replaced the traditional ideologies in practical politics.[2] This consensus was based first and foremost on the widespread acceptance of Keynesian policies. In subscribing to them, social democrats hoped to bring the economy under political control, to introduce relative equality through economic growth and to ensure the economic foundation of the welfare state. Keynesianism provided a formula for compromise with the major non-socialist forces. As Hall has put it, 'full employment and sustained economic growth could be achieved within a capitalist economy through the judicious use of macroeconomic management, without any need to interfere with the managerial prerogatives of private capital. With effective demand management, labour could be guaranteed full employment, while capital retained control over investment.'[3] As a consequence of this, according to Padgett and Paterson, by the 1960s 'the various parties' socialist profiles had been reduced to mere shadows. Revisionist social democracy had come to terms with reformed liberal capitalism.'[4] Christian democrats had gone through a similar development in playing down their initial anti-capitalism and converting to the market economy in the form of the 'social market economy'.[5] However, they had reached this point earlier than the social democrats as their ideological journey had been less far and had started earlier. Conservatives, who at the ideological level had traditionally been hostile to state intervention in the economy and had fiercely defended the right to property, have been pragmatic in these matters to the extent that they were governing parties or considered the acceptance of state intervention, the welfare state etc. as the precondition for electoral success.[6] As Brian Girvin has put it, 'It was as if all parties were now social democratic or Keynesian'.[7] Consequently political competition increasingly revolved around competence and efficiency.

While the 'end of ideology' argument grasped an important aspect of the political development, it did not – as later events demonstrated – give a full picture. As an academic construction it overemphasised the actual degree of consensus between the major political families. The consensus was neither complete nor had it replaced commitments to more ideologically-based policies within the parties. Moreover, all parties had accepted the far-reaching policy consensus in part for electoral reasons rather than because of a genuine change of their ideology.

The economic crisis of the mid-1970s eventually broke this consensus. This article is concerned with how the main political traditions have prescribed the role of the state and how they have have shaped it when in government since the late 1970s. In other words, it will be partly concerned with what parties say and partly with what parties do. Needless to say, that there can be substantial differences between these two.

The actors of this article are the major political families (von Beyme's *familles spirituelles*)[8] and party groupings rather than individual parties. The article concentrates on the communalities and similarities of the parties of each major ideological strand rather than focusing on those aspects which make each party distinctive. Political traditions clearly display differences concerning the role of the state in several respects. Consider, for instance, the different approaches of Christian democratic and secular parties in church-state relations, or between conservatives and liberals concerning civil liberties. However, the socio-economic dimension has been the most important one for structuring European party systems, and party competition still centers around the left-right dimension.[9] In most countries left-right ideological orientations serve as a basic reference point for voters. Thus, for reasons of relevance and space this article concentrates on socio-economic questions. This concentration in turn allows us to ignore differences between political families in other dimensions and to consider only two groupings of parties. They are the moderate parties of the left (which are referred to as social democratic parties in this article) and the major parties of the centre-right and moderate right which are either Christian democratic or conservative.

This article covers six countries, the United Kingdom, France, Germany, Sweden, Spain, and Austria. These not only include the major European countries and representatives of southern, central and northern Europe, but also constitute a fair sample of different reactions to economic and political challenges since the mid-1970s.[10]

After having outlined the parties' positions in the 1960s, the point of departure of this article, it first deals with the development of the conservative and Christian democratic parties. Second, the article analyses the changes in the perception of the proper role of the state that social democratic parties went through. Since relevant changes in social democratic parties occurred later and so far have not been dealt with in great length in the literature, more emphasis will be given to them. Finally, the article compares the current party positions and asks whether a new consensus has emerged.

REDISCOVERING ECONOMIC LIBERALISM: THE CONSERVATIVES AND CHRISTIAN DEMOCRATS

In the 1970s and 1980s Christian democratic and conservative parties adopted or 'rediscovered' neo-liberal economic ideas and since then have departed from the 'social democratic consensus'. This development was led by the British Conservatives. At the programmatical level they made this move under Prime Minister Edward Heath as soon as the early 1970s, only to return to Keynesian policies when faced with economic crisis and resistance from the trade unions. The breakthrough to a point where neo-liberalism was guiding the party's economic programme and practice was made under Margaret Thatcher. In Germany the CDU in the mid-1970s began to stress the genuinely liberal elements of its traditional social-market economy model and eventually could join forces with the FDP in the *Wende* of 1982.[11] In France it was 1981 when RPR leader Jacques Chirac discovered the evils of state interventionism, taxation and regulation. This constituted a severe programmatic change of what had been the most interventionistic of all conservative parties in Western Europe.[12] In Austria the

People's Party (ÖVP) began to adopt neo-liberal economic policies in 1982. Although the ÖVP remained more moderate than many of its European sister parties in detail, it subscribed to the full range of neo-liberal demands.[13] Even before 1982 the chairman of the Swedish conservative party, the Moderata Samlingspartiet, had claimed that it was his party rather than the Liberals, which was most capable of representing the liberal tradition.[14] To be sure, for most of these parties it was not entirely new to subscribe to neo-liberal economic policy proposals. It rather meant the reviving of traditions which had been pushed into the background, mostly in the 1960s. This reorientation of so many West European parties of the centre-right and moderate right was caused by the economic crisis of the 1970s which, by the early 1980s, had clearly shown the *economic* limits of Keynesian intervention and had made neo-liberal policies *politically* viable.

Christian democratic and conservative parties now identified state intervention as a cause or even *the* cause of the economic crisis, a part of the problem and not its solution.[15] Nationalised industries and state subsidies to individual firms were now considered inefficient and an obstacle to the self-adjustment of the market. Too ambitious public policies require too high taxation which in turn produces disincentives. High public debt crowds out private sector demand for credit and hence undermines investment. Although the proposals of conservative and Christian democratic parties do not fundamentally challenge the welfare state, the system is seen as requiring thorough reforms. Welfare state bureaucracies are considered to be distended and inefficient, wasting resources on excessive administration. They are taking care of their own interests rather than those of their clients. Clients are not only not aware of the costs of the welfare services, but they also do not receive those services which they need most. Thus little risks are covered by welfare institutions, while some vital interests are not. Some welfare benefits are provided too generously with the effect of being abused on a large scale. Too generous unemployment payments for instance undermine the motivation of the unemployed to get back to work. This not only boosts welfare spending but also tends to increase the grey sector of the economy, where many unemployed earn additional income.

In short, previous governments demanded too much from the state. Attempts to fulfill these demands have resulted in a vicious circle and have only aggravated the economic problems. In the most pessimistic scenarios, it is not only the initial demands that may be frustrated; political overload may have negative consequences for regime stability.[16]

While these features have been widely shared among the parties under consideration, individual conservative and Christian democratic parties have also been concerned with country-specific features. The most prominent example has been excessive trade union power, targeted in particular by the British Conservatives and, in a very diluted form, by the German Christian democrats.

In order to cope with these problems, conservative and Christian democratic parties have subscribed to a package of policies, including privatization, the reform of the tax system, deregulation and marketisation. Privatization, meaning the withdrawal of the state from industrial ownership, aims at providing better management to the privatised firms, strengthening the market by removing unfair competition conditions and reduce the financial burdens of the state. The reform of the tax system aims at making the economy work by the creation or strengthening of incentives. Deregulation aims at removing regulations which hamper economic activity. Marketisation means the introduction of the market into sectors which remain within the public sector, examples of which are education, health care and housing. All these measures are intended to alter the balance between the public and the private sectors in favour of the latter.

With the taking over of governmental power by conservative and Christian democratic parties since the late 1970s this analysis has guided government policies in the USA and several Western European countries. The most prominent example of the practical relevance of the 'neo-liberal revolution' is the United Kingdom.[17] The policies introduced by the Conservatives represent in the words of John Gray a 'sea change' and bear the 'marks of irreversibility'.[18] Their government record includes a huge privatisation programme, ranging from major industries to council houses, the bringing down of the marginal tax rate and trade union legislation in line with conservative convictions. In Germany the CDU/CSU-FDP coalition has introduced less spectacular reforms; nevertheless it has introduced a new flexibility of labour, and its tax reforms between 1986 and 1990 have reduced the top rate of income tax; net profits of enterprises increased considerably.[19] In France the non-socialist government of 1986–88 privatised numerous firms, reformed the tax system in favour of the wealthy (and thereby reversed the policy of the left) and introduced deregulation.[20] In Austria, although only the junior partner of the SPÖ in government, the ÖVP has since 1987 achieved much of its programme.

However, many of the policies which originally were proposed by conservative and Christian democratic parties have only been partially implemented. It is sufficient to make reference to the United Kingdom and Germany in this context. In Britain privatization (the 'success story' of a thorough implementation of a government programme) has not produced more competition. Social expenditure as a percentage of gross domestic product remained almost unchanged after a decade of Thatcherism,[21] and plans for a radical reform of the National Health Service were scrapped when it became clear that these proposals were unpopular within the Conservatives' own constituency.[22] In Germany the Christian-liberal government has only partially realised the market liberalisation and deregulation which were established as goals of the *Wende* in 1982. The government has achieved more where technological and market change functioned as 'icebreakers': thus neo-liberalism has been much more influential for telecommunications policy than for deregulating shop opening hours.[23] Although the national government implemented its privatisation programme, due to increased activities of other levels of government public involvment in the economy has not been reduced.[24] Similar to the UK, the German welfare state has only been marginally affected by the government's neo-liberal approach.

There are several reasons for not implementing a fully fledged version of the neo-liberal programme. To begin with, there has been a lack of internal agreement within Christian democratic and conservative parties. Although economic neo-liberalism has become the strongest force in many of these parties, its conquest was nowhere total. The parties have remained coalitions of diverse interests. Electoral considerations have been another strong motivation for not introducing neo-liberal policies. Faced with the unwillingness of a majority of voters to accept substantial cuts in the welfare system,[25] conservative and Christian democratic parties as a rule have decided to act as vote-seekers rather than policy-seekers. Moreover, governments for most of the time were not under the 'dictatorship of empty coffers' since economic prosperity (and privatisation revenue) provided sufficient resources, allowing them to postpone unpopular decisions. Finally, the configuration of political institutions – and differences in the strength of political parties within them – have put a limit on neo-liberal reform in several countries.[26]

What is the current outlook of conservative and Christian democratic parties? As all parties would do, they emphasise the achievements of their policies and stress the need to continue with them. In the United Kingdom and Germany, they have interpreted their electoral success over a decade as affirmation of their policies. Similarly, the electoral victories of non-socialists in France and Sweden in the early 1990s have been seen as the popular acceptance of neo-liberal policy proposals. The Spanish conservatives view the substantial improvement in their electoral standing in 1993 in a similar fashion, in particular given the fact that their competitors, the Spanish socialists, were among the first to adapt to neo-liberalism in the West European left. In Austria the ÖVP cannot claim increasing acceptance for neo-liberal policies on the basis of increasing electoral support, but it argues that things have improved since it can exercise influence in government.

Thus neo-liberal economic policies remain on the agenda. Conservative and Christian democratic parties want to continue with their policies and to extend them to areas which so far have been largely excluded from the application of neo-liberal reforms. This includes in particular the provision of *public* services which are seen to be provided without much consideration for efficiency. The reform of the public sector is to be carried out by marketisation and deregulation. Public sector employees are to be exposed to market pressures and consumers of public services are to be charged accordingly. Excessive regulation, that is, regulation 'in which the benefits far outweigh the costs', is to be abolished. Even in the United Kingdom which went farthest down the neo-liberal road, admirers of Mrs Thatcher concede that the problem of excessive regulation 'is if anything getting worse'.[27] Moreover, technological innovation is to be used to spread market-oriented solutions to those fields which had previously been spared because of excessive administrative costs involved in charging the consumers of public services on an individual base. Road pricing by the use of micro-electronics is a case in point. These points are concerned with the extension and intensification of neo-liberal policies. Germany constitutes a special case since reunification with a socialist economy has enormously increased the privatisation potential. In the United Kingdom now even supporters of this course have come to the conclusion that there is a need to reconcile free markets with community and thus to give more emphasis to another strand of conservatism.[28]

LEARNING TO LOVE THE MARKET: THE SOCIAL DEMOCRATS

Traditionally it was an implicit and widspread assumption among social democrats that the degree to which a society was socialist could be measured by the extent of state involvement in the production of goods and services. As David Miller has put it, 'Because socialism was the negation of capitalism, and capitalism relied on the market, state provision in place of market provision became the defining characteristic of socialism in practice.'[29] Thus the number of industries taken into state ownership, the percentage of GNP devoted to the welfare state, etc., could serve as a yardstick for socialism. Many social democratic theorists faced the market and the market economy 'with mental reservations' and have accepted it only 'as a concession to reality'.[30] The policies of social democratic governments in the 1970s corresponded to these perspectives insofar as they were interventionist and increased the size of the public sector, mainly by increasing the tax revenue.[31]

In the late 1970s or in the 1980s social democrats were forced on to the defensive when the limits of Keynesian policies became apparent.[32] They reacted in two ways, with pragmatic policies when they have held governmental office and with programmatic innovation which tries to meet the challenges of a changed economic and political situation when in opposition. Both strategies proceed from an analysis which can be summarised under three points: the recognition that the limits of a national economic strategy are very narrowly drawn, the need to give priority to demand-side and infrastructure policies, and the decreasing viability of traditional social democratic values. The first two of these points are concerned with the *economic* viability of economic policy, the third one faces the *political* feasibility of economic and societal options.

Limits of a national economic strategy. Social democrats have concluded that changes in the world economy have further reduced the leeway of national economic policy. In the 1980s the world economy finally emerged. The mobility of capital has increased enormously, partly due to a deregulation of financial markets. Capital is much more mobile than labour. A government policy which aims at improving the situation of labour has its limits precisely where it causes the flight of capital. Although this dilemma has always existed, it gained a new quality with the deregulation of the financial markets in the 1970s and 1980s.

The need to give priority to demand-side and infrastructure policies. To put it bluntly, social democrats have concluded that Keynesianism does not work any longer in the environment of the 1980s and 1990s. This holds equally true for parties such as the British Labour Party which had to recognize the failure of their previous strategies and parties such as the Austrian SPÖ which had been remarkably successful in applying Keynesian strategies. Social democratic parties now agree that demand-side policies have to be replaced by supply-side policies and public infrastructure programmes. Those of them which are in opposition and therefore do not have to face the problem of financing ambitious infrastructure programmes are more committed to this particular feature.

The viability of traditional social democratic values has been undermined. Over the last two or three decades the core group of the social democrats, the blue-collar workers, has declined in number. Even where social democratic parties have been able to compensate for this by recruiting members and in particular voters from the new middle class their situation has changed as the interest structure of their potential clientele has become more heterogeneous and is affected by two kinds of value change. On the one hand, value change has brought a new individualism. Paradoxically it has been caused partly by the successes of social democracy such as higher levels of education and better conditions of living.[33] Individualism is also strengthened by new forms of labour organisation, including geographical decentralisation by the use of new communication technologies, the use of profit centres and the break-up of large companies into small units, and flexible forms of labour. Besides these long-term developments one single historical event, the collapse of communism in Eastern Europe, contributed to the delegitimisation of economic state interventionism. On the other hand, value change means the emergence of postmaterialism. This means the negation of the traditional pattern of economic growth which has been a cornerstone of the Keynesian strategy of social democrats. It also means an emphasis on a different kind of individualism which rejects large-scale collective solutions.[34]

In responding to this twofold change social democrats can move to the right on the socio-economic left-right scale or move in the post-materialist direction. This puts them in a double squeeze. Value change in the neo-liberal direction not only means that social democrats want to avoid the image of parties of high taxes and low growth. More fundamentally parties of the left began to realise that it would be electorally disastrous to allow their non-socialist competitors to establish a monopoly on advocating freedom. The New Right defines freedom in an exclusively negative way and sees the major threat to it in excessive state activities. In recent years social democrats have become more willing to buy this argument, although they by no means accept it as an exclusive definition of freedom.[35]

Reactions at the Government Level

As governing parties social democrats have incorporated elements of neo-liberal economic strategy in a pragmatic and limited fashion in their policies or refrained from reversing neo-liberal policies, in particular privatisation, which had been introduced by their predecessors in government. The French Socialists abandoned their experiment of 'Socialism in One Country' in 1983 and introduced a policy of budgetary and financial rigour. They worked hard to reestablish company profits, took important steps in the deregulation of the financial and labour markets and did not reverse Chirac's 1986–88 privatisations.[36] Indeed, the government changes beteween socialists and non-socialists in 1986,

1988 and 1993 brought no fundamental policy change nor did electoral campaigns centre around conflicts over policy.

Soon after the Spanish Socialists assumed power in December 1982 they were faced with the failure of Socialist policies in France and Greece and immediately drew the conclusion that Keynesianism in one country was no longer possible.[37] Henceforth the PSOE government 'implemented an economic austerity program more akin to the supply-side policies of Ronald Reagan and Margret Thatcher (than to the French model of 1981), albeit with minor "socialist" correctives'.[38]

In Austria the social democrats have since 1986 subscribed to a 'conservative budget policy', as the Viennese economist Erich Streissler has put it, they have introduced a tax reform which substantially reduced both corporate taxes and the marginal income tax rate. Moreover Austrian social democrats have begun with privatisation and marketisation.[39] All this was not just a demand of the SPÖ's coalition partner, the ÖVP, but was also a result of the party's own economic policy deliberations.

In Sweden it was the social democrats who began with privatisation, paradoxically with industries which had been nationalised by the non-socialist coalition government of 1976–82. Social democrats also reduced the top tax rate, deregulated the financial markets, and began to question whether public services have to be provided by public monopolies.[40] It is even possible to add the British Labour Party to this list if one considers its policy after the IMF crisis in 1976, but the party did not stick to this realistic approach once in opposition.

Programmatic Innovation

At the programmatic level social democratic parties have made the attempt to combine their traditional goals with the market. Originally proposed by a group of British intellectuals, 'market socialism' has entered the programmatic debates of several social democratic parties. According to a theorist of the SPÖ this is the result of a trial and error process, of their own failures and the failures of the conservative economic policy of the 1980s,[41] and can best be described as a 'symbiosis of social democratic and liberal approaches'.[42] An analysis of the Labour Party's Policy Review has characterised it similarly, as 'modernized circumspect revisionism which acknowledges the failure of Keynesianism and in its acceptance of the social and economic changes has lost the optimism and radicalism of revisionism'.[43] The programmatic innovation can be summarised under three headings: review of state activities, marketisation and Europeanisation.

Review of state activities. Social democratic parties have given up the often implicit idea that an increase in the size of the public sector automatically promotes the achievement of social democratic goals, in particular equality. Social democrats no longer unconditionally defend existing state activities. Rather state ownership of industries and banks as well as government programmes and public services are to be reviewed as to whether they are still justified. Existing state activities may either be obsolete or less important than potential new activities. Since social democrats seem to agree that the public sector cannot be extended further, new state activities require the abandonment of existing ones.

Four out of the six social democratic parties to which this article makes reference have modified their programme according to this outline. The 1989 Policy Review of the British Labour Party is the 'most explicit rejection of the policy of expanding public ownership which the Party has ever made'.[44] The 1990 programme of the Swedish social democrats considers increasing expenditure no longer a solution, being neither advisable nor even feasible.[45] The Austrian SPÖ had already considerably reduced its claims about the function of a public sector in the 1978 basic party programme and went further with the new 1989 programme (*Sozialdemokratie 2000*). It states that the efficiency of the public sector has to be checked continuously and that the question of public ownership has to be decided in a non-ideological fashion. Economic policy-makers of the SPÖ have already concluded that there are indeed public services which have become an end in themselves rather than serving a legitimate purpose.[46]

The German SPD also produced a new programme in 1989. However, the party's left was able to exercise considerable influence in this debate and only last-minute efforts by the party leadership prevented a programme which would have fallen behind the Bad Godesberg programme of 1959 regarding state intervention in the economy. The final programme does not say very much about this issue but rather has responded to the second challenge social democratic parties face, postmaterialism. In any case the SPD's 1989 programme has frustrated the ambitions of the party's right to address the 'affluent majority'.[47] In Spain programmatic renewal also did not bring a breakthrough for the party's neo-liberal wing which, however, has been able to determine government policy. Although the *Programma 2000* did not bring the party in line with the government, it remained non-committal and hence does not constrain the government's room for manoeuvre.[48]

Marketisation. Social democratic parties have come to promote or at least to accept market-oriented solutions in those fields where they insist on the state's obligation for providing goods and services. Social democratic ideology determines *where* state intervention is required, but it does not specify *how* this intervention should be carried out. Being ready to use public resources for a certain goal does not imply that the respective goods and services should be provided by the state itself. Social democrats have become willing to consider the full range of alternatives up to total private provision of these goods and services. According to the Labour Party's Policy Review 'the delivery of a particular service has to be discussed pragmatically in terms of whether public or private provision is best in a particular case, rather than in terms of ideological principle'.[49] According to two Austrian cabinet members from the SPÖ only efficiency and effectiveness in the provision of goods and services should be considered when making this kind of decision.[50] And social democratic economic experts have gone so far as to accept that one can normally proceed from the assumption that 'private production is cheaper'.[51] In this new perspective of the left markets are seen as effective information systems and incentive systems. Making use of them does not mean abandoning traditional social democratic goals.[52]

For much of the postwar period competition for the provision of goods and services by the state had been rendered by expanding the public sector. This no longer seems possible since public sector growth reached its political and economic limits in the 1980s. Now it is necessary to choose which demands are to be fulfilled. This, in turn, means that competition for public goods and services becomes sharper. One consequence of this is making minimum winning coalitions in government formation and parliamentary voting more attractive. This argument is potentially important for those political systems which have been characterised by a high degree of consensus and the mutual respecting of the vital interests of the major political forces. In the present situation, it is the improvement of the efficiency of state activities through privatisation and marketisation which can reduce the conflict over the distribution of public goods and services and hence contribute to the maintenance of political consensus.[53]

The willingness of social democrats to review state activities has also been used to attack their main political competitors using their own weapons. In Austria social democrats have suggested policies of rolling back the state which are directed against the ÖVP's clientele, particularly in the agricultural sector.[54] Similarly, a 'deregulation from the left' is to remove pre-modern aspects of economic regulation.[55] It is interesting to see that it is social democrats who have tried to make an issue out of the fact that there are more laws against 'unfair competition' than there are promoting competition.

Europeanisation. Those social democratic parties which traditionally were sceptical or negative about European integration at the beginning of the 1990s have not only accepted integration into the European Community as something which cannot be avoided but have developed positive attitudes toward it. They envisage the EC as a chance to achieve social democratic goals which can no longer be reached by means of national policies. It is the British Labour Party which has made the most dramatic move. It had definitively rejected British membership in the EC in the early 1980s, in particular because EC membership would not have allowed 'socialist reforms' in the United Kingdom. Between 1983 and 1987 the Labour Party developed an ambivalent attitude towards the EC. Although EC membership was accepted this was not without many reservations. Since 1989, however, the Labour Party has been fully committed to European integration. This change reflects the more active role of the EC, but in the first instance it resulted from the prolonged and serious failure of the Labour Party and the unions to succeed in the domestic political arena. Europeanisation for them means a chance to promote what Mrs Thatcher termed 'socialism through the back door', in particular expansive social policies but also control of multinational companies and environmentalism.[56]

Austrian and Swedish social democrats have undergone a similar change though in a more piecemeal fashion and primarily due to other reasons. In the 1960s, the chairman of the Austrian social democrats, Bruno Pittermann, referred to the EEC as the 'capitalists' bloc', too close a relationship with which was not seen as favourable. His successor, Bruno Kreisky, established a pragmatic relationship with the EC and in the 1980s the SPÖ not only led the government which applied for EC membership but also integrated the European flag into the party logo.[57] In Sweden it was a labour government which applied for EC membership in 1991. Both membership applications resulted from the creation of the Single European Market which has put particular pressure on small and export-oriented countries outside the EC. Insofar there is nothing genuinely social democratic in EC integration and indeed the Swedish conservatives and the Austrian Christian democrats have been more committed to it than the social democrats of both countries. Moreover, as has been argued above, internationalisation of the economy also means a shift of power from the trade unions, whose clients are relatively immobile, to capital, which under the conditions of deregulated financial markets can easily be transferred to those countries which seem most attractive. Nevertheless, social democrats have begun to develop perspectives of how EC integration can be employed for their party goals. Reviving their internationalist tradition, social democrats see the EC as a framework which allows effective coordination at the levels of governments and trade unions and which for the first time provides the *possibility* of constituting a 'counter power' to multinational corporations.[58] In other words, the genuine social democratic perspective of EU integration is the chance for 'social democracy in one continent'.

Limits to Neo-Liberal Adaptation

Before dealing with the limits to neo-liberal adaptation it is useful to put it in a historical perspective. Without doubt the changes in the policies and programmes of social democratic parties as outlined above are substantial. They are not so striking, however, in a historical perspective. For the British Labour Party and the French Socialists, which have departed most from their positions of the early 1980s, the new developments meant little more than the return to an old track from which they had temporarily departed. In the Labour Party the early 1980s were the high tide of the left. As a consequence, the 1982 programme was 'almost . . . the left's archetypal platform. It provided the first steps in the transition to socialism with a comprehensive range of policies including a high level of state intervention, economic planning, import controls, an isolationist and neutralist foreign policy based on unilateralism, withdrawal from the EC'. The 1983 manifesto watered down some of these policies but was still 'the most radical set of policies of any European socialist party' and the 1987 manifesto was still committed to policies far left of those which had been advocated by the party over most of the post-war period.[59] Thus the Labour Party's Policy Review of 1989 only meant a return to what the Labour Party had been before losing governmental office in 1979. Similarly, the French Socialists subscribed to a left programme in the 1970s and early 1980s because of the need to have a common platform with the communists which, in turn, had been enforced on them by the French electoral system.[60] In contrast, the Austrian social democrats remained on the track they have followed throughout the postwar period. For them the incorporation of neo-liberal elements meant nothing more than a further step along a direction which was begun in 1945.

The pragmatic policies of social democratic governments were similar to but not identical with the policies carried out by governments under conservative or Christian democratic leadership. Privatisation for instance has been less forcefully introduced by social democrats than conservatives[61] and if a Labour government had come to office in the

United Kingdom in 1992 it would have shelved plans for further privatisation. Although social democratic parties have accepted a bunch of neo-liberal policies when revising their programmes, even those of them which have gone farthest down the neo-liberal road bear important differences with conservative and Christian democratic parties. There are two kinds of limits to a neo-liberal adaptation of social democratic parties: ideological and political limits.

Ideological limits. Social democrats have preserved some reservations about the role of the market. While for the New Right the market is morally right and economically efficient, for social democrats the market is essentially morally neutral; it can function as an efficient means of distributing certain goods, but there is a danger of producing distortions and inequalities.[62] Social democrats' place considerable emphasis on market failure and stress that the market does not provide essential things such as education and training, research and development, health, social services and social security, and it cannot protect the environment.[63] While it is true that conservatives accept state intervention where the market fails to provide the required incentives, for instance to ensure environmental protection, they envisage these interventions as making use of the market mechanism, for example, by taxing energy. Social democrats do not principally reject this, but they are more aware of the consequences for those groups which will not be able to afford increased energy prices because of their basic value of equality.[64] Thus parties of the left realise that in practice they may fail to reach their ideological goals by employing markets. Markets can ensure equality at the starting gate, not equality at the end,[65] in other words equality of opportunity rather than staightforward equality.[66] Moreover not all groups of people are seen to be equally fit for maximising their gains in a market. Thus, empowering ill-informed welfare clients may lead to their exploitation by the producers of welfare services if they are provided in a market environment.[67] Nevertheless, socialist theorists concede that 'some . . . advantages of markets are real'.[68]

When social democrats accept that the public sector cannot grow further or are even willing to accept cuts they are not motivated by the neo-liberal conviction that the smaller the public sector the better. Rather they are concerned with preserving of the public sector what can be preserved. Making the public sector slim is not a goal in itself but rather a means to avoid the conservative backlash. A more effective public sector, the goal of social democrats, does not only serve their immediate goals of providing certain goods and services. It also increases the acceptance for the public sector in a general way and therefore the possibility of providing public goods and services.[69]

Political limits. Even if party theorists and leaders did not have the ideological doubts, the internal power structure of social democratic parties would constitute a severe limit to neo-liberal adaptation. Social democratic parties have become public sector parties also in a sociological sense, that is, that public sector employees are overrepresented among their voters and activists. For this reason social democratic parties have often tended to represent the interests of the producers rather than the consumers of public services.[70] Even if the parties recognise this, overcoming vested interests remains a difficult and often politically costly task. Similarly, the trade unions – in particular those which represent the public sector and declining industries – are less convinced of the merits of incorporating neo-liberal elements in the economic policies of social democratic parties. The more this is the case and the closer the relationships between social democratic parties and trade unions, in particular the more the parties depend on trade unions, the more difficult it is to start with and push through neo-liberal programmatic innovation.[71]

Because of the ideological reservations, the non-ideological nature of accepting neo-liberal policies and the resistance of vested interests within the parties, recent programmes of social democratic parties as well as programmatic statements of their representatives contain many ambiguities. The commitment to check the usefulness of neo-liberal solutions on a case-to-case basis, for instance, leaves much room for interpretation.

CONCLUSION: A NEW NEOLIBERAL CONSENSUS?

This article has been concerned with the role which the major political families in Western Europe prescribe to the state in socio-economic questions. It has outlined the development of conservative and Christian democratic parties on the one hand and social democratic parties on the other since the 1960s, making reference to six countries. The main findings of this article can be summarised under five points.

First, in the 1970s and early 1980s conservative and Christian democratic parties deserted from the 'social democratic consensus' of the 1960s and converted to economic neo-liberalism. Second, in the 1980s and early 1990s social democrats also shifted considerably towards neo-liberal policy options, introducing a new policy convergence with conservative and Christian democratic parties. Third, as a result of these two shifts, compared to the 1960s, the whole political spectrum has shifted to the right. Fourth, the present situation bears similarities with the 1960s insofar as the major political families advocate a set of similar policies. Can one therefore speak of a new – neo-liberal – consensus which has replaced the previous 'social democratic consensus'? Probably yes, if one keeps in mind the qualifications which were made above about the limited extent and internal tensions which characterised the 'social democratic consensus'. About the same can be said about the neo-liberal consensus. Nevertheless it seems that the policy distance between the major political families in socio-economic questions is smaller now than it was in the 1960s. Now all parties believe in a market economy with some social corrective. Social democracy has finally given up its claim to aim at an alternative to capitalism.[72] Fifth, some differences between the political families (and between individual parties of the same family) about the scope of the social corrective to the market and the tasks of state intervention nevertheless still exist. European party politics therefore remain associated with different ideologies and competing policy options. It is only fair to say, however, that it requires close looking and sometimes even a magnifier to pin down these differences between the major political families.

NOTES

1. D.Bell, *The End of Idology* (NY: The Free Press, 1960); see also the subsequent discussion in C.I. Waxman (ed.), *The End of Ideology Debate* (NY: Funk & Wagnalls, 1968).
2. See A. Shonfield, *Modern Capitalism. The Changing Balance of Public and Private Power* (Oxford: OUP, 1965); R. Dahrendorf, *Life Chances: Approaches to Social and Political Theory* (London: Weidenfeld, 1980).
3. P.A. Hall (ed.), *The Political Power of Economic Ideas* (Princeton, NJ: Princeton UP, 1989), p.366; see also A. Przeworski, *Capitalism and Social Democracy* (Cambridge: CUP, 1985), pp.207–211.
4. S. Padget and W.E. Paterson, *A History of Social Democracy in Postwar Europe* (London: Longman, 1991), Ch.1, here p.35.
5. Y. Mény, *Government and Politics in Western Europe* (Oxford: OUP, 1990), p.52; R.E.M. Irving, *The Christian Democratic Parties of Western Europe* (London: Allen & Unwin, 1979), in particular Ch.1.
6. See B. Girvin (ed.), *The Transformation of Contemporary Conservatism* (London: Sage, 1988).
7. Girvin, 'Introduction: Varieties of Conservatism', in Girvin (note 6), p.2.
8. K.v. Beyme, *Political Parties in Western Democracies* (Aldershot: Gower, 1985).
9. S.M. Lipset and S. Rokkan, 'Cleavage structures, party systems, and voter alignments: An introduction', in idem (eds.), *Party Systems and Voter Alignments* (NY: The Free Press, 1967), pp.1–64; I. Budge, D. Robertson and D. Hearl (eds.), *Ideology, Strategy and Party Change: Spatial Analyses of Post-War Election Programmes in 19 Democracies* (Cambridge: CUP, 1987).
10. See, e.g., E. Damgaard, P. Gerlich and J.J. Richardson (eds.), *The Politics of Economic Crisis* (Aldershot: Avebury, 1989).
11. E. Grande, 'Neoconservatism without neoconservatives?', in Girvin (note 6), pp.55–77.
12. V. Lauber, 'Change and continuity in French conservatism since 1944', in Girvin (note 6), p.45.

13. See W.C. Müller, 'Conservatism and the transformation of the Austrian People's Party', in Girvin (note 6), pp.98–119; W.C. Müller, 'Die Österreichische Volkspartei', in H. Dachs *et al.* (eds.), *Handbuch des politischen Systems Österreichs* (Vienna: Manz, 1991), pp.227–46.
14. S.B. Ljunggren, 'Conservatism in Norway and Sweden', in Girvin (note 6), pp.120–44, here p.135.
15. See D.S. King, *The New Right* (London: Macmillan, 1987); N.P. Barry, *The New Right* (London: Croom Helm, 1987); Girvin (note 6), J. Vickers and V. Wright (eds.), *The Politics of Privatisation in Western Europe* (London: Frank Cass, 1989); G.Thompson, *The Political Economy of the New Right* (London: Pinter, 1990); V. Wright (ed.), *Les Privatisations en Europe* (Arles: Actes Sud, 1993).
16. See M.J. Crozier, S.P. Huntington and J. Watanuki, *The Crisis of Democracy* (NY: NYUP, 1975).
17. See the contribution of J.J. Richardson to this publication.
18. J. Grey, 'Conservatism, individualism and the political thought of the New Right', in J.C.D. Clark (ed.), *Ideas and Politics in Modern Britain* (London: Macmillan, 1990), pp.87–99, here pp.87–8. On the Conservatives' record in government see, among others, A. Gamble, *The Free Economy and the Strong State* (London: Macmillan, 1988), D. Kavanagh and A. Seldon (eds.), *The Thatcher Effect* (Oxford: OUP, 1989).
19. J. Leaman, 'The Rhetoric and Logic of the *Wende* – A Reply to Douglas Webber', *German Politics* 2/1 (April 1993), pp. 124–35.
20. Lauber, 'Change and continuity in French conservatism' (note 12), pp.50–1.
21. R. Klein, *The Politics of the NHS* (London: Longman, 1989).
22. P. Pierson and M. Smith, 'Bourgeois revolutions?' *Comparative Political Studies* 25/4 (1993), pp.487–520, here p.513.
23. D. Webber, 'Kohl's *Wendepolitik* after a decade', *German Politics* 1/2 (Aug. 1992), pp.149–80.
24. G. Ambrosius, 'Abbau und Ausbau der öffentlichen Wirtschaft in den 80er Jahren', in R. Voigt (ed.), *Abschied vom Staat – Rückkehr zum Staat?* (Baden-Baden: Nomos, 1993), pp. 265–83.
25. See the contribution of E. Tálos and G. Falkner to this publication.
26. See Grey, 'Conservatism . . .' (note 18) and King, *The New Right* (note 15), pp.111–13, 126 on Britain; E. Grande, 'Neoconservatism and conservative-liberal economic policy in West Germany', *European Journal of Political Research* 15 (1987), pp.281–96, Webber, 'Kohl's *Wendepolitik* after a decade' (note 23), and J. Schmid, *Die CDU* (Opladen: Leske + Budrich, 1990) on Germany. For a comparative perspective see Pierson and Smith, 'Bourgeois Revolutions' (note 22).
27. D. Willetts, 'Modern Conservatism', *Political Quarterly* 63/4 (1992), pp.413–21, here p.415.
28. D. Willetts, *Modern Conservatism* (London: Penguin, 1992), Chs.5 and 7. Cf. T. Honderich, *Conservatism* (London: Penguin, 1990), Ch.6.
29. D. Miller, 'Why markets?', in J. Le Grand and S. Estrin (eds.), *Market Socialism* (Oxford: Clarendon Press, 1989), pp.25–49, here p.28.
30. G. Chaloupek, 'Gesamtwirtschaftliche Planung, Interventionismus und Marktwirtschaft', in E. Nowotny (ed.), *Sozialdemokratische Wirtschaftspolitik* (Vienna: Löcker, 1992), pp.153–73, here p.163.
31. See F.G. Castles (ed.), *The Impact of Parties* (London: Sage, 1982); F.W. Scharpf, *Sozialdemokratische Krisenpolitik in Europa* (Frankfurt: Campus, 1987).
32. See Scharpf, *Sozialdemokratische Krisenpolitik in Europa*, Ch.11.
33. E. Nowotny, 'Sozialdemokratische Wirtschaftspolitik: Ein Überblick', in Nowotny (note 30), pp.9–35, here p.17.
34. See R. Inglehart, *Culture Shift in Advanced Industrial Society* (Princeton, NJ: Princeton UP, 1990).
35. D. Miller, 'Why markets?' (note 29), p.32; Nowotny (note 30), p.18.
36. P.A. Hall, 'The state and the market', in P.A. Hall, J. Hayward and H. Machin (eds.), *Developments in French Politics* (London: Macmillan, 1990), pp. 171–87;

P.G. Cerny and M.A. Schain (eds.), *Socialism, the State and Public Policy in France* (London: Pinter, 1985); P.Godt (ed.), *Policy-Making in France* (London: Pinter, 1989); P. Cerny, 'The"Little Big Bang" in Paris: financial market deregulation in a dirigiste system', *European Journal of Political Research* 17/2 (1989), pp.169–92 and C. Howell, 'The dilemmas of Post-Fordism: socialists, flexibility, and labour market deregulation in France', *Politics and Society* 20/1 (1992), pp.71–99; H. Dumez and A. Jeunemaitre, 'Les privatisations en France', in Wright (note 15), pp.105–32.
37. W. Merkel, 'Sozialdemokratische Politik in einer post-keynesianischen Ära?', *Politische Vierteljahresschrift* 30/4 (1989), pp.629–54.
38. D. Share, *Dilemmas of Social Democracy* (NY: Greenwood Press, 1989), p.73.
39. G. Winckler, 'Der Austrokeynesianismus und sein Ende', *Österreichische Zeitschrift für Politikwissenschaft* 17/3 (1988), pp.221–30; W.C. Müller, 'Privatising in a corporatist economy: the politics of privatisation in Austria', in Vickers and Wright (note 15), pp.101–16; D. Meth-Cohn and W.C. Müller, La réalité en face: les politiques de privatisation en Autriche, in Wright (note 15), pp.209–32.
40. T. Tilton, *The Political Theory of Swedish Social Democracy* (Oxford: Clarendon Press, 1991), pp.236–47; J. Pontusson, *The Limits of Social Democracy* (Ithaca: Cornell UP, 1992), pp.115–21; J.-E. Lane, 'Privatisations et dérégulation: Le modéle Suédois en question', in Wright (note 15), pp. 233–53.
41. Nowotny, 'Sozialdemokratische Wirtschaftspolitik' (note 30).
42. E. Nowotny, 'Sozialdemokratie und Staat', in Nowotny (note 30), pp.107–26, here p.126.
43. M.J. Smith, 'A return to revisionism? The Labour Party's Policy Review', in idem and J. Spear (eds.), *The Changing Labour Party* (London: Routledge, 1992), pp.13–28, here p.28.
44. A. Gamble, 'The Labour Party and economic managment', in Smith and Spear (eds.), *The Changing Labour Party*, pp.61–74, here p.65.
45. D. Sainsbury, 'The Swedish Social Democrats and the Legacy of Continuous Reform: Asset or Dilemma?', *West European Politics* 16/1 (Jan. 1989), pp.39–61, here p.49.
46. Ederer and Lacina, 'Markt, Staat, Sozialdemokartie', in Nowotny (note 30), pp.53–62, here p.60.
47. See P. Lösche and F. Walter, *Die SPD: Klassenpartei – Volkspartei – Quotenpartei* (Darmstadt: Wissenschaftliche Buchgesellschaft, 1992), pp.125–31; S. Padgett, 'The German Social Democrats. A Redefinition of Social Democracy or Bad Godesberg Mark II?', *West European Politics* 16/1 (Jan. 1993), pp. 20–38.
48. R. Gillespie, ' "Programma 2000": The Appearance and Reality of Socialist Renewal in Spain', *West European Politics* 16/1 (Jan. 1993), pp.78–96.
49. Gamble, 'The Labour Party and economic management', in Smith and Spear (note 43), pp.61–74, here p.66.
50. Ederer and Lacina, 'Markt, Staat, Sozialdemokratie' (note 46), pp.60–1.
51. Chaloupek, 'Gesamtwirtschaftliche Planung' (note 30), pp.168–9.
52. J. Le Grand and S. Estrin, 'Market socialism', in idem (note 29), p.3; Miller, 'Why markets?' (note 29), p.28; B. Gould, *A Future for Socialism* (London: Cape, 1989), pp.95–6.
53. Chaloupek, 'Gesamtwirtschaftliche Planung', p.169.
54. See, e.g., Ederer and Lacina, 'Markt, Staat, Sozialdemokratie', p.55.
55. P. Szopo, 'Deregulierung in Österreich: Problematik und Ansätze', *Wirtschaft und Gesellschaft* 12/1 (1986), pp.43–61.
56. S. Tindale, 'Learning to Love the Market: Labour and the European Community', *Political Quarterly* 63 (1992), pp.276–300; S. George and B. Rosamond, 'The European Community', in Smith and Spear (note 43), pp.171–84.
57. See D.M. Schulz, 'Austria in the International Arena: Neutrality, European Integration and Consociationalism', in K.R. Luther and W.C. Müller (eds.), *Politics in Austria: Still a Case of Consociationalism?* (London: Frank Cass, 1992), pp.173–200 (also *WEP* 15/1, Jan. 1992).

58. Nowotny, 'Sozialdemokratische Wirtschaftspolitik', pp.27–30; Chaloupek, 'Gesamtwirtschaftliche Planung', p.170. For an early German perspective see P. Glotz, *Manifest für eine neue Europäische Linke* (Berlin: Sieder, 1985). See C. Lemke and G. Marks, 'From decline to demise? The fate of socialism in Europe', in C. Lemke and G. Marks, *The Crisis of Socialism in Europe* (Durham: Duke UP, 1992), pp.1–20, here pp.15–16 for a pessimistic assessment of the chances for European cooperation of Labour.
59. M.J. Smith, 'The Labour Party in Opposition', in Smith and Spear (eds.), *The Changing Labour Party* (note 43), pp.3–12, here pp.6 and 10.
60. See S. Hazareesingh, *Political Traditions in Modern France* (Oxford: OUP, 1994).
61. W. Merkel, 'Verstaatlichung, Privatisierung und Sozialdemokratie: ein westeuropäischer Vergleich', in H. Abromeit and U. Jürgens (eds.), *Die politische Logik wirtschaftlichen Handelns* (Berlin: Sigma, 1992).
62. Smith, 'A return to revisionism?' (note 46), p.24
63. See, e.g., Gamble, 'The Labour Party and economic management' (note 44), p.67; Smith, 'A return to revisionism?', p.24.
64. Ederer and Lacina (note 46), pp.56–7.
65. Estrin and Le Grand, 'Market socialism' (note 52), p.8
66. D. Rae *et al.*, *Equalities* (Cambridge, MA: Harvard UP, 1981).
67. J. Le Grand, 'Market, Welfare, and Equality', in Le Grand and Estrin (note 29), pp. 193–211, here.
68. Ibid., p.198
69. See Ederer and Lacina (note 46), p.60.
70. Cf. Nowotny (note 42), p.118; Ederer and Lacina (note 46), p.58; H. Kitschelt, 'Class Structure and Social Democratic Party Strategy', *British Journal of Political Science* 23 (1993), pp. 299–337.
71. T.A. Koelble, 'Recasting social democracy in Europe: A nested games explanation of strategic adjustment in political parties', *Politics and Society* 20/1 (1992), pp.51–70.
72. See D. Meth-Cohn, 'Der Abbau der Verstaatlichungsidee in der SPÖ und der Labour Party', *Österreichische Zeitschrift für Politikwissenschaft* 17/3 (1988), pp.249–62; S.M. Lipset, 'No Third Way: a comparative perspective on the left', in H.-D. Klingemann, R. Stöss and B. Wessels (eds.), *Politische Klasse und politische Institutionen* (Opladen: Westdeutscher Verlag, 1991), pp.57–106.

FURTHER READING

Many publications deal with the most recent period of development of conservative and Christian democratic parties (i.e., since the late 1970s). The most comprehensive in terms of geographical coverage and various dimensions of conservatism is Brian Girvin (ed.), *The Transformation of Contemporary Conservatism* (London: Sage, 1988). The following three books mainly focus on Anglo-Saxon countries: Desmond S. King, *The New Right* (London: Macmillan, 1987); Norman P. Barry, *The New Right* (London: Croom Helm, 1987); Grahame Thompson, *The Political Economy of the New Right* (London: Pinter, 1990). The most recent comparative study is Paul Pierson and Miriam Smith, 'Bourgeois revolutions?', *Comparative Political Studies* 25/4 (1993), pp. 487–520.

In contrast, the most recent period of ideological and political change of social democratic parties (i.e., since the 1980s) has not yet received much coverage. Stephen Padgett and William E. Paterson, *A History of Social Democracy in Postwar Europe* (London: Longman, 1991) is a must for an overview of the whole postwar period. Fritz W. Scharpf, *Crisis and Choice in European Social Democracy* (Ithaca: Cornell UP, 1991) is a sophisticated analysis of the social democrats' economic policy until the early 1980s. A relatively recent and comprehensive account is Seymour M. Lipset, 'No Third Way: a comparative perspective on the left', in Hans-Dieter Klingemann, Richard Stöss and Bernhard Wessels (eds.), *Politische Klasse und politische Institutionen* (Opladen: Westdeutscher Verlag, 1991), pp.57–106.

The Role of the State within Social Policy

GERDA FALKNER and EMMERICH TÁLOS

This study gives an overview of the considerable modifications of the role of the state in the field of social policy since the 1980s. Social measures are more oriented towards economic considerations than in the phase of expansion of the welfare state in the postwar decades. The increased heterogenity of the labour market and in working conditions has increasingly been reproduced within social security. A shift between the three essential factors of social reproduction (state, market, family) is reflected by the shrinking coverage of social security and the increased risk of poverty within the welfare systems. Last, but not least, considerable changes at the procedural level of social regulation have focused on the decentralisation of regulation (collective agreements, enterprise level agreements, and individual agreements).

Despite the divergence in aims and structures of the West European welfare states there was a clear trend towards broadening state regulations during the first postwar decades. Social scientists have particularly emphasised the expansion of social security systems in terms of inclusion of new groups and of the increase of social security expenditures.[1] No less important were changes in working conditions and industrial relations. These were based on substantial measures (e.g., working time reductions, protection from dismissal) as well as procedural regulations (e.g., introduction and extension of co-determination, standardisation of collective bargaining).[2] Both working conditions (with the exception of Great Britain) and social security were subject to a high degree of regulatory density and intensity. The regulatory activities of the welfare state crucially contributed to improving and standardising of the social reproduction conditions of the workforce as well as of the population in general.

The expansion and differentiation of welfare policies took place, especially from a contemporary perspective, during a long phase of prosperity, with economic growth as well as increases in incomes and jobs.[3] The relationship between economic development and the development of the welfare state was not of a unilateral nature: the welfare state contributed, in all its dimensions, to economic and social stabilisation.[4]

Politics corresponded to the economic context of the welfare state. Reform of living and working conditions made up a central aspect of political options for social democrats and the trade unions, which had, after 1945, achieved the status of major political actors. The extension of the welfare state has to a large extent been shaped by this factor.[5] Another decisive factor was the widespread political consensus (not only on the 'left' of the political spectrum) on the extension of the welfare state – regardless of all differences about its shape.

In comparison with previous decades it is possible to detect change on several levels since the 1980s. Welfare state economies are now faced with significant problems and challenges which contrast with the prosperous postwar phase. Obvious indicators are, besides a mass production and mass consumption crisis, lower growth rates, the pressure of intensified international competition and uncertainty, structural problems, and, last but not least, consistent mass and long-term unemployment.[6] The burden of economic problems and the concomitant efforts to restructure production and work organisation provide the background for social policy since the 1980s. Generally, the policy is intended to give employers more leeway and to decrease their costs.

This is to be seen, on the one hand, in the break-up of political consensus over the necessity and functionality of the welfare state and, on the other hand, in the growing criticism of traditional welfare regulation. Parallel to these calls for change slogans such as like 'Mehr Markt – weniger Staat', 'mehr Markt am Arbeitsmarkt', 'deregulation and flexibilisation' are becoming more credible.[7]

Meanwhile structural problems of the welfare state have become visible alongside changed economic conditions. Thus, in the field of social security, problems of financing as well as problems of exclusion and risks of poverty have appeared. With regard to working conditions there is a gap between the de facto plurality of forms of work and the standardised regulations often oriented towards the Standard Employment Relationship ('*Normalarbeitsverhältnis*'[8]). Furthermore there is a discrepancy – at least from the demand-side economists' view – between regulation at the legal level and the desired or necessary flexibility of working conditions.

In short, the burden of increased economic and social problems, the structural problems of the welfare state as well as changes in social policy options have provided the background for changes in welfare policy.

It is these changes which are the topic of our contribution. First, we shall summarise the social policies which have been implemented since the 1980s in eight West European countries which are distinctive in size as well as in structure of the welfare system (employment oriented, citizenship oriented or a type combining both principles). Second, we shall analyse, from a comparative perspective, the trends in central subfields of social policy, including (a) equal treatment; (b) regulation of working hours and of 'atypical' forms of work and protection from dismissal; (c) unemployment and pension insurance schemes. Finally, we shall try to answer the question whether the role of the state in social policy since the 1980s has been characterised by continuity or change.

DEVELOPMENTS IN SELECTED COUNTRIES

Sweden

Until recently Sweden belonged to the most advanced and stable welfare states. Current developments, however, show that not only the environment of the Swedish welfare system has changed but the social policy agenda as well. Restrictions of benefits as well as challenges to labour law regulations have become part of the political agenda. The state's role in securing and regulating economic and social living conditions inside and outside the workplace was modified later than in many other countries. During the 1980s, only few such aspects (which were counterbalanced by progress in other fields) were to be found.

(a) The legal bases of the *policy of equal treatment* and of measures altering the traditional split of roles and tasks between the sexes were already in place in the 1970s. In 1980 the 'Law on Equality of Women and Men at the Workplace' came into force and combined the prohibition of discrimination with requirements for employers actively to promote equality. To secure implementation, the Equal Opportunities Commission and the Equal Opportunities Ombudsman were introduced. In 1991 these rules were altered so that companies now have to facilitate the combination of work and parenthood for women and men and to prevent sexual harassment at the workplace.[9] The fact that the duty for the employer to work actively on equality in the enterprise has been lifted[10] may be seen as a step backwards. Besides incentives for a decrease in labour market segregation Swedish policy also includes specific legal measures that make it easier to fulfil both family and employment commitments. The 'parent insurance', introduced in 1974, represents a first step towards a continuing extension of maternity leave to a parental leave system.[11] Although plans for prolonging parental leave from 15 to 18 months (1990) respectively to 24 months (1992) were postponed, the 1980s brought a significant extension of parental leave in case of a child's sickness (from 60 to 90 days per child and year).

(b) Swedish labour law was mainly developed during the 1970s (protection from dismissal 1974, Shop Steward Law 1974, Law on the Working Environment 1977, Law on Paid Holidays 1978).[12] Some smaller alterations were made during the 1980s (under the conservative coalition governments): a certain liberalisation of the rigid protection from dismissal took place in 1982 with the admission of probationary fixed-term contracts. Hand in hand with the codification of dispersed legal regulations concerning annual working time, a regulation of overtime work for part-time workers as well as increased flexibility as to working hours were adopted in 1982. Flexible working hours may now be negotiated within the national collective agreement by employers and employees themselves. In autumn 1992 a major austerity package was presented which included among other things a cut in paid holidays of two days per year. At the same time a review of labour law (with such points of discussion as, for example, protection from dismissal) was announced.[13]

(c) No serious changes were made in Sweden during the 1980s in the field of *social security* (i.e., unemployment and pension schemes). Examples of partial modification are the increase in prescription charges for patients within the health insurance system, the reduction of the level of partial pensions (withdrawn by the Social Democrats during the mid-1980s) and the reform of the widow's and widower's as well as the orphan's pension (giving priority to the support of children).[14]

In addition to health insurance, where the Social Democrats had already cut benefits in 1991, the new Centre-Right coalition (partly in co-operation with the Social Democrat opposition) intends to reduce the budget deficit by taking steps in the fields of retirement and unemployment insurance. The planned separation of the cost of both health and work injuries insurance from the Swedish national budget would have significant effects on social security. The introduction of a cut in sick pay and the abolition of payments for the first day that an employee reports ill were already agreed upon by the end of 1992. For 1993 cuts in benefits, non-indexation of the top level of benefits and the introduction of five so-called *karensdagar* – unpaid qualifying days for receipt of benefits – are envisaged for the unemployment insurance. No less important are the plans for pension insurance: the retirement age is to be raised from 65 to 66 years and benefits are to be cut. Moreover, a reduction of compensation in partial pension insurance from 60 to 62 years is again on the agenda.[15]

Italy

In Italy the welfare state continued to be expanded during the 1970s. This included, for example, the universalisation of the health service in 1978, going beyond the traditional orientation towards salaried employment. The 1980s brought some further modifications to the traditional regulations. Plans for significant measures in pension insurance were proposed by the Amato government within the framework of the 'Urgency Programme' aimed at cutting the budget deficit.

(a) In contrast to other EC-member states Italy had already passed a law comprehensively redefining the *positions of men and women* in labour and social security law in 1977.[16] A law passed in 1991 goes even further by providing positive action to ensure equality. Such initiatives by public bodies, unions and/or enterprises receive financial support from the Ministry of Labour. At the same time a national commission was established to promote the implementation of equality and equal opportunity.[17]

(b) During the 1980s modifications to the Italian regulation of employment conditions focused on such aspects as protection from dismissal and on working hours. The prevalent pluralisation of work forms was legalised: a law passed in 1984 legalised part-time work in all forms.[18] In 1988 part-time and flexitime work was also legalised for public services. An exception is the prohibition of temporary agency work, which is still in force, though under debate.

The existing ban on night work for women was relaxed in 1987 and legal changes allowing for alterations in collective agreements were introduced. Moreover, as in other countries, collective bargaining played an important role in the flexibilisation of working hours. Reductions in working hours were exchanged for greater flexibility for the companies.[19]

The conclusion of fixed-term contracts of employment for limited periods each year[20] had already been made possible by a law-decree of 1977 but only for the trade and tourism sectors, and was extended to all other economic sectors in 1983. Furthermore a law of 1987 broadened the possibilities for fixed-term contracts: additional reasons for the determination of such contracts may be determined by collective agreement. With regard to young people fixed-term working or training contracts, for periods of two years, were first allowed in 1986. A law passed in 1990 points in the opposite direction and extended protection from dismissal to employees of small enterprises.[21]

(c) Despite increasing rates of unemployment the Italian *unemployment insurance* with its extremely low benefit rates, which until 1988 amounted to only 800 lire per day,[22] was only gradually improved. A law adopted in 1988 provides for a compensation rate of 7.5 per cent of the average daily salary. Yet when confronted with major labour market problems, the government, in March 1993, announced, besides an active employment policy, a rise in unemployment benefits.[23]

While the 1980s brought improvements in the field of social and minimum pensions, the early 1990s, as in Sweden, saw serious proposals to cut benefits. Public employees' privileges in pension insurance are to be abolished. For 1993 early retirement in the private as well as the public sector is to be stopped and no further increase in any pension scheme is to take place until 1994. Further important proposals concern the raising of the retirement age, for men from 60 to 65 years, for women from 55 to 60, a reduction in early retirement benefits, a step-by-step extension of eligibility requirements for pensions from 15 to 20 years and the calculation of pensions on the basis of 10 instead of 5 years.[24]

Germany

The 1980s brought an end to the expansion phase of the German welfare state. Significant and durable changes in social security and labour law were introduced (e.g., loosening of protective measures, cuts in benefits). Expansionary and positive measures are to be found solely in the field of equal treatment.

(a) In fulfilling EC directives Germany passed an *Equal Treatment* Law in 1980. During the past few years some attempts to improve and widen it have been made. One example is a draft bill (1990) which aimed at establishing codification of procedures in cases of discrimination at job entry or at promotion as well as non-discriminating job offers. A recent draft law by the minister of women's affairs aims at promoting equality in the public services and protecting women from sexual harassment at the workplace.[25]

b) Although the conservative-liberal coalition's option of *flexibilisation* was also realised in other fields (Protection of Young Workers at Work Act 1984, a law on fixed-term contracts at universities 1985),[26] the Employment Promotion Act 1985 represents the most significant development. Thus, non-standardised forms of contracts of employment and working conditions were regulated with the explicit goal of creating more favorable conditions for flexibilisation of work. The regulative action dealt with part-time work (placing it on an equal footing with full-time jobs), job-sharing and work-at-call.

At the level of collective bargaining a reduction of working time was exchanged for flexibilisation.[27] The possibility of limiting the scope of protection from dismissal via the legalised fixed-term contracts is closely connected with the promotion of working-time flexibilisation. In the case of newly hired persons dismissal is possible now for the first 18 months, in the case of new smaller size enterprises (with fewer than 21 employees) for two years. The relaxation of regulation affecting enterprises was also achieved by lessening obligations arising out of the 'Sozialpläne'[28] and by not counting short-term employees as staff when the number of staff members would decide on the applicability of regulations (e.g., concerning protection from dismissal).[29]

(c) Whereas the steps taken in labour law aimed at relaxing traditional requirements, German activity, during the 1980s, in the field of *social security* fought the financing problems at a time of increasing unemployment, more early retirements and demographical changes as well as new political priorities (budget consolidation, more flexibility for enterprises). Contrary to the field of labour law the traditional orientation towards the Standard Employment Relationship in social security was not only upheld but was even strengthened to some extent (e.g., by the introduction of better unemployment benefits for longer working careers, tightened principles of insurance and equivalance in pensions insurance).

By the early 1980s the social-liberal coalition had already changed the eligibility criteria and prolonged the period of suspension from unemployment benefits for those who refuse suitable employment. The conservative-liberal government cut benefits even further: The ratio of earnings replacement for single people was cut by 5 percentage points for insurance benefits and by two percentage points for assistance benefits.[30] The largely suspected abuse of benefits was a subject of legal action (e.g., 8th amendment to the Employment Promotion Act 1987, introduction of a social security identity-card 1989). Related to the so-called *Solidarpakt*[31] the government is considering, besides fighting 'abuse', new plans for cuts in unemployment benefits.[32]

In the field of pension insurance specific measures were taken by the 1983 law concerning independent artists, the 1985 amendment concerning the survivors' pensions and the granting of credit for years of childcare, the 1987 law on partial pensions for old aged persons and promotion of consecutive entry into retirement. Far-reaching steps were taken with the social insurance pension reform,[33] which was agreed upon in 1989 and has been in force since 1992. The central aspects of this reform are the linking of pensions to the development in net salaries, the prolongation of working life, with a step-by-step rise of the retirement age to 65 years from 2001 on, a rise in benefits for later pension entry, and a cut in benefits for early retirements. The resulting savings are considered sufficient for consolidating the financial situation of the insurance system despite a cost push resulting from demographic developments. The introduction of minimum standards was explicitly rejected by the German government.

Austria

Since the 1980s developments in Austria with respect to its employment-oriented social security system[34] may be characterised as 'adaptation' to international developments on the one hand (e.g., equal treatment policy) and to changing political options and economic and social conditions on the other (in the field of unemployment and retirement insurance policy). The change in direction seen in other countries has been more moderate in Austria. This has certainly been favoured by relative economic success as well as favourable labour market developments, political conditions in which the main parties and interest groups co-operated, and the considerable room for manoeuvre allowed within the framework of labour regulations.

(a) As already exemplified by the very first *Equal Treatment* Law of 1979, Austrian policy during the 1980s was mainly characterised by its adaptation to the higher standards of the EC and some other European countries.[35] The goal of equal treatment was gradually extended from equal pay to other more specific aspects of work. In 1985 a prohibition of discriminating job offers and equal treatment for fringe benefits and in professional training were introduced. The year 1990 saw the extension of the equal treatment principle to personnel recruitment, dismissal and promotion regulations, as well as the establishment of an Ombudsperson for equality matters.

Equality was also promoted outside the traditional field of equality rules, with the introduction of parental leave which can be taken alternately by one of the parents or divided between them (from 1989 for one year and since 1990 for two years). The most recent package of equality-oriented reforms passed in December 1992 has its roots in work by the Ministry of Women's Affairs as well as in a Constitutional Court's ruling removing the unequal pension age for men and women on the one hand, and in adaptations to the corresponding EC rules on the other. Adaption of certain laws was also made necessary as Austria is a signatory of the European Economic Space Treaty. This package contains, for example, the extension of the equal pay principle to work of equal value, the prohibition of indirect discrimination and a raise in indemnities.

(b) Regarding the regulation of *contracts of employment and working conditions* there was no significant change to the legal norms.[36] Change did, however, occur in regulation of temporary agency work in 1989, the extension of possible exemptions from the ban on women's night work in 1986 and the prolongation of the opening hours in commercial trade. This does not mean, however, that the international trend of deregulation and flexibilisation has left Austria untouched at all, especially as the following changes to working time have occurred. In contrast to earlier periods, since the 1980s, there has been a broad consensus that any reduction should be negotiated between the major interest groups and not be fixed by law. Since 1985, as in many other countries, there have been agreements on increasing flexibilisation on the part of enterprises[37] in return for a reduction in working time beyond the legally fixed level of 40 hours (which has been in force since 1975). 'Atypical' forms of work and of contracts of employment have also increased in Austria but to a lesser extent than in other countries. This development is a way of circumventing labour law ('flight out of labour law')[38] without explicitly changing its standards. Austrian labour law gives enough opportunities for this: for example, there are no barriers establishing fixed-term contracts when hiring employees or justifying dismissals by economic crisis. According to Runggaldier, Austrian labour law has so far proven to be flexible enough to meet the special requirements of major economic crises or of crises of individual enterprises.[39]

(c) The direction of developments in the field of *unemployment insurance* has not been uniform.[40] Since 1987 various amendments to the respective laws have brought some improvements, as for example in 1988 when the 'full earning clause' ('*Vollverdienstklausel*')[41] was abolished. Further examples include the extension of unemployment benefits to economic crisis regions, the introduction of a uniform net compensation rate in unemployment benefits and the prolongation of the duration of benefits according to the age of the recipient. However, benefits were also reduced: unemployment benefits are now suspended for as long as one receives holiday compensation or dismissal compensation. The level of '*Notstandshilfe*'[42] was cut from 95 to 92 per cent of unemployment benefits. The period of exclusion from benefits ('*Sperrzeiten*') if suitable work is rejected and the qualifying period for the entitlement to unemployment benefits for young people were extended.

Compared with these measures concerning unemployment benefits the development within *pension insurance policy* has largely been of a uniform nature: in accordance with the priority given to budget consolidation, amendments in the 1980s have led to a strengthening of the insurance principle. This has been achieved, on the one hand, by cuts in '*Soziale Komponenten*' such as the elimination of the 'basic amount' in 1984, the elimination of the time spent at school or university is as being relevant for the calculation of benefits and, on the other hand, by changes in the calculation basis for benefits with the introduction of linear rates of increase and a prolongation of the period of calculation in 1988.[43] The effect of these measures is a reduction in the level of pension benefits.

The most recent modifications are similar to the German reform: gradually raising the retirement age for women (between 2018 and 2028), raising pension benefits according to the net compensation rate instead of the practised adaptation to the gross earnings developments, introducing flexible pensions and reducing benefits for those taking early retirement. Moreover, time spent for raising children is now to be included in calculating pensions. An expansionary social security innovation is the introduction of an attendance allowance for people with disabilities and frail elderly people, with seven categories according to the degree of need.[44]

Great Britain

The Thatcher government – despite all the attacks on existing standards (labour law, social insurance, influence of the unions) – had to give up its initial plan for a far-reaching retreat of the state from the field of social security. Under the pressure of public opinion only gradual changes were introduced. Despite the political option of deregulation the Thatcher government did not refrain from the use of regulation for achieving its goals within the fields of income policy, labour market policy, union legislation, and taxation (e.g., the burden of taxes increased for everybody except the highest 5 per cent of income earners[45]). Even within social policy the 'retreat of the state' occurred only partly with traditional forms of regulation being replaced by newer ones. The result was a new group of 'winners', those who were already wealthy.[46]

(a) With respect to *equal treatment policy* Great Britain has, since the 1980s, implemented only the relevant EC directives: equal pay for work of equal value in 1983, equal treatment within the state social security system in 1985, no more exceptions for small enterprises and annulling discriminating collective agreements in 1986, equal treatment in statutory systems of social security in 1989. In part this was done only after rulings by the European Court of Justice. Besides, a brochure was published against sexual harassment suggesting proceeding informally in such cases.[47]

(b) British *labour law*, which by international comparison had traditionally been quite poor, was under Thatcher cut back even further. Protection against dismissal was progressively weakened (in 1980, 1984,

1985 and 1989), and only employees who have been working for at least two years with the company are entitled to receive a written explanation for their dismissal. It should be said that administrative approval for dismissal had never been necessary in Britain.[48]

Concerning working hours there was no need for further flexibilisation by the Thatcher administration, since no general legal limitation existed. However, for part-time employees a 1985 Act provided for a flexible 13 weeks period of calculation of work allowing for 16 to 29 hours per week. Job-splitting was even promoted by the introduction of financial incentives. For fixed-term contracts restrictions had never existed in Great Britain.

With regard to remuneration the Wages Act, in 1986, brought about a loss in influence for the Wages Councils, as, in the first instance, young people were excluded from the scope of minimum pay regulations. The hiring of young people at very low salaries was even promoted by state subsidies to the employer. In 1992 Wages Councils were abolished so that legal statutory minimum pay no longer exists: 'The government believes that decisions on pay are best left to employers and individual employees.'[49] Consequently, there is a strong tendency towards individual agreements between employers and employees.[50]

Improved rights for the labour force were, during the Thatcher period, almost exclusively brought about by EC directives. Such directives included protection of employees' rights in cases of company takeovers, employers' insolvency, mass redundancies and the protection of pregnant and nursing mothers.

(c) In the field of *social insurance* the Thatcher government changed flat rate benefits for special groups into discretionary loans and increased social control over the poor.[51] Under the conditions of high unemployment, which reached 13.5 per cent in 1985 though it had been reduced by statistical changes, the British government increased the pressure to accept any offer of work. This was brought about by abolishing income-related supplementary benefits in 1982 and by real cuts in benefits and supplements, for instance, via non-indexation, taxation of benefits, longer periods of non-eligibility in cases of rejection of suitable work, the obligation to seek work actively in order to qualify for benefits. With regard to the contributions, more of the cost was placed on employees and households while companies were relieved.

The planned abolition of SERPS (State Earnings Related Pension Scheme), which had only been introduced during the 1970s, did not succeed. Instead it was made less attractive by cuts in benefits, by restricted criteria of eligibility and by incentives for 'contracting out' of statutory systems and opting for company schemes.[52]

France

During the last decade French economic and social policy has been characterised by a series of almost contradictory activities.[53] The brief initial phase after the change of power in 1981, which lasted until mid-1982, saw nationalisation programmes and 'social growth', that is an increase in demand brought about by an increase of mass incomes and social benefits. Austerity measures intended to save and stabilise the economy followed. The 'Delors plan' with its restrictive budget, demand and income policies attempts to abolish the automatic adaptation of incomes to changes in price levels. Since 1984 a policy of privatization, deregulation and liberalisation has been followed mainly in anticipation of the EC internal market programme and increased pressure brought about by international competition.[54] Since March 1986 French social policy has aimed principally at loosening mandatory labour regulations.[55]

(a) In contrast to Great Britain, French *equal treatment policy* went beyond the EC directives (implemented in 1981, 1983 and 1989) and was innovative in the early 1990s by adopting a law on sexual harassment.[56] Employers have to give an annual report on the position of women in their company to the works council, and since 1990 the social partners have been obliged to negotiate measures to combat any shortcomings. In 1984 the French government set up a scheme of parental leave without pay for two years and the possibility of working part-time because of family commitments.

Although the ban on women's night work had already been partially lifted in 1987, in cases where national interest and collective agreement allow it,[57] it was a French case which caused the European Court of Justice to declare that a ban on nightwork for only one of the sexes was a forbidden form of discrimination.[58]

(b) In the field of regulation of *working conditions*, the announcement of a reduction of working hours to 35 hours and the establishment of 39 hours per week by law at the same time as increasing minimum incomes enormously are to be mentioned. Simultaneously, some flexibilisation followed: overtime work does not now require administrative approval but may be exchanged for extra time off as long as the total of 130 hours per year is not passed. Weekly working hours are adaptable by collective agreement. Such agreements have to take place at least annually and negotiate the effective duration and shaping of working hours, but may also decide on a ban on Sunday and night work.

In 1987 flexibilisation was even extended by the so-called Séguin Act:

collective agreement may now increase the weekly working hours up to a limit of 44 hours as long as the annual average of 39 hours per week is not exceeded. Possible exceptions from the ban on night and Sunday work were increased and cyclical models of working hours for shift work were allowed.[59]

Fixed-term contracts had, in France, already been restricted since the 1970s. In 1982 they were allowed under certain specified and exceptional circumstances for up to one year only, as was temporary agency work. Regarding the financial implications of employment contract termination they were put on an equal footing with traditional contracts.[60] Those regulations were extended for two years in 1985 and 1986 but may be loosened even further by collective agreement. In this arena the possibility of allowing contracts of employment with seasonally flexible working hours also exists.[61] In 1990, the maximum duration of fixed-term contracts was, following a collective agreement, restricted again to 18 months and termination payments were introduced.[62] Part-time work has been promoted financially since the mid-1980s and may, since 1991, be pursued as an individual right.

France made significant steps towards flexibilisation also in protection from dismissal. Since 1986 no administrative approval has been necessary for dismissal for economic reasons, and even in cases of mass redundancies the reasons given are not subject to control any more.[63] In 1987 individual dismissal was further simplified and accelerated.[64]

Innovative steps were made in the field of labour law in 1984, primarily by the introduction of leave in order to create an enterprise or for personal training. After two years with a company, employees are entitled to redundancy payment. In 1987 and 1988 laws providing for a quota of 5 per cent of employees to be disabled workers were passed.[65] The regulative activity of the French government regarding a ban on smoking at the workplace remains unique in Europe.[66]

(c) After significant increases in benefit for the poorest pensioners as well as for handicapped persons and the inclusion of the unemployed in the health insurance system by the new socialist government in 1981, the French *social insurance policy* mainly fought financial crisis. Thus cuts in benefits, tightened eligibility criteria and fees for clients were introduced. Furthermore, the pressure to accept work was increased in 1992 and unemployment figures were 'reduced' by excluding people on training courses.[67]

These deteriorations in the provision of welfare benefits were countered to some extent by new or prolonged minimal benefits which were introduced in 1982 and 1985 in the framework of the unemployment insurance.[68] The '*revenu minimum d'insertion*' (RMI), in force since

1988 as a part of a package fighting poverty, points in the same direction.[69]

The Netherlands

With its system of 'people's insurances', social insurance for employed people and private insurance, the Dutch social system integrates the whole population. Since the 1970s there has even been a form of guaranteed minimum income insofar as all minimum benefits and supplements are bound to the minimum salary and thus to the general development of incomes.[70] During the 1980s no major change in this system occurred, but automatic indexation of benefits and of minimum income were not implemented while the conditions of eligibility were tightened. The door was opened for this by a continuing debate on the abuse of social benefits.

(a) With respect to *equal treatment* of the sexes the Netherlands had, during the 1980s, to implement the relevant EC directives. This meant a considerable change for a system which had often discriminated against women by connecting benefits to the qualification as 'head of family' or by paying benefits intended for the whole family to the father. Thus, women had to be put on an equal footing in respect of working conditions (1980), pensions and unemployment benefits[71] (1985) as well as within the health insurance system (1988). Full compliance with EC law has not yet been reached in view of the ban on female night work which was only partly removed in 1985.[72] Since 1987 partnership (also homosexual partnership) has been treated on equal terms as marriage with regard to pension insurance.

(b) Deregulation has hardly affected Dutch *labour law*. But the debates in this direction which have been taking place since 1985 have led to a cut in protection from dismissal in 1989.[73]

However, new protective measures for employees were introduced during the 1980s. The law on working conditions for contracts not falling under collective agreements was passed in 1980, temporary agency work now needs ministerial approval (1980 and 1985). Employee participation in the enterprise was regulated in 1981, in 1986 a law on the employment of disabled workers was passed and in 1988 the legal minimum holidays were extended. However, the indexation of incomes was delayed several times or not fulfilled in certain cases at all. In 1983 the minimum income for young people was even cut.

(c) With a programme entitled 'Compass 81' the Van Agt government initiated a series of cuts in *social insurance* at the beginning of the 1980s. These steps were continued under the Lubbers government. On several occasions savings were brought about by cuts in minimum benefits and by tightening the eligibility criteria. Indexation was constantly delayed or diminished until, in July 1991, a new flexible indexation law was passed allowing for non-indexations for various reasons.[74]

Like other European countries the burden of contributions was shifted to employees and households in the Netherlands in order to strengthen companies for international competition. More pressure to accept work was even put on handicapped people. The disability retirement benefit is, since mid-1991, for people under 50 only awarded for a short time.[75] As days of sick leave were thought to be too numerous the government first intended to deduct one holiday from annual leave for each first day of sick leave, but then invited the social partners to agree on it.[76] Current Dutch policy focuses on increasing the gap between social benefits and salaries in order to make employment 'more attractive'.

Spain

Spain holds a special position amongst European welfare states, because the 1980s were still years of the basic shaping of the social security system. Financial problems and from 1985 onwards also increasing European integration produced a pressure for a consolidation which tended towards cuts in social benefits, lower labour costs and increased flexibility.

(a) *Equal treatment* and equality of the sexes were written into the Spanish Constitution in 1978. During the 1980s Spain had to implement the details of the EC directives on equal treatment. Measures which went even further were part of a plan for equal opportunities passed in 1987. In 1989 parental leave was prolonged to 16 weeks and the employee statute of 1980 was amended in order to grant a right to be protected from sexual harassment.[77]

(b) The basic *labour acts* of the nascent Spanish democracy aimed at flexibility from the very beginning. This is to be seen before the background of the extremely rigid labour market regime under the Franco dictatorship. This flexibilisation aimed at reaching an equilibrium on the labour market.[78]

During the 1980s further steps towards liberalisation were taken. In 1984 fixed-term contracts were permitted as an employment promotion measure for periods not exceeding three years. The employer was given further scope in determining how, when and where employees are to be used. Collective agreements may now divide working hours flexibly over the whole year and hiring of part-time employees was made easier. Since 1986 it is possible to 'pay' over-time by shortening working hours correspondingly, but there has been a decrease in maximum for extra-hours. The result of this policy is an extreme increase in 'atypical' forms of work (e.g., between April and June 1986 almost 50 per cent of all work placements).[79]

A speciality of Spanish labour law is that administrative approval is still needed for dismissals and temporary agency work is prohibited.

(c) Contrary to the field of labour law, Spanish measures following the international trend of the 1980s started only very late in the field of *unemployment* and *pension insurance*. By the early 1990s significant improvements to the initial 'basic law of public social insurance' of 1963 had taken place. They comprised the inclusion of new groups in 1986 and the introduction of new benefits for older workers and long-term unemployed in 1987, 1989 and 1990. However, Spain has begun to exert more pressure on the unemployed by cutting the duration or the level of benefits and by strengthening the conditions of eligibility. This has mainly been justified by pointing to the pressures of European integration.[80]

Within pension insurance the financial crisis had already led to the introduction of saving measures in the second half of the 1980s, even if an automatic annual increase in rents parallel to consumer prices was agreed upon in 1985.[81] Private and statutory forms of pension insurance have been promoted since 1987.

WELFARE STATES IN COMPARISON: TRENDS OF SOCIAL POLICY

The postwar period of general expansion of the welfare state had by no means removed differences in the pace, level or shape of measures in the individual states. Furthermore, developments during the past decade have not been solely of a convergent nature. Differences are to be found not only between countries but also between the subfields of social policy.

(a) For *equal treatment* a clear trend of regulation is visible. With regard to remuneration, working conditions and social security this has been due to the respective EC directives. The principle of equal treatment has been extended to more and more aspects of employment and to all forms of employment contracts. More recent aspects of equal opportunities policy are positive action and protection from sexual harassment, both of which are to be found in some of the countries covered by this article. Furthermore, measures which aim at better co-ordination of private and professional life (e.g., parental or child care leave) were introduced.

(b) In the *regulation of working hours and 'atypical' forms of work* it became clear that social changes should not only be seen in the light of legal changes alone. Obviously the terms 'regulation' and 'deregulation', used so frequently by social scientists, need more interpretation and differentiation.

In general, a significant extension of 'atypical' forms of work can be seen in all of the countries analysed and elsewhere, too. This includes part-time work in general inclusive of special forms such as job sharing, work-at-call, so-called petty employment not qualifying for social insurance in some countries and employment-like forms of independent work.[82] Consequently, traditional welfare regulations as such have, de facto, been weakened, in particular concerning the extent of their coverage. Nevertheless, there are diverse forms of reaction to this phenomenon in the field of social policy legislation reaching from non-regulation, as in Austria, to legalisation with the goal of promoting such phenomena as in Germany, and even deliberate attempts to undermine traditional full-time employment as in Great Britain. Regulation of 'atypical' forms of work may have a deregulating character insofar as legal measures support the erosion of 'typical' forms of protected full-time employment. This is disturbing, as traditionally welfare states have linked guarantees of protection and financial security to full-time employment.[83]

The notion of 'deregulation' is often exclusively used to describe those legal activities which hamper the protective and insurance functions of the welfare state. It does, however, neglect the fact that relevant changes may also be brought about by other means. Developments in Germany, where regulations on protection from dismissal were not altered as such, indicate a weakening of such protection being brought about by 'regulating' fixed-term contracts, for which protection from dismissal is not applicable. Returning to our case studies, it should be mentioned that there are also attempts to 'liberalise' protection from dismissal itself in some countries, most notably in Sweden and Italy.

A second crucial aspect is that collective bargaining has become the central method of promoting more pluralisation and flexibilisation of working conditions and thereby denying recourse to legal action. This has been the case both where law-making activities have given more leeway to the social partners, and where this development took place by non-decisions, without any formal amendment to labour law (e.g., Austria).

(c) *Unemployment insurance* trends, excluding the effects of 'non-decision making', have taken the form of slight modifications to the existing regimes. Obvious tendencies were the tightening of eligibility criteria and cuts in the level of benefits. While they had already taken place in most of the countries by the end of the 1980s, Sweden and Italy only recently began cutting benefits. Improvements to the social systems are less significant. Examples of improvements include the increase in duration of benefits which have been tied to the length of employment in several countries and the implementation of a minimum level of support in France (RMI). Developments in Austria have tended to be of contradictory nature. Cuts in benefits have taken place parallel to improvements.

In all of the countries the question of individual responsibility for unemployment has played a part in debates despite the obvious deterioration of the labour market situation. There is also a strong tendency to force people into accepting more or less any job on offer, thus not taking into account their qualifications and previous position, particularly in Great Britain. A sign of the current social and political treatment of mass unemployment may be seen, furthermore, in the cosmetic changes to figures brought about by changed modes of statistical registration and calculation (Great Britain, France, Austria).

In the field of *social insurance financing* the argument of international competition, especially by making reference to the European Internal Market, has often been used to put more of the cost onto employees and households while relieving companies. As part of economising measures, legal minimum wages and minimum benefits, to the extent they exist at all, have been cut by not adapting them to the general price development.

Pension insurance has been faced with a similar range of problems. These include rising life expectancy, budgetary crisis, unemployment, and a growing gap between revenues and expenditures. Most of the countries analysed have taken similar steps in facing these problems, including eligibility restrictions, recalculation of benefits, and changes in retirement age and financing methods. Given the proposed goal of relieving the state budget and of avoiding increases in contributions, especially employers' contributions, the 'solution' of cutting benefits was taken. This is true even for the former 'model' Sweden. Together with these deteriorations in the state-regulated social security system, in some countries other forms of insurance on company or private levels have been promoted. The partial reprivatisation of social security is appearing in diverse forms, ranging from the introduction of company pension schemes and their financial support as in Austria to the possibility of contracting-out of the state pension system as in Great Britain.

A CHANGING ROLE OF THE STATE WITHIN SOCIAL POLICY?

Even if welfare state benefits and services have been cut to some extent, their principal structural elements have remained the same throughout the 1980s and the first years of the 1990s. Furthermore, a specific aspect of state regulation, equal treatment policy, has only been developed to its full extent during this phase, as was the Spanish social security system, since Spain was a latecomer to the democratic welfare states. In other words, despite visible changes in several subfields of social policy there are significant continuities in state regulation. This is underlined by qualitative as well as quantitative indicators. None of the welfare regulations has been replaced by pure market mechanisms. Neither the broad-based spectrum of state regulation in the field of labour law (with the exception of working hours) nor has the traditional structure of social security have been fundamentally questioned. A series of recent measures have even followed more traditional lines (e.g., the improvements of survivors' pension in Germany). The constant involvement of the state in securing social reproduction is also visible in the almost unchanged ratio of social expenditure to gross national incomes.

Nonetheless it is obvious that since the 1980s a remarkable change has taken place, consisting of, at times drastic, modifications to particular regulations as well as a change in the traditional role of the state in social policy in general. The crucial points of this change may be described as follows:

– The role of the state within social policy is *connected more closely to economic conditions* and the substantial reshaping of social measures is oriented towards economic interests/considerations to a larger extent than before. This is to be seen in the context of the increased internationalisation of the economy which leaves less room for national strategies in economic and social policies. In other words, the corresponding relationship between economic development and the welfare state during the Fordist phase of postwar development has developed into a hierarchical one in which the economic aspect is of greater importance than the social one. This has been expressed by restrictions in entitlement to benefits, by cuts in benefits, by linking improvements to cuts and by widening the employers' scope for making decisions.

– Several recent social policy activities, as well as non-decisions on explicit questions of regulations, have reproduced the increased *heterogenity* on the labour market and in working conditions. Traditional welfare regimes were oriented towards generalised standards and generalised norms, achieved in part by the introduction of universal systems as well as by the constant extension of addressees and of the scope of welfare regulations. By contrast, there has been a stronger orientation towards differentiation of state regulations since the 1980s. This is partly connected to the limitation of the coverage offered by labour and social security law. At the same time the Standard Employment Relationship has been on the decrease, and is no longer a guiding principle of state regulation. At the level of legislation this is exemplified in the increased possibility of 'atypical' forms of work, in exemptions from the coverage of existing norms, or in the renunciation of social regulation as for example on 'negligible' work of only few hours per week and in the limitation of insurance obligations.

– So far there has, to some extent at least, been a *shift between the three essential factors of social reproduction* (state, market, family). This is reflected by the shrinking coverage of social security (in some countries the number of excluded people, that is those with fewer working hours, has increased enormously) and the increased risk of poverty within the welfare system. Economically uneven conditions have thus become, to a larger extent, the decisive factor in determining the distribution of welfare benefits. For countries with dominant employment-oriented social security schemes it is nothing new for inequalities in incomes to be reproduced within the system of benefits. However, the situation in the 1980s was different to previous periods insofar as the shift towards more private spheres of action (market and family) was partly initiated and encouraged by state intervention, and in part promoted by state inactivity. State intervention has included measures restricting the eligibility for benefits, binding them even closer to the integration in the labour market, cutting the level of benefits and promoting alternative forms of insurance such as company insurance and contracting-out schemes. State inactivity has two major aspects, refusal to extend welfare benefits to new groups and rejecting the introduction of minimum benefits. Exceptions are constituted by Spain which extended its old age pension system, and France which introduced minimum unemployment benefits.

– Considerable procedural changes in social regulations have been concentrated on decentralising them. Compared with the intensive use of legislation securing social reproduction by most of the states during the postwar period, recent years have seen increased importance given to subordinate institutions such as collective agreements, enterprise level agreements, and individual agreements. This has been achieved by renouncing modifications to traditional social regulations (e.g., the upholding of legislation restricting working hours that leaves enough space for further negotiations at lower levels in Austria) as well as by the legal extension of the non-legislative institutions' importance (e.g., the explicit transfer of the fixing of flexible working hours to collective agreements or plant-level agreements).

To summarise, it is important to note that even though there is still a great deal of continuity in the state's role in social policy, this role has been considerably modified. The above examples of administrative and legal steps taken since the 1980s do not appear to justify talk of a basic and fundamental transformation of the traditional welfare systems but they do need to be interpreted as a significant change in the state's role compared with the phase of expansion during the immediate postwar decades. An important impetus for this development has certainly been the continuing process of European integration: 'Quite apart from its specific social policy provisions, the European Union Treaty signed in Maastricht . . . is already having an enormous effect on employment and industrial relations in the Member States. This is because of the strict limits on public spending deficits and debt which are prerequisites for entry into the Economic and Monetary Union. For most States, meeting these conditions means a great reduction in public expenditure on social matters and on public sector employment.'[84]

The main problem within this change is the increased selectivity of the welfare state expressed by exclusion and the increased risk of poverty. We do not think that the changes, detailed above, have already brought about an adequate balance between individual liberty and collective security or between flexibility and state regulation.[85] Hence, a rebalancing seems to be necessary in the view of current as well as future social challenges such as pluralisation of work and ways of life in a time of increased individual pressure (mobility, qualification, risk of unemployment) and uncertainty.[86] Appropriate measures could be the state regulation of 'atypical' forms of work and the introduction of generally applicable minimum standards in social security.

NOTES

1. Cf. Jens Alber, *Vom Armenhaus zum Wohlfahrtsstaat* (Frankfurt: Campus, 1982), p.151.
2. Cf. Ulrich Mückenberger, 'Zur Rolle des Normalarbeitsverhältnisses bei der sozialstaatlichen Umverteilung von Risiken', in Christoph F. Büchtemann and Helmut Neumann (eds.), *Mehr Arbeit durch weniger Rechte?* (Berlin: Sigma, 1990), pp.172–3.
3. Cf. Burkart Lutz, *Der kurze Traum immerwährender Prosperität* (Frankfurt: Campus, 1984), pp.196–228.
4. Cf. Bob Jessop, 'Der Wohlfahrtsstaat im Übergang vom Fordismus zum Postfordismus', *Prokla*, Vol.16 (Dec. 1986), pp.12–13.
5. Cf. Manfred Schmidt, *Sozialpolitik* (Opladen: Leske, 1988), pp.152–3.

6. Cf. Peter Flora 'Introduction' in Peter Flora (ed.), *Growth to Limits*, Vol.1 (Berlin: de Gruyter, 1986), pp.xxi–xxvi; Bob Jessop, 'Der Wohlfahrtsstaat im Übergang vom Fordismus zum Postfordismus', pp.13–15.
7. Cf. Emmerich Tálos, 'Umbau des Wohlfahrtsstaates', *Österreichische Zeitschrift für Politikwissenschaft* 22/1 (March 1993), pp.39–42.
8. A 'Standard Employent Relationship' is characterised by an unlimited, permanent and full-time employment completely covered by social insurance and labour law.
9. Cf. *European Industrial Relations Review* 17/209 (June 1991), p.9.
10. Cf. Teresa Kulawik, 'Gleichstellungspolitik in Schweden', *WSI-Mitteilungen* 45/4 (April 1992), p.234.
11. Cf. Emmerich Tálos and Gerda Falkner, 'Politik und Lebensbedingungen von Frauen. Ansätze von 'Frauenpolitik' in Österreich', in Emmerich Tálos (ed.), *Der geforderte Wohlfahrtsstaat* (Vienna: Löcker, 1992), pp.202–3.
12. Cf. 'Die Tarifparteien auf dem schwedischen Arbeitsmarkt', *Recht der Arbeit* 41/2 (1988), pp.109–14.
13. Cf. *European Industrial Relations Review* 18/216 (Jan. 1992).
14. Cf. Peter A. Köhler, 'Reform der Hinterbliebenensicherung in Schweden', *Deutsche Angestelltenversicherung* 38/5 (1991), pp.167–73.
15. Cf. Swedish Ministry of Finance, Press Release, 11 Jan. 1993; Joint Statement by the Swedish Government and the Swedish Social Democratic Party, 20 Sept. 1992.
16. Thomas Simons, 'Gleichberechtigung von Mann und Frau im italienischen Arbeits- und Sozialrecht', *Recht der Arbeit* 37/1 (1984), pp.30–41.
17. Cf. *European Industrial Relations Review* 17/208 (May 1991), *Info MISEP* No.34 (Summer 1991).
18. Cf. EC-Commission, *Bericht über die soziale Entwicklung 1986, 1987, 1988*.
19. Cf. G. Pera, 'Der Prozeß der Neuregelung des italienischen Arbeitsrechts', *Zeitschrift für ausländisches und internationales Arbeits- und Sozialrecht*, Vol.1 (July–Sept. 1987), p.300.
20. Herbert Kronke, *Regulierungen auf dem Arbeitsmarkt* (Baden-Baden: Nomos, 1990), p.83.
21. Roland Abele, 'Neue Regelung des arbeitsrechtlichen Kündigungsschutzes', *Recht der internationalen Wirtschaft* 37/3 (1991), pp.188–96.
22. Deviating from this there is a financial support of 80 per cent of the gross wage for industrial workers not on a fixed term contract who are dismissed for local or regional crisis.
23. Cf. *Standard*, 8 March 1993.
24. Cf. *European Industrial Relations Review* 18/223 and 225 (1992).
25. Cf. *Frankfurter Rundschau*, 15 Jan. 1993.
26. Cf. Ulrich Mückenberger, 'Deregulierung des Arbeitsrechts', *Kritische Justiz* 18/3 (1985), pp.255–71.
27. Cf. *Chronik zur Arbeitsmarktpolitik*, No.17 (July 1984); *Bericht über die soziale Entwicklung* 1989, p.V–5, EG-Commission.
28. Employers are obliged to compensate employees for economic disadvantages in case of restructuring of or shutting down the enterprise.
29. Cf. 'Beseitigung von Einstellungsbarrieren', *Chronik zur Arbeitsmarktpolitik*, No.18 (Oct. 1984); Mückenberger, 'Deregulierendes Arbeitsrecht', pp.258–61.
30. Cf. Johannes Frerich, *Sozialpolitik* (München: Oldenbourg, 1987), pp.508–10.
31. An arrangement to support the new German *Länder* who belonged to the GDR until 1989.
32. Cf. *Frankfurter Rundschau*, 25 Feb. 1993.
33. Cf. Friedbert W. Rüb and Frank Nullmeier, 'Alterssicherungspolitik in der Bundesrepublik', in Bernhard Blanke and Helmut Wollmann (eds.), *Die alte Bundesrepublik*, Leviathan Sonderheft, No.12 (Opladen: Westdeutscher Verlag 1991), pp.437–62.
34. Cf. Emmerich Tálos, 'Sozialpolitik', in Herbert Dachs *et al.* (eds.), *Handbuch der politischen Systems Österreichs* (Vienna: Manz, 1991), pp.528–9.

35. Cf. Tálos and Falkner (note 11), pp.205–14.
36. Cf. Runggaldier, 'Auswirkungen wirtschaftlicher Schwierigkeiten auf die Arbeitsbedingungen', in Hans Floretta (ed.), *Österreichische Landesberichte zum XIII. Internationalen Kongreß für das Recht der Arbeit und der sozialen Sicherheit in Athen* (Vienna, 1991), p.21.
37. Cf. Tom Schmid, 'Arbeitszeitpolitik', in Emmerich Tálos (ed.), *Sozialpartnerschaft. Kontinuität und Wandel eines Modells* (Vienna: Verlag für Gesellschaftskritik, 1993), pp.190–1.
38. Klaus Firlei, 'Flucht aus dem Arbeitsrecht', *Das Recht der Arbeit*, Vol.40 (Vienna 1987), p.272.
39. Runggaldier (note 36), p.33.
40. Cf. Emmerich Tálos and Bruno Roßmann, 'Materielle Sicherung im Wohlfahrtsstaat. Am Beispiel der Pensions- und Arbeitslosenversicherung', in Tálos (note 11), pp.51–2.
41. This clause had meant that women whose husbands have a full–time job lose their entitlement on 'Notstandshilfe'. This regulation had therefore discriminated against women.
42. Contrary to the unemployment insurance benefits, the subsequent 'Notstandshilfe' is a means-tested and in principle unlimited assistance benefit.
43. Cf. Tálos and Roßmann (note 40), pp.46–7.
44. Cf. Kurt Pratscher, 'Sozialhilfe: Staat-Markt-Familie', in Tálos (note 11), pp.91–4.
45. Cf. Uwe Kühnert, '*Soziale Aspekte des Thatcherismus in Großbritannien*', *IPW Berichte*, No.5 (1990), pp.21–2.
46. Cf. Bob Jessop, 'Thatcherismus und die Neustrukturierung der Sozialpolitik – Neoliberalismus und die Zukunft des Wohlfahrtsstaates', *Zeitschrift für Sozialreform*, Vol.11, (Nov./Dec. 1992), p.725.
47. Cf. Commission of the European Communities, *MISEP basic information report*, Vol.38 (1988), p.13.
48. Cf. Michael Emerson, 'Regulation or Deregulation of the Labour Market', *European Economic Review*, Vol.32 (1988), p.789.
49. *European Industrial Relations Review* 19/228 (Jan. 1993), p.25.
50. Cf. Commission of the European Communities, *Erster Bericht über die Anwendung der Gemeinschaftscharta der sozialen Grundrechte der Arbeitnehmer*, KOM(91) 511 endg., Brussels (5 Dec. 1991), p.275.
51. Cf. Paul Spicker, 'Großbritannien: Armut im Lande des 'Welfare State', *Kölner Zeitschrift für Soziologie und Sozialpsychologie*, Sonderheft 32 (1992), pp.187–90.
52. Cf. Richard Perry, 'United Kingdom' in Flora, *Growth to Limits* (note 6), Vol.2, p.229.
53. Cf. Henrik Uterwedde, 'Wirtschafts- und Sozialpolitik unter Mitterrand 1981–1991', *Aus Politik und Zeitgeschichte*, No.47–48 (15 Nov. 1991), p.16.
54. In addition to a significant decrease in company taxes a stabilisation of employers' contributions to social security took place. The cost of manpower was decreased by selective financial incentives such as the exemption from social contributions for new posts. Cf. Uterwedde, p.19 (note 53).
55. Cf. Christina Reiland, 'Die Neuregelung der Kündigung aus wirtschaftlichen Gründen im französischen Recht', *Zeitschrift für internationales und ausländisches Arbeits- und Sozialrecht*, Vol.3 (1989), p.328.
56. Cf. *European Industrial Relations Review*, Vol.226 (Nov. 1992), p.6.
57. Cf. EC-Commission (ed.), *Bericht über die Soziale Entwicklung* 1987, V–21; Hans Jürgen Sonnenberger and Reinhard Damann, 'Die Reformen des französischen Arbeitsvertragsrechts 1986/87', *Recht der Internationalen Wirtschaft* 34/5 (1988), p.351.
58. Cf. Case C-345/89 of 25 July 1991.
59. Cf. EC–Commission (note 57), V–7.
60. Cf. Jörg Langer, 'Die neue Arbeitszeitordnung in Frankreich', *Recht der internationalen Wirtschaft*, Vol.29 (Feb. 1983), pp.102–3; Peter Klima, 'Gesetzliche Neuregelung

der Arbeitsverhältnisse auf bestimmte Dauer in Frankreich', ibid., Vol.28, (June 1982), pp.411–12.

61. Cf. Francis Kessler, 'Kündigungsschutzrecht in der Europäischen Gemeinschaft', (*Zeitschrift für ausländisches und internationales Arbeits- und Sozialrecht*, Vol.5 (1991), p.396; Lothar Hirschberg, 'Arbeitszeitrecht in Frankreich', ibid., Vol. 3 (1989), p.291.
62. Cf. Otto Kaufmann, 'Revenu minimum? d'insertion in Frankreich. Wegweiser für neue Formen der sozialen Sicherheit'?, *Zeitschrift für Sozialhilfe und Sozialgesetzbuch* 29/8 (1990), p.394.
63. Cf. EC-Commission (note 57), V–23.
64. Bériaud argues that the flexibilisation of French labour law turned out not to be an efficient means of fight against unemployment: in fact stable working relations were turned into unstable ones (Cf. Jean-Marc Bériaud, 'Die Flexibilisierung im französischen Arbeitsrecht', *Zeitschrift für ausländisches und internationales Arbeits- und Sozialrecht*, Vol.1 (1987), p.273).
65. Cf. EC-Commission, *Berichte über die soziale Lage* (1984) V–8 and (1988) V–23.
66. Cf. *European Industrial Relatios Review* 18/222 (July 1992), p.7.
67. Cf. ibid. 18/217 (Feb. 1992), p.4.
68. Cf. Rudolf Hanke, 'Französische Kehrtwende', *Bundesarbeitsblatt* 34/10 (Oct. 1983), p.9.
69. Cf. *Internationale Revue für Soziale Sicherheit*, Vol.40 (1987), p.194 and Vol.42 (1989), p.243.
70. Theo Berben and Joop Roebroek, 'Das Stufenparadoxon – Sicherung des Subsistenzminimums und Einführung eines Grundeinkommens in den Niederlanden', in BMAS (ed.), *Basislohn/Existenzsicherung/Garantiertes Grundkeinkommen für alle?*, Forschungsberichte aus Sozial- und Arbeitsmarktpolitik, No.16 (Vienna, 1987), p.125.
71. But on this occasion the duration of unemployment benefit was cut for everybody under 35 years of age in return, cf. EC-Commission, *Bericht über die soziale Entwicklung* (1985), VIII–12.
72. Cf. EC-Commission, *Berichte über die soziale Entwicklung* (1985), V–22 and (1986) V–27).
73. Cf. *European Industrial Relations Review*, Report, 15/1 (1989), p.45.
74. Cf. ibid., 17/210 (July 1991), p.8 and 212 (Sept. 1991), p.7.
75. Cf. *Neue Zürcher Zeitung*, 19 July 1991.
76. Cf. *European Industrial Relations Review* 17/215 (Dec. 1991), p.7.
77. Cf. Commission of the European Communities, *Erster Bericht über die Anwendung der Gemeinschaftscharta der sozialen Grundrechte der Arbeitnehmer*, KOM(91) 511 endg., Brussels (5 Dec. 1991), p.256.
78. Cf. EC–Commission, Spanien: Institutionen, Verfahren und Maßnahmen, *MISEP Basisinformationsbericht* (1988), p.24.
79. Cf. EC-Commission, *Berichte über die soziale Entwicklung* (1986, V–7); Juan Antonio Sagardoy Bengoechea, 'Flexibilität des Arbeitsrechts', *Zeitschrift für ausländisches und internationales Arbeits- und Sozialrecht*, Vol.1 (1987), p.366.
80. Cf. *European Industrial Relations Review* 18/220 (1992), p.12.
81. Cf. EC-Commission (ed.), *Berichte über die soziale Lage* (1986), VIII–8.
82. Cf. Doris Bollinger, Wolfgang Conetz and Birgit Pfau-Effinger, 'Atypische Beschäftigung', in Klaus Semlinger (ed.), *Flexibilisierung des Arbeitsmarktes* (Frankfurt: Campus, 1991).
83. Cf. Bernd Keller, 'Noch mehr De-Regulierung oder stärkere Re-Regulierung?' *WSI-Mitteilungen*, Vol.43 (June 1990), p.367.
84. *European Industrial Relations Review* 18/220 (1992), p.1.
85. Ulrich Mückenberger and Simon Deakin, 'From deregulation to a European floor of Rights: Labour Law, flexibilisation and the European single market', *Zeitschrift für ausländisches und internationales Arbeits- und Sozialrecht*, Vol.3 (July–Sept. 1989), pp.154 and 196–7. Klaus Nielsen, 'Towards a Flexible Future – Theories and Politics',

in Bob Jessop, Hans Kastendiek, Klaus Nielsen and Ove K. Pedersen (eds.), *The Politics of Flexibility* (Aldershot: Elgar, 1991), p.9.

86. Wolfgang Zapf *et al.*, *Individualisierung und Sicherheit* (München: C.H. Beck 1987), p.138.

FURTHER READING

Developments in social policy up to the early 1980s are dealt with in the country studies in Peter Flora (ed.), *Growth to Limits* (Berlin: Walter de Gruyter, 1986, 4 vols.). A most useful source on changes in social and labour law within West European countries is the *European Industrial Relations Review*. Some reports published periodically by the EC Commission provide information on recent developments in the various EC Member States, e.g., in the fields of social security and labour law (reports on the implementation of the Social Charter; annual report on the social conditions within the EC) or labour market policy (MISEP information reports, annual Employment in Europe report).

The Rise of the Regulatory State in Europe

GIANDOMENICO MAJONE

Privatization and deregulation have created the conditions for the rise of the regulatory state to replace the dirigiste *state of the past. Reliance on regulation – rather than public ownership, planning or centralised administration – characterises the methods of the regulatory state. This study examines the growth of regulation in Europe, at the national and Community levels. It stresses the advantages of this mode of policy making, but also recognises its problems. It is suggested that political accountability can be ensured by a variety of substantive and procedural controls, among which judicial review is especially important. Executive oversight and co-ordination may be improved by using new tools of public management like the regulatory budget or the regulatory clearing house.*

REGULATION AND THE REDRAWING OF THE BORDERS OF THE STATE

A paradoxical consequence of the international debate about privatization and deregulation has been to focus the attention of European policy makers and scholars on regulation as a distinctive mode of state intervention in the economy and society. In the words of a legal scholar, regulation has become the new border between the state and the economy, and the battleground for ideas on how the economy should be run.[1] A political scientist observes that regulation is a pervasive and widely accepted phenomenon in all advanced countries.[2] According to an economist, the regulation issue – what, how, and at what level of government to regulate – is the core of the compromise between the European Community and its member states that made the Internal Market programme possible.[3]

This consensus on the significance and distinctiveness of regulation is a relatively new phenomenon. Until recently, European scholars devoted little attention to the special features of regulation that distinguish it from other modes of policy making. Thus, while the American deregulation movement was preceded and prepared by decades of intensive research on the law, economics and politics of the regulatory process, in Europe the terms 'deregulation' and 'privatization' gained sudden currency – even in Great Britain the words were scarcely heard of before 1978 – with hardly any intellectual preparation.

The academic and political debate in the United States has been greatly facilitated by the fact that the meaning of regulation is fairly clear within the framework of American public policy and administration (see below). By contrast, European scholars tend to identify regulation with the whole realm of legislation, governance, and social control. Such a broad use of the term makes the study of regulation almost coextensive with the study of law, economics, political science, and sociology. If it is true that reductionism is a necessary condition of scientific progress,[4] it is not surprising that the analysis of regulation as a particular type of policy making is still in its infancy in Europe.

The relative neglect of regulatory analysis in the past corresponded to the low visibility of regulatory activities. While in the United States the tradition of regulation by means of independent agencies combining legislative, administrative, and judicial functions goes back to the Interstate Commerce Act of 1887 – and even earlier in states like Wisconsin, Massachusetts and New York – the tendency in Europe has been to treat regulatory issues as either purely administrative, and so tasks for central departments or ministries, or as judicial, and so matters for determination by courts or court-like tribunals. In Britain, for example, tribunals like the Railway Commission (created in 1873),

> proved so common that by 1933 the regulation of British public utilities was viewed by some as considerably impaired by this reliance on the quasi-judicial method and by the resulting failure to develop the administrative commission. What was absent was a powerful agency that applied a special expertise, employed its own secretariat and regulated (in the sense of imposing a planned structure on an industry or social issue). Regulators, instead of instituting action, responded to the competing proposals of private interests.[5]

Even these timid beginnings of an autonomous regulatory function were forgotten in the era of nationalisations and municipalisations. In most countries of Europe, public ownership of key industries such as like railways, telecommunications, electricity, gas, water and other natural monopolies was supposed to protect the public interest against powerful private interests. In this respect, nationalisations and municipalisations were the functional equivalent of American-style regulation. Indeed, at one level, this equivalence is so close that it is possible to

TABLE 1

COMPARING TWO TYPES OF GOVERNMENT FAILURE

Failures of Economic Regulation	Failures of Nationalised Industries
Capture of regulators by regulated firms	Capture of public managers by politicians and trade unions
Overcapitalisation (so-called Averch-Johnson effect)	Overmanning
Anticompetitive regulation	Public monopolies
Vague objectives ('regulate in the public interest')	Ambiguous and inconsistent goals given to public managers
Poor coordination among different regulators	Poor coordination among different public enterprises
Insufficient political accountability of independent regulatory agencies	No effective control over public enterprises by Parliament, the courts, or the sponsoring minister

establish a one-to-one correspondence between typical forms of 'regulatory failure' and certain well-known problems of public ownership, as shown by Table 1.[6]

Because of these analogies, it has been argued that there is no great difference between public monopolies, like the European Post and Telecommunications Ministries, and privately owned but publicly regulated monopolies like the American Telephone and Telegraph Company before deregulation. However, this argument overlooks one important point: the purpose of public ownership was not simply to regulate prices, conditions of entry and quality of service, but also to pursue many other goals including economic development, technical innovation, employment, regional income redistribution, and national security. While nationalisations and other traditional forms of direct state intervention were thus justified by appealing to a variety of often conflicting goals, regulation has a single normative justification: improving the efficiency of the economy by correcting specific forms of market failure such as monopoly, imperfect information, and negative externalities.

Because regulation is more narrowly targeted, and because many of the traditional goals of nationalisations have become obsolete or can be pursued more efficiently by other means, privatisations tend to strengthen, rather than weaken, the regulatory capacity of the state. The British experience, for all its imperfections, is quite instructive in this respect. Paralleling the sale process of industries such as British Telecommunications and British Gas has been the development of a whole new regulatory structure.[7] This structure rests on a body of economic law involving specific obligations and license conditions placed on the privatized industries, and on a new breed of regulatory agencies – the regulatory offices (ROs). The ROs combine several functions: they regulate prices; they ensure that the privatized firms comply with the terms of their licenses; they act as a channel for consumer complaints and as promoters of competition in the industry they regulate. Detected instances of monopoly abuse are referred to the Office of Fair Trading and to the Monopolies and Mergers Commission (MMC).

Thus, privatization has led to a considerable widening of the scope of agencies to promote competition. Now the MMC has a direct role in the regulation of utilities, while prior to privatization it did not have the competence to examine the potentially anti-competitive practices of the nationalised industries. Regulation of the competitive behaviour of the privatized industries is further strengthened by the availability of the competition law of the European Community (EC) which offers considerably more powerful remedies than are available under British law.[8] Similarly, in America newly deregulated industries have lost their pre-existing statutory immunity from anti-trust laws, and despite major changes in the telecommunications sector, important segments of the industry remain regulated.[9] In sum, neither privatization nor deregulation have meant a return to *laissez-faire* or an end to all regulation. Privatization changes the role of the state from a producer of goods and services to that of an umpire whose function is to ensure that economic actors play by the agreed rules of the game. Deregulation often means less restrictive or rigid regulation: a search for ways of achieving the relevant regulatory objectives by less burdensome methods of government intervention, as when command-and-control methods are replaced by economic incentives. Thus, neither American deregulations nor European privatizations can be interpreted as a retreat of the state, but rather as a redefinition of its functions. What is observed in practice is a redrawing of the borders of the public sphere in a way that excludes certain fields better left to private activity, while at the same time strengthening and even expanding the state's regulatory capacity in other fields like competition or environmental and consumer protection.

NORMATIVE AND POSITIVE THEORIES OF REGULATION

In order to explain the sudden growth of administrative regulation, as well as the lateness of its arrival on the European political stage, it is important to specify more precisely the basic characteristics of this mode of policy making. As noted above, within the framework of American public policy and administration, regulation has acquired a meaning which is often imperfectly understood in Europe. To use Philip Selznick's formulation,[10] regulation refers to sustained and focused control exercised by a public agency over activities that are socially valued. The reference to sustained and focused control by an agency suggests that regulation is not achieved simply by passing a law, but requires detailed knowledge of, and intimate involvement with, the regulated activity. This requirement will necessitate, sooner or later, the creation of specialised agencies entrusted with fact-finding, rule-making, and enforcement.

The emphasis on socially valued activities excludes, for example, much of what goes on in the criminal justice system: the detection and punishment of illegal behaviour is not, *per se*, regulation in the sense in which the term is used here. On the other hand, market activities can be 'regulated' only in societies that consider such activities worthwhile in themselves and hence in need of protection as well as control. If the first part of Selznick's definition reminds us of the different institutional traditions of the United States and Europe, and specifically of the lack of a tradition of independent regulatory bodies in Europe, the second part reminds us of important ideological differences in the past. As discussed above, nationalisations may be viewed, in important respects, as the functional equivalent of American-style regulation. The fact remains that nationalisations were not undertaken in order to support the market by improving its efficiency, but rather to replace market criteria by political and administrative ones. The first wave of nationalisations coincided with the first worldwide depression of the capitalist economy (1873–96) which shattered popular and elite support of the market for almost one century. The late Peter Jenkins[11] exaggerated only slightly when he wrote in 1988 that only now, for the first time in this century, the governing classes of Europe no longer assume that socialism in some form is what history has in store.

By contrast, the American rejection of nationalisation as an economically and politically viable option expressed a widely held belief that the market works well under normal circumstances and should be interfered with only when it does not function properly. The normative theory of regulation expresses this belief in analytic terms. According to this theory, public regulation of economic activity is justified only when the market is incapable of producing a social (Pareto) optimum. This occurs when some form of market failure is present: monopoly power, negative externalities, inadequate or asymmetrically distributed information, public goods. Regulation should be used to increase the efficiency of the economy by correcting market failures, but not for other purposes, however legitimate. For example, income redistribution should be achieved through social policy, not through regulation. An important recent development is the recognition that market failures provide only a *prima facie* case for intervention, since the costs of public intervention may exceed the benefits. Hence 'regulatory failure' must also be considered (see Table 1).

A frequent criticism of the market-failure approach is precisely that it is a normative, not a positive, theory. It provides a basis for identifying situations where the government ought to do something, tempered by considerations of regulatory failure. Many political scientists and economists argue that analysts should focus their attention not on normative issues but on describing the consequences of government programmes and the nature of the political processes that produce such programmes. Normative analysis, it is said, is irrelevant since policy outcomes depend, not on norms or ideas of the public interest, but on factors such as the rules of the political process, the incentives facing various participants in the process, and the changing configurations of power and interests in society.

According to the positive theory, as formulated by George Stigler among others, regulation is not instituted in the public interest, that is, for the protection and benefit of the public at large or some large subclass of the public, but is acquired by an industry and is designed and operated primarily for its benefit.[12] How else could one explain the price and entry regulation of basically competitive industries such as airlines, trucking, banking and telephone services, or the anti-competitive licensing of so many professions and trades? The positive theory has greatly enriched our understanding of the regulatory process, but has not made the normative theory obsolete. As always in the social sciences, the distinction between normative and positive is much less sharp than positivists used to think.[13]

In a useful survey paper on 'Regulation in Theory and Practice', Joskow and Noll call 'normative analysis as a positive theory' (or NPT) the theory which regards market failure as the motivating reason for the introduction of public regulation.[14] The characterisation is appropriate, since the normative theory is often successful in explaining the origin and development of many regulatory policies. As Peltzman[15] writes:

> If there is an empirical basis for the NPT's continuing attraction for economists, it is probably its apparent success as an entry theory. Consider Hotelling's classic statement in 1938 of the

> natural monopoly version of the NPT. In this purely theoretical piece, railroads and utilities are presumed, without much evidence, to be the main real-world examples of natural monopoly. They also occupied most of the regulatory (including public ownership) effort when Hotelling wrote. The correspondence between the NPT and the real-world allocation of regulatory effort seems striking. Now consider the postwar expansion of regulation. In terms of the resources involved, the biggest single chunk is probably accounted for by environmental regulation, where the externalities aspect of the NPT scores another success.

In Europe, too, as we shall see in the following pages, much of the recent growth of regulation can be explained in normative, public-interest, terms. But even when regulation is best explained by the political or economic power of groups seeking selfish ends, those who attempt to justify it must appeal to the merits of the case. Legislators, administrators, scholars, and the public at large wish to know whether the regulation is justified. All of them seek standards against which to judge the success of a policy and the merits of specific programmes initiated within the framework of that policy.

THE GROWTH OF REGULATION IN EUROPE

Administrative regulation – economic and social regulation by means of agencies operating outside the line of hierarchical control or oversight by the central administration – is rapidly becoming the new frontier of public policy and public administration throughout the industrialised world. The absence of an efficient regulatory framework is increasingly seen as a major obstacle to modernisation. Thus, as a 1993 issue of *The Economist* points out, one of the serious problems of privatization in Russia is that there is no regulatory system to control trading in vouchers or shares. This 'regulatory black hole' has already claimed many victims among uninformed investors, and creates an irresistible temptation for any swindler.[16]

The growth of administrative regulation in Europe has greatly accelerated during the last two decades. In France, for example, the expression 'autorité administrative indépendante' was used for the first time by the law of 6 January 1978 creating the Commission Nationale de l'Informatique et des Libertés, but several independent regulatory agencies already existed prior to that date: the Commission de Contrôle des Banques created in 1941 and transformed into the Commission Bancaire by the law of 24 January 1984; the Commission des Opérations de

Bourse (1967), whose powers have been significantly extended by the law of 2 August 1984; the Commission des Infractions Fiscales (1977); the Commission des Sondages (1977); the Médiateur (1973), the only single-headed regulatory agency created so far in France. Today there are almost 20 independent agencies including, in addition to those already mentioned, the Commission d'Accès aux Documents Administratifs (1978), the Commission de la Sécurité des Consommateurs (1983), the Conseil de la Concurrence (1986), and the Commission de Contrôle des Assurances (1989).[17]

In Britain, too, the 1970s have been a period of significant innovation, especially in the area of social regulation. The Independent Broadcasting Authority (1972), the Civil Aviation Authority (1972), the Health and Safety Commission (1974), the Equal Opportunities Commission (1976), and the Commission for Racial Equality (1976) are only some of the regulatory bodies created in this period.[18] Despite the hostility of Conservative governments toward any kind of 'quangos', regulatory agencies were set up in the 1980s and early 1990s, partly because it was realised that in many cases privatization would only mean the replacement of public by private monopolies unless the newly privatised companies were subjected to public regulation of profits, prices, and entry and service conditions. Hence the rise of a new breed of regulatory agencies, the regulatory offices: Office of Telecommunications (1984), Office of Gas Supply (1986), Office of Water Services (1989), Office of Electricity Regulation (1990).

Parallel, if slower, institutional developments are taking place in all other European countries, and the reasons given for the rise of the independent agencies are strikingly similar from country to country. These functional explanations are also strongly reminiscent of the arguments of earlier American writers. Thus it is said that agencies are justified by the need of expertise in highly complex or technical matters, combined with a rule-making or adjudicative function that is inappropriate for a government department or a court; that an agency structure may favour public participation, while the opportunity for consultations by means of public hearings is often denied to government departments because of the conventions under which they operate; that agencies' separateness from government is useful whenever it is hoped to free government administration from partisan politics and party political influence. Agencies are also said to provide greater continuity and stability than cabinets because they are one step removed from election returns; and the exercise of a policy-making function by an administrative agency should provide flexibility not only in policy formulation but also in the application of policy to particular circumstances. Finally, it is argued that independent agencies can protect citizens from bureaucratic arrogance and reticence, and are able to focus public attention on controversial issues, thus enriching public debate.[19]

The growth of administrative regulation in Europe owes much to these newly articulated perceptions of a mismatch between existing institutional capacities and the growing complexity of policy problems: policing financial markets in an increasingly interdependent world economy; controlling the risks of new products and new technologies; protecting the health and economic interests of consumers without impeding the free flow of goods, services and people across national boundaries; reducing environmental pollution. It is sufficient to mention problems such as these to realise how significant is the supranational dimension of the new economic and social regulation. Hence the important role of the European Community (now Union) in complementing the regulatory capacities of the member states.

THE EUROPEAN COMMUNITY AS REGULATOR

Apart from competition rules and measures necessary to the integration of national markets, few regulatory policies or programmes are explicitly mentioned in the Treaty of Rome. Transport and energy policies which could have given rise to significant regulatory activities, have remained until lately largely undeveloped. On the other hand, agriculture, fisheries, regional development, social programmes and aid to developing countries, which together account for more than 80 per cent of the Community budget (see Table 2), are mostly distributive or redistributive rather than regulatory in nature.

This budget of almost ECU 47 billion represents less than 1.3 per cent of the gross domestic product (GDP) of the Community and less than 4 per cent of the central government spending of member states. Given such limited resources, how can one explain the continuous growth of Community regulation, even in the absence of explicit legal mandates? Take the case of environmental protection, an area not even mentioned by the Treaty of Rome. In the two decades from 1967 to 1987, when the Single European Act finally recognised the authority of the Community to legislate in this area, almost 200 directives, regulations, and decisions were introduced by the Commission. Moreover, the rate of growth of environmental regulation appears to have been largely unaffected by the political vicissitudes, budgetary crises, and recurrent waves of Europessimism of the 1970s and early 1980s. From the single directive on preventing risks by testing of 1969 (L68/19.3.69) we pass to 10 directives/decisions in 1975, 13 in 1980, 20 in 1982, 23 in 1984, 24 in 1985

TABLE 2

THE EC BUDGET BY MAJOR CATEGORIES OF EXPENDITURE (1990, ECU)

Administration – Total	1,529,765,860
Operations	
Agricultural market guarantee	26,452,000,000
Guidance (agricultural structures)	2,073,475,000
Fisheries	376,100,000
Regional development and transport	5,209,700,000
Operations in the social sector	3,672,885,000
Energy, technology, research, nuclear safeguards, information market and innovation	1,763,478,000
Repayments and aid to member states	2,335,091,812
Co-operation with developing countries	1,503,590,000
Other expenditures	1,000,000,000
Operations – Total	44,386,319,812
Commission – Total	45,916,085,672
Other institutions	847,661,982
Grand Total	46,763,747,654

Source: *Source: The Community Budget: The Facts in Figures* – 1990 ed., Luxembourg: Office for Official Publications of the European Communities, p.62.

and 17 in the six months immediately preceding passage of the Single European Act.

The case of environmental regulation is particularly striking, partly because of the political salience of environmental issues, but it is by no means unique. The volume and depth of Community regulation in the areas of consumer product safety, medical drug testing, banking and financial services and, of course, competition law is hardly less impressive. In fact, the hundreds of regulatory measures proposed by the Commission's White Paper on the completion of the internal market[20] represent only the acceleration of a trend set in motion decades ago. The continuous growth of supranational regulation is not easily explained by traditional theories of Community policy making. At most, such theories suggest that the serious implementation gap that exists in the European Community may make it easier for the member states, and their representatives in the Council, to accept Commission proposals which they have not serious intention of applying. The main limitation of this argument is that it fails to differentiate between areas where policy development has been slow and uncertain (for example, transport, energy or research) and areas such as environmental protection where significant policy development has taken place even in the absence of a clear legal basis.

Moreover, existing theories of Union policy making do not usually draw any clear distinction between regulatory and other types of policies. Now, an important characteristic of regulatory policy making is the limited influence of budgetary limitations on the activities of regulators. The size of non-regulatory, direct-expenditure programmes is constrained by budgetary appropriations and, ultimately, by the size of government tax revenues. In contrast, the real costs of most regulatory programmes are borne directly by the firms and individuals who have to comply with them. Compared with these costs, the resources needed to produce the regulations are trivial.

It is difficult to overstate the significance of this structural difference between regulatory policies and policies involving the direct expenditure of public funds. The distinction is particularly important for the analysis of Community policy making, since not only the economic, but also the political and administrative costs of enforcing EC regulations are borne by the member states.[21] As already noted, the financial resources of the Community go, for the most part, to the Common Agricultural Policy and to a handful of distributive programmes. The remaining resources are insufficient to support large-scale initiatives in areas such as industrial policy, energy, research, or technological innovation. Given this constraint, the only way for the Commission to increase its role was to expand the scope of its regulatory activities.

Another important element in an explanation of the growth of Community regulation is the interest of multinational, export-oriented industries in avoiding inconsistent and progressively more stringent regulations in various EC and non-EC countries. Community regulation can eliminate or at least reduce this risk.

A similar phenomenon has been observed in the United States, where certain industries, faced with the danger of a significant loss of markets through state and local legislation, have strongly supported federal regulation ('preemptive federalism'). For example, the American car industry, which during the early 1960s had successfully opposed federal emission standards for motor vehicles, abruptly reversed its position in mid-1965: provided that the federal standards would be set by a regulatory agency, and provided that they would preempt any state standards more stringent than California's, the industry would support federal legislation.

Analogous reasons explain the preference for Community solutions of some powerful and well-organised European industries. Consider, for example, the 'Sixth Amendment' of Directive 67/548 on the classification, packaging, and labelling of dangerous substances. This amending Directive does not prevent member states from including more substances within the scope of national regulations than are required by the Directive itself. In fact, the British Health and Safety Commission proposed to go further than the Directive by bringing intermediate products within the scope of national regulation. This, however, was opposed by the chemical industry, represented by the Chemical Industries Association (CIA) which argued that national regulation should not impose greater burdens on British industry than the Directive placed on its competitors. The CIA view eventually prevailed.

Similarly, German negotiators pressed for a European-wide scheme that would also provide the framework for an acceptable regulatory programme at home, wanted a full and explicit statement of their obligations to be defined at the EC level. Moreover, with more than 50 per cent of Germany's chemical trade going to other EC countries, German businessmen and government officials wished to avoid the commercial obstacles that would arise from divergent national regulations.[22]

The European chemical industry had another reason for supporting Community regulation. In 1976 the United States, without consulting their commercial partners, enacted the Toxic Substances Control Act (TSCA). The new regulation represented a serious threat for European exports to the lucrative American market. A European response to TSCA was clearly needed, and the Community was the logical forum for fashioning such a response. An EC-wide system of testing new chemical substances could serve as a model for negotiating standardised requirements covering the major chemical markets. In fact, the 1979 Directive has enabled the Community to speak with one voice in discussions with the United States and other Organization For Economic Co-operation and Development (OECD) countries, and has strengthened the position of the European chemical industry in ensuring that the new American regulation does not create obstacles to its exports. There is little doubt that the ability of the Commission to enter into discussions with the USA has been greatly enhanced by the Directive, and it is unlikely that each European country on its own could do so effectively.[23]

EXPLAINING REGULATORY POLICY MAKING IN THE EC

In the preceding section I have considered three variables that are clearly important for explaining the growth of EC regulation: the tightness and rigidity of the Community budget; the desire of the

Commission to increase its influence by expanding its competencies; and the preference of multinational firms for dealing with a uniform set of rules rather than with 12 different national regulations. However, these variables are not sufficient to explain the willingness of the member states to surrender important regulatory powers to supranational institutions, nor the ability of the Commission to introduce significant innovations with respect to the policies of the member states.[24]

As already suggested, available theories of policy making in the Community do not explain why the member states would be willing to delegate regulatory powers beyond the level required by an integrated market; nor can they explain the policy entrepreneurship of the EC Commission. This is because such theories stress the dominant role of the member states in all stages of the policy process, from initiation (which comes from the heads of state or governments in the European Council) to formal adoption (the prerogative of the Council of Ministers), to implementation (in the hands of the national administrations).

A model capable of explaining the above mentioned phenomena must come to grips with two issues that have been overlooked by the traditional theories: first, problems of 'regulatory failure' in an international context, which limit the usefulness of purely inter-governmental solutions; and, second, the fact that regulation, as a very specialised type of policy making, requires a high level of technical and administrative discretion.

To start with the first issue, market failures with international impacts, such as transboundary pollution, could be managed in a co-operative fashion without the necessity of delegating powers to a supranational level, *provided* that national regulators were willing and able to take into account the international repercussions of their choices; that they had sufficient knowledge of one another's intentions; and that the costs of organising and monitoring policy co-ordination were not too high. These conditions are seldom, if ever, satisfied in practice. Experience shows that it is quite difficult to verify whether or not inter-governmental agreements are being properly kept. Because regulators lack information that only regulated firms have, and because governments are reluctant, for political reasons, to impose excessive costs on industry, bargaining is an essential feature of the process of regulatory enforcement. Regardless of what the law says, the process of regulation is not simply one where the regulators command and the regulated obey. A 'market' is created in which bureaucrats and those subject to regulation bargain over the precise obligations of the latter.[25] Because bargaining is so pervasive, it may be impossible for an outside observer to determine whether or not an international regulation has been, in fact, violated.

When it is difficult to observe whether governments are making an honest effort to enforce a co-operative agreement, the agreement is not credible. For example, where pollution has international effects and fines impose significant competitive disadvantages on firms that compete internationally, firms are likely to believe that national regulators will be unwilling to prosecute them as rigorously if they determine the level of enforcement unilaterally rather than under supranational supervision. Hence the transfer of regulatory powers to a supranational authority like the European Commission, by making more stringent regulation credible, may improve the behaviour of regulated firms. Also, because the Commission is involved in the regulation of numerous firms throughout the Community, it has much more to gain by being tough in any individual case than a national regulator: weak enforcement would destroy its credibility in the eyes of more firms. Thus it may be more willing to enforce sanctions than a member state would be.[26] In fact, the Commission has consistently taken a stricter pro-competition stance than national authorities such as the British Monopolies and Mergers Commission, the German Bundeskartellamt, or the French Conseil de la Concurrence.

In short, the low credibility of inter-governmental agreements explains the willingness of member states to delegate regulatory powers to a supranational authority. At the same time, however, governments attempt to limit the discretion of the Commission by making it dependent on the information and knowledge provided by national bureaucrats and experts. We must now explain how the Commission often manages to overcome these limitations.

The offices of the Commission responsible for a particular policy area form the central node in a vast 'issue network' that includes not only experts from the national administrations, but independent experts (also from non-EU countries), academics, public-interest advocates like environmentalists and leaders of consumer movements, representatives of economic and professional organisations and of regional bodies. Commission officials listen to everybody – both in advisory committees, which they normally chair, and in informal consultations – but are free to choose whose ideas and proposals to adopt. They operate less as technical experts alongside other technical experts, than as policy entrepreneurs, that is, as 'advocates who are willing to invest their resources – time, energy, reputation, money – to promote a position in return for anticipated future gain in the form of material, purposive, or solidary benefits'.[27]

In his study of policy innovations in America, Kingdon identifies three main characteristics of successful policy entrepreneurs: first, the person must have some claim to be taken seriously, either as an expert, as a leader of a powerful interest group, or as an authoritative decision maker; second, the person must be known for his political connections or negotiating skills; third, and probably most important, successful entrepreneurs are persistent.[28] Because of the way they are recruited, the structure of their career incentives, and the crucial role of the Commission in policy initiation, Commission officials usually display the qualities of a successful policy entrepreneur to a degree unmatched by national civil servants. Actually

> the Commission officials' typical motivational structure is quite different from that of the average national government official. While the staff of the national governments is often recruited from persons who tend to be – compared with their peers who choose an industrial career – solid, correct, security-oriented, conservative, risk-averse and often somewhat narrow-minded, the Commission recruits its staff from people who are highly motivated, risk oriented, polyglot, cosmopolitan, open-minded and innovative . . . From the beginnings in the 1960s and up to the present, it has indeed been officials of a special type who chose to leave the relative security of their national administrations to go to Brussels to do there a well-paid but extremely challenging job . . . The structural conditions of recruitment and career favour a tendency to support new ideas and to pursue a strategy of innovative regulation which attempts to go beyond everything which can presently be found in the Member States.[29]

Because of this tendency to favour innovative regulatory solutions, even national experts may find the Community a more receptive forum for their ideas than their own administration. A 1989 directive on the safety of machinery (89/392/EEC) offers a striking example of this phenomenon. The crucially important technical annex of the directive was drafted by a British labour inspector who originally sought to reform the British regulatory approach. Having failed to persuade the policy makers of his own country, he brought his innovative ideas about risk assessment to Brussels, where they were welcomed by Commission officials and eventually became European law.[30]

Moreover, what is known about the *modus operandi* of the advisory committees suggests that debates there follow substantive rather than national lines. A good deal of *copinage technocratique* develops between Commission officials and national experts interested in discovering pragmatic solutions rather than defending political positions. By the time a Commission proposal reaches the political level, first in COREPER (the committee of permanent representatives of the member states) and then in the Council of Ministers, all the technical details have been worked out and modifications usually leave the essentials untouched. The Council may, of course, delay a decision or reject the proposal outright, but these options are becoming increasingly problematic under the qualified majority rule and the 'co-operation procedure' between the European Parliament and the Council introduced by the Single European Act. Fitting together all the variables introduced in this and the preceding section – budget constraints, bureaucratic and economic interests, the poor credibility of purely intergovernmental arrangements and, last but not least, the highly technical nature of most regulatory policy-making – we begin to understand not only the origin and growth of Community regulation, but also its increasingly innovative character.

THE PROBLEM OF POLITICAL ACCOUNTABILITY

We just noted the significance of administrative and technical discretion for EC policy-making. Of course, regulatory discretion has important institutional and political implications also at the national level. One obvious consequence is the creation of specialised agencies such as the French *autorités administratives indépendantes* and the British regulatory offices mentioned above. Such agencies are independent of the central administration, and hence of civil service rules, and often combine legislative, judicial, and executive powers – rule making, adjudication, and enforcement, in the terminology of American administrative law – in more or less narrowly defined areas of policy making.

As already suggested, such institutional arrangements represent an important departure from European constitutional and administrative traditions. The implicit, and in some cases explicit, model is the American independent regulatory commission (IRC). The IRCs were created by Congress to ensure agency independence from presidential control and short-term political considerations. Although they cover an extremely wide range of administrative activities – from the control of prices, routes and service conditions of railway companies by the Interstate Commerce Commission created in 1887 to the licensing of nuclear power plants by the Nuclear Regulatory Commission created in 1975 – all IRCs share some organisational characteristics that are meant to protect their decisional autonomy: they are multi-headed, having five or seven members; they are bipartisan; members are appointed by the president with the consent of the Senate and serve for fixed, staggered terms. Unlike the single-headed line agencies, the IRCs operate outside the presidential hierarchy in making their policy decisions. As the US Supreme Court asserted in *Humphrey's Executor vs. United States* (1935) commissioners can be removed from office only for official misbehaviour, not for disagreement with presidential policy.

In the course of their century-old history, IRCs have been often criticised for violating the principle of separation of powers, for their lack of political accountability, and for an alleged tendency to be captured by private interests. Not surprisingly, the same criticisms are heard now in Europe. Here, regulatory agencies are still seen as 'constitutional anomalies which do not fit well into the framework of controls, checks and balances',[31] even as challenges to basic principles of democracy and of the *Rechtsstaat*.[32] To be sure, it is no easy task to fit the new institutions into the constitutional framework of countries where the diffraction of state power is seen as a direct challenge to parliamentary sovereignty and to the principle of a rigid separation of powers. Expressed in traditional terms the dilemma is: either the regulatory agencies are part of the state administration, and then they cannot be independent; or else they are independent, but in this case to whom are they accountable?

It is impossible to escape this dilemma without questioning the relevance of traditional notions such as the constitutional axiom of the tripartite separation of powers, or the political principle that governmental policy making ought to be subject to control only by persons accountable to the electorate. It is certainly not a coincidence that similar issues are being raised in the ongoing debate about the proper scope of judicial review and judicial policy making. The rise of judicial review in Europe shows that the triad of government powers is no longer considered an inviolable principle. At the same time, courts find their policy making role enlarged by the public perception of them as guarantors of the substantive ideals of democracy when electoral accountability in all spheres of government seems to be waning.[33] What connects the discourse about administrative regulation with that about judicial review and policy making is the issue of the role of non-majoritarian institutions in democratic societies. Again, it is no mere coincidence that the same country has developed both the most advanced system of judicial review and the most extensive network of regulatory institutions.

The American experience shows that a highly complex and specialised activity like regulation can be monitored and kept politically accountable only by a combination of control instruments: legislative and executive oversight, strict procedural requirements, public participation and, most importantly, substantive judicial review. Measured against these standards, regulation in Europe is seen to be highly discretionary, suffering from weak accountability to Parliament, weak judicial review, absence of procedural safeguards, and insufficient public participation.[34]

The issue of the political accountability of regulators, who are neither elected nor directly responsible to elected officials, is particularly visible at the EU level precisely because of the central importance of regulatory policy-making in the Community system. However, the remedies should not compromise the effectiveness of the supranational institutions. The comparative advantage of EU regulation lies mainly in the relative insulation of Community regulators from the short-run political considerations and pressures which tend to dominate national policy-making. As was noted above, the Commission has more to gain by being tough in any individual case than a national regulator. This is because the Commission is involved in the regulation of firms throughout the Community, so that weak enforcement would destroy its credibility in the eyes of more firms. For the same reason, the Commission is less likely to be captured by a particular firm or industry than a national regulator. In the language of James Madison, the insulation of the Commission from day-to-day politics is an important safeguard against national and sectoral 'factionalism'.

In fact, as I have shown elsewhere,[35] many of the arguments developed along Madisonian lines by the American advocates of an 'independent fourth branch of government' – the regulatory branch – apply, *mutatis mutandis*, in the context of the European Union and its member states. These writers acknowledge that government by judges and technocratic experts raises serious issues for democratic theory, but point out that government by elected officials, too, suffers from defects. For example, in seeking re-election legislators engage in advertising and position taking rather than in serious policy making, or they design laws with numerous opportunities to aid particular constituencies. Thus, re-election pressures have negative consequences for the quality of legislation. On the other hand, pro-regulation scholars ask, if the courts require the regulatory process to be open to public inputs and scrutiny and to act on the basis of competent analyses, are the regulators necessarily less accountable than elected politicians?.[36]

The procedural remedies suggested here are also relevant to the problem of the 'democratic deficit' of the EU. For example, it is well known that the Treaty of Rome does not structure the executive power of the Community in a single way, applicable to all instances of legislation needing further execution. Instead, it has been left to the Council, in its capacity as legislative decision maker, to organise, case by case, the executive process.[37] This ad hoc approach is the very negation of the idea of transparency which plays such a large role in the current discussion of regulation. The adoption of something like an Administrative Procedures Act for the European Union could do more to make public accountability possible than the wholesale transfer of traditional party politics to Brussels. Any progress along such lines at Union level would have positive spillovers for the member states where, as we saw, the accountability of regulators is still an open issue. The fact that regulation is relatively more important at EU than at national level, makes the Union an ideal laboratory for the study of the problems of the regulatory state. This can be seen also by examining the issue of co-ordination and executive control – the second key issue of regulatory policy-making.

CO-ORDINATION AND CONTROL

An important characteristic of regulatory policy making is the absence of a regulatory budget procedure. Because, as was shown above, the size of regulatory programmes is not significantly constrained by legislative appropriations and by the level of tax revenues, as in the case of non-regulatory programmes, no mechanism exists for regulation that requires policy makers throughout the government to solve the two-level budget problem – how much to spend during a given period and then how to allocate this total amount among alternative uses – which is addressed by any government in its direct expenditure activities. The result is both economic inefficiency and inadequate political oversight.

These defects of the regulatory process are, again, particularly evident in the case of EU rule-making. Thus budgetary discipline is even weaker than at the national level since the burden of implementing Union regulations is carried by the governments of the member states. Also, because of the absence of a central political authority, regulatory issues are dealt with sector by sector, with little attempt to achieve overall policy coherence. Even within the same sector it would be difficult to maintain that regulatory priorities are set in a way that explicitly takes into consideration either the urgency of the problem or the benefits and costs of different proposals. The piecemeal procedure of the Commission in proposing new regulatory measures has resulted in directives in areas where harmonisation is a low priority, while neglecting other areas which need a considerable amount of harmonisation.

Since the lack of budgetary discipline is a basic reason for the structural defects of the regulatory process, one should attempt to create control mechanisms similar to those traditionally used in the case of direct public expenditures. This simple idea has led several analysts of the American regulatory process to propose the introduction of a *regulatory budget*. In its basic outline the regulatory budget would be established by Congress and the President for each agency, perhaps by starting with a budget constraint on total private expenditures mandated by regulation, and then allocating the budget among the different agencies. By setting a budget constraint on mandated private expenditures, the regulatory budget would clarify the real costs to the economy of adopting a regulation and encourage cost effectiveness. The knowledge that agencies would be competing against each other would lead them to propose their 'best' regulations in order to win presidential and congressional approval. Simultaneous consideration of all new regulations would permit an assessment of their joint impact on particular industries and the economy as a whole.[38]

Serious technical difficulties (e.g., estimating the full social cost of regulations, especially when the regulations restrict outputs or behaviour rather than merely requiring outlays for compliance) have to be resolved before the regulatory budget could actually be implemented. Nevertheless, because the budget is such a useful analogy for highlighting the defects in the current regulatory process, a promising approach consists in developing methods of regulatory oversight and control that incorporate budget concepts in a workable fashion.

One possible model suggested by the analogy with the budgetary process, deserves special investigation: a *regulatory clearing-house*. In the EU context, such a clearing house should be located at a sufficiently high level in the Union bureaucracy, possibly in the office of the President of the Commission. Directorates-General would be asked to submit annually draft regulatory programmes to the clearing house for review. When disagreements or serious inconsistencies arise, the President or a 'working committee on regulation' would be asked to intervene. By extending centralised control over the regulatory agenda of the Directorates-General, this review process would help the Commission shape a consistent set of regulatory measures to submit to the Council and the Parliament. The usefulness of the procedure as a tool of managerial control could be increased by co-ordinating the regulatory review with the normal budgetary review, thus linking the level of budgetary appropriations to the cost-effectiveness of the various regulatory programmes.

One key function of such a clearing-house system, in addition to providing for greater coherence, would be to flesh out the concept of subsidiarity: only through systematic review of all proposals put forward by the various Directorates-General will the Commission be able to determine when action by the Union is necessary. Obviously the idea of a regulatory clearing-house system would be useful also for the member states, as one way of reducing the negative consequences of the diffraction of state power which is one of the significant characteristics of the regulatory state.

CONCLUSION: THE PARADOXES OF PRIVATIZATION, DEREGULATION AND RE-REGULATION

At the beginning of this analysis we noted that European scholars and policy makers began to recognise regulation as a distinct mode of policy making only after deregulation became a popular theme of political discourse. This is only one of several paradoxes, real or presumed, that seem to characterise the development of regulation in Europe during the past two or three decades. Thus, the privatization and/or deregulation of potentially competitive industries have not meant the end of all regulation; on the contrary, they have created the conditions for the rise of a regulatory state to replace the *dirigiste* state of the past. Where competitive conditions did not yet exist, as in the case of telecommunications, only public regulation could ensure that privatisation did not simply mean the replacement of public monopolies by private ones.

Often, deregulation is only a first step towards re-regulation, that is, regulation by other means – economic incentives instead of administrative rules, statutory instead of self-regulation – or at different levels of government – for example, at Community rather than national level. This paradoxical combination of deregulation and re-regulation is what is usually meant by regulatory reform.

On the other hand, the experience of countries such as Britain shows that old habits of secretiveness and ministerial interference, characteristic of the management of nationalised industries, continue to persist even after privatization. Serious flaws in the design of institutions to regulate the newly privatized industries can be detected in the choice of a non-participatory model, with none of the public hearings and other procedural characteristics of US regulation; in the creation of a system of agencies linked to particular industries, rather than the pattern of commissions regulating a range of utilities in order to reduce the risk of agency capture; and in the fact that government departments still preserve important regulatory powers, so that the operations of agencies are often dependent on prior decisions of the minister laying down the principles to be applied. The danger, Tony Prosser concludes, is that these powers of direction 'could be abused to exert behind-the-scenes pressure on the regulation in much the same way as pressure was put on the nationalised industries by government, precisely the situation which the privatization programme is supposed to render impossible'.[39]

Also the stupendous growth of EU regulation has a certain paradoxical quality. By imposing a tight and rigid budget, the member states no doubt wished to restrict as much as possible the competencies and decisional autonomy of the Commission. Accustomed to think of state power primarily in terms of the power of taxing and spending, national leaders did not apparently realise that regulatory activities cannot be controlled by means of the traditional budget constraints: only a 'regulatory budget' could introduce the necessary discipline. In the absence of a regulatory budget procedure, the rule-making power of the Union has proved well-nigh irresistible. Moreover, the growth has been qualitative as well as quantitative. As noted above, in some areas of economic and social regulation EU directives go beyond the levels achieved by the legislation of the most advanced member states. This is another paradox, at least for theories claiming that member states control all stages of Union policy making.

Finally, the terms of the debate about the 'democratic deficit' of the Union are often paradoxical when not simply hypocritical. Problems of political accountability can be perceived most clearly at Union level precisely because regulation is at the core of EU policy making. Yet the frequent criticisms that Union institutions lack direct democratic legitimacy also apply to many national institutions, including courts and independent regulatory agencies. The problem of a 'democratic deficit' concerns all regulatory states, not just the Union. The problem has no simple solution, but it can be mitigated by a variety of substantive and procedural means ranging from judicial review to the 'regulatory budget'. The shift to regulation at the national and supranational level is an attempt to improve the procedural and substantive rationality of public policy in a dramatically changing world. However, the changing role of the state raises new conceptual and practical issues that are still poorly understood, let alone resolved.

NOTES

1. Cento Veljanovski, 'The Regulation Game', in Veljanovski (ed.), *Regulators and the Market* (London: Inst. of Economic Affairs, 1991), pp.3–28.
2. Kenneth Dyson, 'Theories of Regulation and the Case of Germany: A Model of Regulatory Change', in Dyson (ed.), *The Politics of German Regulation* (Brookfield, VT: Dartmouth, 1992), pp.1–28.
3. Jacques Pelkmans, 'Regulation and the Single Market: An Economic Perspective', in H. Siebert (ed.), *The Completion of the Internal Market* (Tübingen: J.C.B. Mohr, 1989), pp.91–117.
4. Jon Elster, *Explaining Technical Change* (Cambridge, UK: CUP, 1983).
5. Robert Baldwin and Christopher McCrudden, *Regulation and Public Law* (London: Weidenfeld, 1987).
6. Giandomenico Majone and Antonio La Spina, 'Lo Stato Regolatore', *Rivista Trimestrale di Scienza dell'Amministrazione* 13/3 (1991), pp.3–62.
7. Cento Veljanovski, *Selling the State* (London: Weidenfeld, 1987).
8. Ibid, pp.165–73.
9. Giandomenico Majone, 'Introduction' in G.Majone (ed.), *Deregulation or Re-Regulation?*, (London: Pinter Publishers, 1990), pp.1–6.
10. Philip Selznick, 'Focusing Organizational Research on Regulation', in R.G. Noll (ed.), *Regulatory Policy and the Social Sciences* (Berkeley and Los Angeles: Univ. of California Press, 1985), pp.363–67.
11. Peter Jenkins, *Mrs.Thatcher's Revolution* (Cambridge, MA: Harvard UP, 1988).
12. George J. Stigler, 'The Theory of Economic Regulation', *Bell Journal of Economics and Management Science*, 6/2 (1971), pp.114–41.
13. Giandomenico Majone, *Evidence, Argument and Persuasion in the Policy Process* (New Haven, CT: Yale UP, 1989).
14. Paul J. Joskow and Robert G. Noll: 'Regulation in Theory and Practice: An Overview', in G. Fromm (ed.), *Studies in Public Regulation* (Cambridge, MA: MIT Press, 1981), pp.1–65.
15. Sam Peltzman, 'The Economic Theory of Regulation after a Decade of Deregulation', in *Brookings Papers in Economic Activity* (Washington, DC: The Brookings Instn., 1989), p.17.
16. *The Economist*, 27 Feb. 1993, pp. 89–90.
17. Marie-José Guédon, *Les Autorités Administratives Indépendantes* (Paris: Librairie Générale de Droit et de Jurisprudence, 1991).
18. Baldwin and McCrudden (note 5).
19. Catherine Teitgen-Colly, 'Les Autorités Administratives Indépendantes: Histoire d'une Institution', in Claude-Albert Colliard and Gérard Timsit (eds.), *Les Autorités Administratives Indépendantes* (Paris: Presses Universitaires de France, 1988); Giulio Vesperini, 'Le Funzioni delle Autorità Amministrative Indipendenti', *Diritto della Banca e del Mercato Finanziario* 4/4 (1990), pp.415–19; Baldwin and McCrudden (note 5), pp.4–9; Guédon (note 17), pp.16–27.
20. Commission of the European Communities, *Completing the Internal Market*, COM(85)310, final, (Luxembourg: Office for Official Publications of the European Communities, 1985).
21. Giandomenico Majone, 'Market Integration and Regulation: Europe after 1992', *Metroeconomica* 43/1–2 (1992), pp.131–56, and, 'Regulatory Federalism in the European Community', *Government and Policy*, Vol.10 (1992), pp.299–316.
22. Ronald Brickman, Sheila Jasanoff, Thomas Ilgen, *Controlling Chemicals* (Ithaca, NY: Cornell UP, 1985).
23. Ibid, p.277.
24. Giandomenico Majone, 'The European Community between Social Policy and Social Regulation', *Journal of Common Market Studies* 31/2 (1993), pp.153–70.
25. Alan Peacock (ed.), *The Regulation Game* (Oxford: Basil Blackwell, 1984).

26. Kristos Gatsios and Paul Seabright, 'Regulation in the European Community', *Oxford Review of Economic Policy* 5/2 (1989), pp.37–60.
27. John W. Kingdon, *Agendas, Alternatives and Public Policies* (Boston: Little, Brown, 1984), p.188.
28. Ibid., pp.189–90.
29. Volker Eichener, *Social Dumping or Innovative Regulation?* Working Paper SPS No.92/28, (Florence: Eur. Univ. Inst., 1992).
30. Ibid, p.52.
31. Veljanovski, *Regulators and the Market* (note 1), p.16.
32. Teitgen-Colly (note 19), p.49.
33. Mary L. Volcansek, 'Judges, Courts and Policy-Making in Western Europe', *West European Politics* 15/3 (July 1992), p.5.
34. Tony Prosser, 'Regulation of Privatized Enterprises: Institutions and Procedures', in Leigh Hancher and Michael Moran (eds.), *Capitalism, Culture and Economic Regulation* (Oxford: Clarendon Press, 1989), pp.135–65; Baldwin and McCrudden (note 5); Veljanovski (note 1).
35. Giandomenico Majone, 'Controlling Regulatory Bureaucracies: Lessons from the American Experience' in Hans Ulrich Derlein, Ita Gerhardt and Fritz W. Scharpf (eds.), *Systemnationalität und Partiellintereste* (Baden-Baden: Nomos, 1994), pp.291–314.
36. Susan Rose-Ackerman, *Rethinking the Progressive Agenda* (NY: The Free Press, 1992).
37. Koen Lenaerts, 'Some Reflections on the Separation of Powers in the European Community', *Common Market Law Review* Vol. 11 (1991).
38. Robert E. Litan and William D. Nordhaus, *Reforming Federal Regulation* (New Haven, CT: Yale UP, 1983).
39. Prosser (note 34), p.147.

FURTHER READING

After a late start, relative to the United States, the literature devoted to various aspects of economic and social regulation in Europe is growing at a very fast rate. Most authors are legal scholars or economists, but political scientists, and even sociologists are beginning to make significant contributions. The following books provide, in different ways, useful introductions to the subject.

Robert Baldwin and Christopher McCrudden, *Regulation and Public Law* (London: Weidenfeld, 1987).

The first part of the book is a good general study of regulatory agencies, with particular attention to questions of expertise, efficiency and political accountability, and to the impact of judicial review. The second, and longest, part contains nine case studies of British regulatory agencies. The concluding chapters examine the relationship between regulation and public law, and provide suggestions for further readings.

Leigh Hancher and Michael Moran (eds.), *Capitalism, Culture and Economic Regulation* (Oxford: Clarendon Press, 1989).

A valuable collection of essays on various aspects of economic regulation. The authors attempt to relate regulation to broader themes of political economy and sociological analysis. The chapter by Tony Prosser on the regulation of privatised industries is especially relevant to some of the themes of this contribution.

Keith Hawkins and John M.Thomas (eds.), *Making Regulatory Policy* (Pittsburgh, PA.: University of Pittsburgh Press, 1989).

A multidisciplinary collection of essays by American and British scholars. The contributions focus on knowledge and discretion in regulatory policy-making, on the influence of various constituency groups on regulatory programmes, and on problems of implementation.

Giandomenico Majone (ed.), *Deregulation or Re-regulation? Regulatory Reform in Europe and the United States* (London: Pinter Publishers, 1990).

Regulatory reform – a combination of deregulation and re-regulation – is examined by American and European scholars in a variety of areas ranging from transportation and telecommunications to product safety, environmental taxes and the regulation of new medical drugs. The volume stresses the important role of the EC in regulatory reform.

Alan Peacock (ed.), *The Regulation Game* (Oxford: Basil Blackwell, 1984).

After a general introduction to the theory of regulation and a methodological discussion of the problems of measuring compliance costs, the volume examines how British and German companies bargain with government over the substance of regulation in the field of health and safety at work. Interviews with firms and other empirical data are used to illustrate propositions concerning 'negotiated compliance'.

Francis Snyder (ed.), *European Community Law*, Volumes I and II (Aldershot: Dartmouth, 1993).

This very extensive collection of readings about European law in context, includes several papers on Community regulation.

Cento Veljanovski, *Selling the State* (London: Weidenfeld, 1987).

One of the first book-length accounts of privatization in Britain, written in a lively style that makes it particularly appealing to the non-specialist. The relationship between privatisation and regulation is discussed at length. Chapter 7, on regulating the private utilities, and Chapter 8 on the rise of regulatory agencies, are particularly useful.

Cento Veljanovski (ed.), *Regulators and the Market* (London: The Institute of Economic Affairs, 1991).

The volume examines developments of economic regulation in the UK by letting the regulators themselves assess the achievements and problems of their agencies.

The interested reader should also consult the indices of journals such as *Journal of Common Market Studies*, *Journal of Public Policy*, *Oxford Review of Economic Policy*, *Economic Policy* and *Common Market Law Review*.

Reshaping the State: The Implications for Public Administration

VINCENT WRIGHT

Reshaping the states of Western Europe has direct implications for their respective public sectors. Broad convergent pressures have led to largely similar reform programmes. However, differences remain across Western Europe in the nature, style, timing and pace of the reforms. These differences may be explained by analysing the nature of the pressures, the size and scope of the traditional public sector, the ambitions of governments, as well as their ideological commitment and political durability, and the domestic political opportunity structure. The reform programmes being pursued in several countries are characterised by contradictions, paradoxes and problems.

The process of reshaping the state, described in the Introduction, has had inevitable consequences for public enterprises, for intergovernmental relations and for central public administrations. The latter are the principal focus for this study which begins by describing the pressures which are redefining those administrations. Some have already been outlined in the Introduction. The general and broadly convergent programmatic response across Western Europe to these pressures is then presented. The differences between the programmes are then briefly explored and explained. Finally, the contradictions, paradoxes and problems of the various programmes are examined. The general argument is that the convergent pressures which are reshaping the states of Western Europe, combined with other convergent pressures, have inevitable direct or indirect effects on their public administrations, squeezing governments into reforms which are broadly and increasingly similar. However, significant differences remain in the nature, intensity, timing and pace of the reforms. These differences may be explained in terms of the opportunities afforded by the politico-institutional and cultural environment in which they are being pursued. Furthermore, many of the reforms, which are flawed in several ways, may have unanticipated and unwelcome consequences.

PRESSURES FOR PUBLIC SECTOR REFORM

Since the early 1980s administrative reform has been placed firmly on the agenda of most West European states. Thus, the 1992 Organization for Economic Co-operation and Development (OECD) Report on *Public Management Developments* reveals an almost frenetic quality about the reform programmes. The United Kingdom was, characteristically, in the vanguard of the movement, with reforms on all fronts, and particularly in the extension of the 'Next Steps' initiative. Its Irish neighbour saw the signing of an accord outlining 'fundamental structural reforms' between the government and the social partners. In Northern Europe, the new government in Finland promised administrative reform and established a permanent ministerial committee to oversee it, whilst the Danish government issued another set of reform proposals, and the new coalition government in Sweden committed itself to renewing and limiting the public sector, to extending market mechanisms into that sector and to enhancing evaluation procedures. The two traditional models of political accommodation – the Netherlands and Austria – were each proposing important reform programmes: the former, in the name of 'Fewer Civil Servants but a Better Service' (a perennial dream), was pushing a new programme of decentralisation and efficiency; the latter passed legislation which transferred certain public tasks to private firms. In Germany, the politically delicate decision to transfer 10 of the 18 Federal ministries to Berlin was taken. In France, the recently created Committee on Evaluation selected five major policy areas to investigate, and the Post and Telecommunitions organisation was split into two separate public establishments. In Belgium, a Royal Decree was issued transferring new powers to the Communities and Regions, and an Act was passed which transformed the status of some public enterprises, providing managers greater autonomy and giving them the right to raise private capital. Southern Europe was not spared: in Italy, a 'global strategy' of reform was launched; in Greece, a Modernisation Programme was promulgated by the New Democracy government; in Spain, the ministries were restructured (to take account of the impact of European integration) and an agreement was reached with the unions on the need for administrative modernization; in Portugal, a major evaluation of public-sector salary structures was undertaken.

A reading of the OECD reports of recent years reinforces the impression of extensive administrative reform. Furthermore, these reforms have been undertaken by Right-wing governments (UK, Greece, Norway) by coalitions (Germany, Italy, the Netherlands) or by Socialist or Social Democratic governments (Spain, Sweden, France).

It would appear, therefore, that Western Europe has truly entered 'the age of administrative reform' after years of sporadic, pragmatic and limited change, often internally engendered. Perhaps this is not surprising, since the states of Western Europe are being squeezed by convergent and interconnected pressures for change. Some of these have been mentioned in the Introduction to this collection, but they are worth emphasising, because each is pregnant with administrative implications. These pressures may be summarized as follows:

– *internationalisation* of industrial and financial markets, which is creating great problems of international, transnational or cross-border administrative co-ordination, and which is provoking in some sectors a mismatch between nationally-based administrative structures, procedures and personnel and the administrative management of new internationalised regulatory requirements. Moreoever, internationalisation has sometimes involved increased connections between firms (joint ventures, share swaps, research or marketing agreements, minority stakes) not only in different countries but also amongst public and private enterprises. This increasing foreign/national, public/private hybridisation – often encouraged by West European governments – is blurring not only the identity but also the lines of accountability for public administrators.[1]

– *Communitarianisation*, which has involved the increasing regulatory creep of Brussels into sectors (such as citizenship, the environment, consumer protection and even social cohesion) previously exclusively domestic, thus raising issues of information and administative co-ordination, as well as complex personnel and 'administrative culture' questions. The European Union has indirect implications for national public sectors notably through the consequences of monetary convergence (with its requirements of greater budgetary discipline), its competition policy (which harbours long-term consequences for protected national public sectors), its extended regulated policy areas, and its increasing implementory role.[2] Membership of the Union has both reactive administrative implications (adjustments to the impact) and active ones (creating new administrative bodies to exploit the potential of the Union). The latter may be seen most notably at regional level.[3] The impact of the Union may be seen most dramatically in the implementation of Article 48 of the Treaty of Rome and the celebrated decision of the Court (*Commission v Belgium*, 17 December 1980) which opened up many – indeed, most – national public-sector posts to citizens of other member states. A member state can reserve for its own citizens only those posts which require 'participation, direct or indirect, in the exercise of public power' and functions which have as their object 'the safeguarding of the general interest of the state and of other public bodies'. Of course, this does not mean that national administrations have been Europeanised in their composition. But certain posts have – often reluctantly – been opened up in many countries where a sacrosanct principle established that only national citizens could serve the state.

– *economic and financial pressures*, caused by problems of public debt and public deficits, of state revenues and fiscal resistance, and which have had a direct impact on administative budgets and personnel. This is probably the greatest single pressure – *l'aguillon de base* – for reform, and this has been openly confessed by several governments.[4] 'The party is over' slogan of late-1970s Britain has found a direct translation – 'la festa è finita' in 1994 Italy. And it is not only the British Conservative government that has insisted that the public sector give 'value for money' by increasing its efficiency.

– *the general paradigm shift*, with its strong ideological prejudice against the state, big government, bloated bureaucracies, universalistic solutions. In terms of the administration, the paradigm has been fed not only by Chicago-style market-oriented economics, but also by public choice theories (with their simplistic notions of bureaucratic behaviour), by principal-agent theory, by new theories of property rights and by economic analyses of the failure of the public sector.[5] One of the keys to an understanding of this paradigm shift is the move to the idea that the citizen, a problematic concept for the neo-liberal, is an individual consumer or customer of public services, and is entitled to certain standards of service tested by performance scrutiny. This move from the 'age of the captive client to the age of consumerism' is fraught with consequences for the traditional public service paradigm.[6]

– *the changing policy agenda in many West European countries*, with the increasing political salience of problems such as the environment, drug-trafficking, law and order, many of which require new national cross-border or international administrative bodies and cooperation, and many of which necessitate bureaucratic expansion.[7]

– *the rapidly changing political environment*, especially in Germany which is faced with the mammoth task of absorbing the five Eastern *Länder*, in Italy which is changing Republics in unpredictable circumstances, in Spain which is witnessing the increasingly dynamic and autonomous activities of certain regions, and in Belgium which has seen the almost total disintegration of traditional administrative structures under the impact of the enduring conflict between the Flemish and the Walloons.

– *technological change*, – the explosion of so-called convergent information technologies (CIT) involving an increasingly intimate relationship between telecommunications, computer data processing and office automation products. The full implications for the public sector have yet fully to be realised, let alone absorbed, but the impact is already being felt on traditional state bureaucratic hierarchies, organisational structures, working practices and skills, personnel management and service delivery.[8] New technology is also transforming the nature of some public-sector industries, rendering notions of natural monopoly obsolete, and turning single-product nationally-based firms into multi-product, internationalised groups which are more difficult to administer.

– *the democratic pressure*, with its many and potentially conflicting strands and demands: more and better yet cheaper services; greater effectiveness yet great transparency and access; quicker decisions yet more citizen participation and consultation, self-management and industrial democracy; greater representativeness (for women, ethnic groups, racial minorities, underprivileged classes, handicapped people) yet entry and promotion to the administration by merit. Each of these demands is problem-ridden.[9] It is far from clear, for instance, what is meant by 'representative bureaucracy', the meaning of which has changed over time and which currently includes conflicting exigencies. Yet these demands impact upon the administration – and in predictably unpredictable, unambiguously ambiguous and unquestionably questionable – fashion, increasing the sense of disorientation which afflicts public administrations in many countries.

These pressures have been felt at the level of all the European states, and have had indirect but automatic repercussions for their public sectors. Two other major common pressures have more specifically affected those sectors:

– *generalised disgruntlement at the performance of the public sector* which has taken different and conflicting forms across Western Europe, and often within each country of Europe. The public sector is allegedly either too powerful and too intrusive or too weak and too ineffective, either too politicised and too beholden to politicians or too independent and not sufficiently sensitive to the demands of its political masters. In almost all countries it is also accused of profligacy, inefficiency, opacity, and in some it is justifiably indicted as corrupt. It is scarcely surprising that some public choice theories, with their criticisms of the intrinsic propensities of self-serving bureaucrats, should become the fashionable philosophical underpinnings and rationalisation for the various reform programmes. Nor is it surprising that critiques of state interventionism (based on its inherent inefficiency compared with the market) become intermingled with those of bureaucracy (rooted in self-serving officials seeking only to expand their empires and to maximise their budgets). It is no less surprising that politicans, looking for scapegoats for their own failures and in their search for easy remedies to problems inherent in the management of expanding demands on the state with increasingly limited means, should all too readily accept part or whole of the neo-liberal critique of the public sector. Certainly, if the public sector could not be abolished or radically slimmed down (and many thought it could) it had to be reformed. This desire for reform has been shared by governments of all political hues and has found a favourable echo amongst some modernizing elites within the public administration. These are sometimes econocrats, brought up on a diet of classical economics and are untainted by the rule-bound instincts of lawyers or the lazy scepticism induced by the study of history or political science. In some cases they are bureau-shaping officials (to borrow Patrick Dunleavy's description) often more interested in policy formation and control rather than the less exalted task of implementing it. In many cases, however, they are public officials dedicated to public service and keen on improving it.[10] Whatever the reason, many have needed no encouragement to react to the following pressure.

– *the so-called managerial revolution* which has radically called into question traditional procedures, techniques and styles, and which claims that efficiency lies in smaller, more decentralised, more flexible, more specialised, and more autonomous managerial units run by flattened hierarchies with a higher degree of participation of the lower echelons. For Osborne and Baebler, who in their post-modernist critique, vulgarised the new views in their best-selling *Reinventing Government*,[11] the great centralised hierarchically-structured and integrated public organisations, bound by multiple layers or regulations, which had emerged during the period of the growth of government, of mass production, and paternalism and of uniformity, are no longer appropriate in an era of flexibility, choice and personal responsibility. Curiously, the same point was being made several years earlier by certain Swedish Social Democrats![12] Traditional public administration was also, according to the critics, managerially flawed because of its obsession with abiding by rules and regulations and with respecting due process. Indeed, it is alleged that for many public sector officials, good administration lies in the uniform and inflexible application of the law and of established procedures. Insufficient attention is paid to goals, outputs, performance. Given the increasing capacity of the public sector to define such goals, and measure outputs and performance this was not only regrettable but inexcusable.

Moreover, there were apparently successful experiments being carried out in public-sector reduction and reform in one European country, which was becoming the model for several of its neighbours. Britain's privatization programme – and particularly its lucrative outcome – has inspired many of its revenue-starved European neighbours (the 'privatization industry' has become one of Britain's few succesful exporters), and its radical pursuit of 'new public management' strategy (see below), based on private-sector techniques and styles, has also been carefully studied in many European states (notably the Netherlands, Denmark and Norway). Policy emulation is particularly clear in the Spanish and Italian reform programmes, both of which have been defined by ministers well acquainted with foreign experiences: the Spanish Minister for Administrative Reform, an academic, carefully studied the programmes of Sweden, the Netherlands, France and the United Kingdom, whilst the Italian Minister, another academic, is a leading expert on European administration. New Public Management (NPM) is rooted in attention to substance and not process, in constructing and assessing specific rather than general objectives and goals, in treating people as customers, in encouraging competition betwen service providers, in decentralising decision making, in improving financial management techniques, in introducing efficiency indicators and corporate planning methods, and in exploiting private human resource management practices and information services.[13] It has become a new policy fashion or fad, a pervasive *Zeitgeist* diffused by international bodies (such as the OECD), national governments,[14] business schools, armies of consultants and research institutes, but the key to its success lies in the propitious nature of the political terrain which it has penetrated.[15]

The public sector, as the major agent of the state, is, therefore, caught at the cross-roads of these muiltiple, conflicting and largely convergent pressures. Pressures on the state are automatically translated into pressures on the public sector. And there is evidence that convergent pressures are leading to convergent programmatic ambitions and outcomes.

PROGRAMMATIC RESPONSES

As noted at the beginning of this contribution, since the early 1980s, Western Europe appears to be caught in a frenzy of administrative reform activity. However, it is useful to distinguish between the various types of reform programmes:

– *reforms which are part of an outgoing process of generally internally-induced modernisation.* These would include the progressive and piecemeal adjustment to membership of the European Union and to increasing internationalisation[16] and the progressive, if problematic, introduction of new technologies.[17]

– *reforms which are introduced by governments in reaction to specific political pressures.* These would include the dramatic restructuring of the central administration in Belgium (where ministries have been split on linguistic grounds), the purge and reorganisation of the East German administration following reunification, and the creation of centrally located horizontal and vertical bodies of intergovernmental relations in regionalising countries such as Spain and Italy.

– *reforms which are introduced by governments in piecemeal, pragmatic and instrumentalist fashion* – which is the case in most countries for reforms affecting organisational structures.

– *reforms which are necessitated by the management of the above reform programmes.* Thus, the privatization of public monopolies in the United Kingdom has led to the creation of regulatory agencies, whilst decentralisation – one of the major politico-administrative responses to pressures on the state – has often demanded considerable administrative reforms at the national level.[18] Technological innovations are both a response to, and a source of administrative reform.

– *reforms which belong to a comprehensive programme and which are part of a wider programme of political change.* In some senses, the British reform programme – arguably the most radical in Western Europe – has never been structured by an overarching strategy. Rather it was stumbled into, was developed on the hoof, and was fed by its own apparent success. The reasons for the programme were often invented after implementation. At a more profound level, however, it could be argued that the programme has assumed a coherence and rationalisation which is embedded in that wider set of anti-state instincts and prejudices which have informed the British Conservative government since 1979. Like Sweden after 1982 public sector reform appears to have moved from being an 'ad hoc activity' to being a 'public policy' (in the terms of March and Olsen).[19] Overall programmes often underpinned by anti-statism, albeit in attenuated form, may be seen in the reforms of the first Lubbers cabinet (1982–86) in the Netherlands, and of the 1983 Conservative-Liberal government in Denmark. The same cannot be said of the wide-ranging programmes of the Spanish Socialists [the 1992 *Plan de Modernización de la Administración del Estado* contained no fewer than 204 separate proposals], of the Rocard government in 1989 in France (which wished to move from an 'administration de procédure' to an 'administration de responsabilité'), of the November 1990 programme of the newly elected Social Democratic government in Norway, of the Swedish Social Democrats who returned to power in 1982 after six years of right-wing coalition power and who in 1985 presented a comprehensive reform package, or of '*la cura Cassese*', the radical reform programme [the *Indirizzi per la modernizzióne delle amministrazioni pubbliche* proposed 36 reform ambitions under ten main headings], of the 1993 Ciampi government in Italy, and named after the minister responsible for the '*pachetto*'. In all these cases, the desire was not to dismantle or weaken the state apparatus, but to streamline and modernise it, either as part of a more far-reaching state modernisation programme or for purely instrumental reasons.

What programmes of administrative reform are being pursued in Western Europe? According to the country studied they may involve either marginal adjustment or radical change, involve several interconnected levels, and they may be summarised as follows:[20]

I. *Reduction in the size, resources and scope and direct leverage of the national public sector.* This may be seen in attempts – not altogether successful – to reduce or to stabilize the number of civil servants (see Statistical Annex after the notes). This policy has been pursued notably by Greece (the New Democracy government in 1992 committed itself to a policy of 'one replacement for every two retired officials'), Portugal (which had witnessed an explosion of numbers during the 1970s and 1980s), Finland (the 1992 budget aims at reducing the size of the state administration by 5 per cent by 1995), the Netherlands (which, in 1992, targeted a reduction of 9,000 by 1994), Sweden (with its ambitious Plan of October 1990 designed to reduce the national public administration by 10 per cent over a three year period), France (which in 1987 decided to reduce the number of intakes even into ENA, its elite administrative training school, by half), and now Italy. Similar squeezes on personnel numbers may be seen in Denmark and, to a lesser extent, in Austria and Germany. The champion butcher is, of course, the United Kingdom which saw a reduction in the number of civil servants of 46,602 (or 7.3 per cent) to 554,212 in 1987–93, although the reality is less dramatic than the figures and the government suggest.[21]

The squeeze in resources has affected all national public sectors, forcing many into policies of cut-back management.[22] The aggregate data do, however, disguise considerable variations across policy areas, and, in any case suggest that radical ambitions have not always been translated into effective outcomes.

The scope of the public sector has been reduced most markedly by the policy of privatization, especially in the industrial domain. The United Kingdom and France have the most radical industrial privatizers, although other countries, after a reluctant and sluggish start, are extending the limits and accelerating the pace of their privatization drives.[23]

However, privatization, in the sense of the wholesale transfer to the private sector, has been much less apparent in the public services and welfare state areas, although some limited policies have been undertaken in the United Kingdom[24] and in the Netherlands.

The attempt to reduce the scope of the public sector may also be seen in the policies of deregulation or more especially of debureaucratisation – the scrapping of rules and regulations which have grown in number and complexity and which are either obsolete or hamper the pursuit of a government policy. Amongst the most notable debureaucratisation campaigns have been those of Germany (the Federal Government established in 1983 a Committee charged with the task of identifying useless regulations), and Britain (President of the Board of Trade Michael Heseltine's 1993 promise of 'a bonfire of regulations' is but the latest step). In Portugal, in October 1990, the Cavalo Silva government even established a National Day for Debureaucratisation, to be celebrated every last Tuesday of October, with the aim of raising awareness of the problem and to produce initiatives to solve it. As in many other countries, a project team has been created to monitor progress – or lack of it. In Britain seven such teams were established in 1993.

The size, resources and scope of the national public sector have also been reduced – often sharply – by decentralisation policies, either to the regions (Belgium, Spain, Italy), or to the departments and municipalities (France, Norway, Sweden, Denmark). The notable exception is the United Kingdom which has lived through a period of unprecedented centralisation.

Reducing the direct leverage of the State has taken several forms, most notably in the policies of disguised privatization (granting greater autonomy to state public enterprises and privatizing their management or objectives – a policy seen in almost all countries which retain an extensive public sector) and of policy delegation either to independent administrative or regulatory bodies or to 'third sector' bodies. The 1980s and early 1990s have seen the proliferation of independent administrative regulatory authorities which fall outside the state administration, traditionally defined, or local government, and which are entrusted with public tasks. Thus, financial and insurance markets, competition policy and broadcasting are increasingly regulated by such bodies and not directly by state administrations.[25]

Policy deregulation may also be seen in the widening range of public tasks undertaken by third sector bodies – non-profit generally – which are 'private agents of public policy'[26] delivering 'government by proxy'[27] in areas such as education, health and pensions.[28] Such bodies have always played a prominent policy-making role in countries such as

Germany and the Netherlands. They are now spreading to Southern Europe.

II. *Improving the monitoring capacity of the administration by reforming budgetary, planning and evaluation procedures of the public sector* – in an attempt to achieve better value for money, based on the three 'Es': economy, efficiency and effectiveness. This is closely linked with marketisation, management and technological reforms. At bottom, it involves the tightening of financial controls and accountability, and improved auditing and evaluation of more precisely defined objectives, often in the form of contracts.[29] As any British academic will testify, evaluation has become a policy craze since the mid-1980s.

But no other European country has escaped the mania. Even Switzerland, the least reformist of West European countries, has joined the monitoring bandwagon (since the measures taken in February 1990). Scores of bodies have been strengthened or established to carry out auditing and evaluation: the Audit Commission (1983) in Britain for local government and then the National Health Service, followed by the National Audit Office (1984) for central government; the Risk Revision Verket in Sweden; the Conseil Scientifique de l'Evaluation, the Comité interministériel de l'évaluation, and the Fonds national de développement de l'évaluation in France; the newly created (1993) office in the Corte dei Conti in Italy.[30] In some cases, those bodies even establish the performance indicators to be tested (the case of the British Audit Commission).

III. *Improving the management of the public sector* which has remained either an incremental and *ad hoc* process or has developed into part of a wider and allegedly coherent management 'revolution'. The British Conservatives have pursued the New Public Management (NPM) strategy with the greatest zeal, starting with the Rayner scrutinies of individual departments and the Griffiths Report (1983) on the need to introduce managers into the National Health Service and then the Financial Management Initiative and then broadened out to encompass broader objectives. They have also provided it with a belated intellectual and ideological underpinning.[31] Yet Swedish Social Democrats and Spanish and French Socialists, untainted by the same ideological motivations, have been only slightly less zealous. NPM has become an ideology in itself – and a dominant one in many political circles and public management schools – and is slowly being diffused across Western Europe: by 1991 the first timid steps were being taken in Italy. Many of the dominant features of NPM spring from the wider reform programme, and may be summarised in the following way:[32]

– *Fragmentation*: this may be seen at several levels. In the first place, it may be seen at the level of policy-making, with the separation of policy decision from policy execution. A small group of central administrative decision makers should be served by a host of devolved and autonomous (in operational and budgetary terms) agencies. This system of internal self-government or agencification has long historical roots in Sweden, has been adopted in the Netherlands (with the 1983 report *The Improvement of Performance in Government Organisations*), in Denmark, and in France. Measures designed to enhance autonomy for the managers have also been introduced in Austria, in Italy (since December 1992) and Spain (the 1992 Budget Act established two pilot agencies, one in the tax collection service, the other in the postal services). In Norway, the new Social Democratic government decided, in November 1990, to grant greater autonomy for day-to-day operations to existing agencies.

This policy of splitting delivery of services from policy making through autonomous agencies has received its most forceful expression in the United Kingdom, with the introduction of the *Next Steps Initiative* in 1988. Launched in 1988, with the Vehicle Inspectorate, it involved 49 agencies embracing a third of the Civil Service by the end of 1991. By the end of 1993 there were over 90 agencies and 44 candidates had been identified. It was hoped that by the end of 1995 four fifths of the civil servants would have been transferred to agencies.[33] The purchaser/provider divide – another, but related form of fragmentation – is clearly evident in local government and in the National Health Service which has witnessed the creation and rapid growth in the number of self-governing hospital trusts and fund-holding family practitioners which have been encouraged to opt out of local authority control. In this disaggregated administrative world, integrated hierarchies have given way to independent agents whose relations are regulated by contracts. The public service has thus taken on the appearance of constituting a nexus of contracts or treaties.[34]

– *Regulation:* the aim of the public sector is not provision but regulation: hence, the spread and increasing influence of regulatory agencies. To ensure their independence they are separated from clients and providers.

– *Competition:* this is induced by outright privatization, deregulation, or within the public sector by marketisation, based on internal markets (as in the health services of the United Kingdom, the Netherlands and Germany), contracting out and tendering (often obligatory), vouchers. By March 1994, market testing in the United Kingdom had put the jobs of 25,000 civil servants up for competition,[35] and great swathes of the public sector (including not only catering, computer service, car pools and property management, but also more delicate areas such as helicopter maintenance and ship repairs for the armed forces, the running of the Treasury's economic model, amphibious training courses for the Royal Marines, passport production, and security for the Royal Armouries) had been subject to market testing and competitive tendering. The idea is to construct surrogate or social markets which duplicate in the public sector, as far as possible, those pressures for efficiency and quality which exist in the private sector.

– *'Hands-on' management* enjoying greater visibility, accountability and discretion.

– *Precision:* NPM is management by objectives or precise corporate plans, defined by contract, and based on explicit targets, measures or indicators of performance. It has been widely introduced from Thatcherite Britain to the Spain of Felipe Gonzáles.[36]

– *Output orientation:* emphasis is shifted from processes to *results*, with rewards, including pay, linked to performance. Evaluation becomes a key element in NPM.

– *Privatization* of management personnel, styles and procedures (total quality management, quality circles, flexibility in hiring and firing, incentives and sanctions). The traditional ethic of public service is to be replaced by one based on entrepreneurship, personal initiative and risk taking.[37]

– *Parsimony:* in resource allocation, with greater sensitivity to cost cutting and financial discipline.

– *Customerisation:* the task of the public sector is not to cater for the citizenry but to serve 'customers' – sometimes according to quality contracts as in the UK's *Citizen's Charter* of July 1991 or the *Charte des services publics* of March 1992 in France.

IV. *Dismantling the traditional statutory framework for civil servants which was based on*:

– *Permanence:* officials on short-term contracts increased sharply everywhere but especially in countries such as France (they tripled between 1981 and 1991 to reach 150,000 in that year).

– *Tenure:* it is now easier to dismiss civil servants in several countries such as France (since the Act of 30 July 1987) and Italy where the *posto sicuro* is no longer *sicuro* as a result of a decision of December 1993. A 1994 plan emanating from the British Efficiency Unit which is attached to 10 Downing Street envisages compulsory redundancies for underperformers and officials 'surplus to requirements'.

– *Full-time work:* part-time workers are now beginning to be recruited in several Western European countries.

– *Equal pay for people of the same rank:* performance-related pay is now a common feature of European bureaucracies, including Britain, Austria, Sweden, France, Spain, Portugal, Greece, Denmark and the

Netherlands. The Norwegian decision of 1992 to pay 450 senior public managers according to individual performance contracts is but one of several such plans. This growing individualisation of the public sector is matched by its officially encouraged Balkanisation – and not only in its organisational structures. The very notion of a unified civil service – *un grand service public* – is under threat. And if national pay bargaining – one of the expressions of its unity – remains intact in most countries, there are clear signs of erosion in others.[38]

– *A sharp public-private distinction:* not only are public management training programmes being organised by private bodies (as in France, for example) or are increasingly imbued with a private-sector logic (as in the UK), but attempts are being made to attract private sector managers into the public service: attempts have been made to open up the ENA in France to the private sector, and in the United Kingdom the Efficiency Unit, in November 1993, suggested that most senior public administrative posts be advertised and made competitive – a plan welcomed by Prime Minister John Major.[39]

V. *Democratize the public sector* in a variety of ways: enabling greater consultation in public enquiries; ensuring greater, if not equal opportunities in recruitment or and promotion with the administration and especially amongst its elites (ENA in France, the *cuerpos superiores* in Spain) for women, working-class people, ethnic or linguistic minorities, and the physically handicapped; providing the lower echelons of the administration with some say in decision making through the introduction of quality circles. There have even been tentative experiments in workplace democracy and co-determination in a few countries.

VI. *Render the public sector more user-friendly*, by greater openness, personal visibility, responsiveness and accountability. Reforms under this heading include the naming of officials (personalisation), the simplification of administrative procedures by reducing the number involved, by reducing the number of signatures required for any one transaction (as in Greece), or by the 'single-window' campaigns in France and Italy aimed at eliminating some units within a department involved in issues to the user. They would also include giving citizens greater access to their own records and to government information (Information Acts have been passed in almost all countries) and strengthening complaints institutions and procedures.[40] In certain countries a real effort has been made to improve the image of the administration through well-orchestrated public relations campaigns, and some public management courses underline the 'customerisation' development of the sector. In Ireland, workshops have been organised to sensitise public managers to the needs of their 'clients'.

VII. *Reorganizing the structures of the public sector.* The response to the above changes has required a certain capacity for institutional innovation and renovation: ministry reduction, reshuffling and creation (new ministries for environmental affairs, for women's affairs and for administrative reform); new state-controlled regulatory and coordinating agencies at international, EU and national level; the new independent administrative bodies; new semi-autonomous agencies within the departments; new bodies to encourage technological change (such as the French Comité interministériel de l'Informatique et de la Bureaucratique dans l'Administration); new or reinforced auditing or evaluation bodies (see above); a proliferation of instruments to foster and monitor administrative reform, [*cellules de modernisation* in Belgium, the General Office of Public Administrative Service Inspectors (IGSAP) in Spain, the Central Productivity Observatory in Germany, the Government Commissioner for Administrative Reforms in the Netherlands; the Efficiency Unit at 10 Downing Street, the Public Competition and Purchasing Unity at the Treasury, and more recently, in the United Kingdom the Citizens' Charter Unit, the Office of Public Service and Sciences in the United Kingdom]. In truth administrative organisational environment has defied all attempts at simplification, and agencification (see below) has merely added a few complex dimensions.

VIII. *Transforming the culture of the public sector* in accordance with the old adage about making 'the business of government less unbusinesslike'. The public sector should be 'entrepreneurial' in spirit, led by a breed of more 'robust public servants', and served by officials who are sensitive to the private sector and to its 'customers', who are keener on economics than on law, who are more concerned about cash flows and balancing income and expenditure and who prefer the market to formal rules and competitiveness to bureaucratic order. In the words of the Spanish Socialist's reform programme of 1989, but which could have been voiced by any Thatcherite, the administration should 'pride itself on getting results' and rid itself of its 'old legal culture'.[41] Or, to quote the Swedish Social Democratic government's ambition: there was a need to move from 'an authority culture to a service culture'.[42]

'Downsizing', 'resource-squeeze', 'cut-back management', 'economic effectiveness', efficiency, privatization, 'outsourcing', 'marketisation', 'new managerialism', 'contractorisation', 'competition', 'customarisation', 'restructuring', 'democratisation', 'autonomisation', 'agencification' – these are but a few of the many forces currently affecting the public sector. But the extent, intensity, mix, timing and pace differ widely across Western Europe. There is a danger of seeing the administrative world through Anglo-American spectacles: the administrative reform movement – when it exists – has a chequered record on closer inspection.

POLICY DIFFERENCES: TOWARDS AN EXPLANATION

There is a singular lack of reliable comparative data on the administrative reform programmes being carried out across Western Europe.[43] However, a wealth of fragmentary evidence clearly points to major differences in the style, nature, timing, and pace of the programmes. These differences do not appear to be correlated with the political complexion of governments or with the macro-economic performance levels of countries.

In terms of *style*, it would appear that there are marked differences, for instance, between the evolutionary and internally generated programme of the Germans, the reformist and negotiated programme of the French and Spanish, and the imposed radicalism of the British. Differences in the *nature* of the programmes may be seen in their range and composition. As noted above, the British have pursued a wide-ranging strategy of reform and have sought to anchor it in an even wider set of theoretical or ideological rationalizations. Other governments, Lubbers' (1982–86) in the Netherlands, Olof Palme's in Sweden, Rocard's in France, Gonzáles' in Spain and Ciampi's in Italy have also elaborated wide-ranging programmes. In most other countries, however, the reform process has been limited, sporadic and *à la carte*. It has not been driven by some new paradigm or overriding need, but has been reactive, partial and largely instrumental.

Some countries have shared elements of the British package. Others have not. If the Greeks in 1991 and 1992 and the Italians in 1993 joined the British in trying to curb the influence of the unions (over appointments or the financing of their activities) in the public sector,[44] almost all others have had neither the desire nor the means to do so. Other reform programmes have notable omissions or distinctive features compared with the British one. Thus, the Germans, Greeks and Portuguese have not indulged in *Next Steps*-type budgetary decentralisation. The Greeks, French and Spanish have tried to introduce more participation into certain levels of decision making – hardly a characteristic of the British reforms.

Amongst the specific features of each reform programme have been the new Recruitment Law in Austria in 1989 (designed to depoliticise the public sector), the strengthening of the Court of Accounts in Italy (to combat corruption), the important reforms in the system of administrative justice and the emphasis placed on the introduction of information technology in France in the 1980s, the creation of ministerial private offices (or *cabinets* on the French model) in Greece under the Pasok government, and the 1984 return of the Spanish public administration which unified several administrative *cuerpos*, the decision of the Portuguese government to provide money for advanced training programmes for its public sector managers – either in national or foreign institutions.

The different *timing* of the programmes is clear by looking at the policies of resource squeeze. Whilst in Britain the 'party' was declared to be 'over' by a pre-1979 Labour government, the *fiesta* roared ahead in Spain, Portugal and Greece until the late 1980s or early 1990s (there was a very sharp increase in spending all three countries during the period of transition). And whilst several countries attempted to reduce or peg the number of civil servants from the early 1980s, similar policies came late in countries such as Portugal.[45]

In terms of the pace of reforms, there are very clear differences between the sustained frenzy of the British programme and the sporadic or cautious attitudes of most European countries. The Italians, after an apprehensive and fitful approach to reform, have now decided to push forward rapidly with a comprehensive reform of the country's labyrinthine, chaotic and gargantuan administration: the '*pacchetto Cassese*' contains elements aimed at increasing performance control, flexibility, mobility, visibility and accountability within the public administration and at eliminating or reducing corruption, clientelism, automatic promotion based on seniority, absenteeism, fringe benefits, pensions and those infamously prolonged coffee breaks.[46] The Greeks, on the other hand, have made noisy declarations of intent which are rarely translated into action.

Explanations for these differences lie at four interlinked levels: pressures; potential; ambitions; perceived political opportunity structures.

Whilst many pressures for reform have been common some have differed in their intensity and in their timing. Thus, the United Kingdom felt the budgetary pressure earlier than most of its European neighbours. The administrative adjustment to the European Community was clearly more demanding in the 1980s for the new member states – Spain, Portugal and Greece – than for the founder members. Furthermore, some countries have clearly felt different pressures: rapid federalisation in Belgium; regionalisation in Italy and Spain;[47] the pressing need to improve the technical quality of management in Greece (hence the creation of a National School of Administration in 1983 to train top officials[48]) and Portugal; the purge or retraining of East German officials and the absorption of the five new *Länder* in Germany.[49]

Depoliticisation has been an issue in France and more especially in

Italy (60 per cent of Italian civil servants have been recruited outside the normal competitive examination system) and Greece (where some 15 per cent of the civil servants have been politically recruited on short-term contracts). In the latter two countries measures have been taken to tighten up recruitment procedures. Both countries have also attempted to abolish the practice of civil servants holding more than one post simultaneously (in the Greek case *inside* the public sector).[50]

Reform programmes are also obviously shaped by what is potentially reformable. If there is no radical industrial privatization in Sweden and the Netherlands it is because neither country has ever had an extensive system of public enterprises. Similarly, the potential for decentralisation has been far greater in Britain, Portugal, Greece and France than in Germany or Denmark. The same may be said of the public administration. Thus, the Swedes and the Danes have not established numerous *Next Steps* autonomous agencies because they already have them (and in some senses pioneered their use), and the Germans, the Danes and the Dutch have not outsourced administrative activities to third sector bodies because they already do so.

Third, differences in programmes clearly spring from different ambitions. It would be entirely mistaken to interpret the absence of radical programmes in most countries as an indication of lack of pressure, potential or political will. Many West European countries have simply defined quite limited ambitions – even when pressures for change are apparent. Hence the Germany government of Kohl, which has only rarely (and recently) indulged in anti-state rhetoric or 'bureaucrat-bashing', has limited itself to only very timid reforms of the central administration. And it did not seize the opportunity of reunification to reorganize the boundaries of either the West or East German Länder (a policy advocated by reformers seeking more 'rational' territorial units). It would be equally mistaken to view all radical programmes as motivated by the same objectives as those of the British Thatcherites or the Danish Conservative government of 1982. Left-wing governments in Spain, France and Sweden were keen on modernising their public administrations not denigrating and dismantling them.[51]

Finally, differences between the programmes have clearly been determined by domestic political opportunity structures. Political will and durability are vital for reforming governments,[52] and these ingredients have frequently been in short supply. Of equal importance is a propitious politico-institutional environment. A quick analysis of the British reform programme underlines this point, since all the elements were favourable to radical policy-making:

– *strong executive leadership* focused around the premiership. This was a factor in countries such as the Netherlands and Denmark. However, a reforming Prime Minister is much more hemmed in by his ministerial colleagues, and exercises little or no administrative/bureaucratic leadership. In other countries, such as Germany, sharp departmental segmentation or compartmentalisation hampers attempts to generalise reform proposals across the entire administration.

– *the backing of government, parliament and majority party.* Elsewhere, reticence or divisions or resistance have frequently been the case. Thus, the German government has been divided over privatization whilst the Swedish Social Democrats were profoundly split over public sector reform.[53] Moreover, in the British system the traditional strict separation between political and administrative personnel has left the public sector unprotected against politically-imposed decisions. In many European countries, civil servants are powerfully represented in the government, in parliament and in the political parties.

– *the absence of constitutional or statutory constraints and developed judicial review.* This is certainly not the case in many West European countries where constitutional inhibitions are all too obvious (Germany and Switzerland, for example) or where judges have placed firm limits on the reformers (e.g., the French Constitutional Council has clearly imposed obstacles to the privatization of certain welfare services and of the prison service). Alternatively there are civil service laws which effectively limit reform ambitions. This is the case in France, Germany, Italy, Austria and Belgium. Perhaps more profoundly, the public sector in the United Kingdom, unlike elsewhere, receives no cultural shield in the form of a developed doctrine of the state and its irreducible and inalienable core and function: there is no equivalent in Britain, for instance, to the Germany constitutional principles of the *Sozialstaat* or of the federal state which effectively place limit on the ambitions of reformers. The history of the United Kingdom has led to an identification of the government with the state, to a deep acceptance of parliamentary sovereignty, and to an 'executive prejudice' – an instinctive acceptance by most elites that the interest of a government, backed by parliament, coincides with that of the state. States with more turbulent histories have erected constitutional or cultural barriers against such notions.

– *the absence of powerful generalised political constraints* which slow down or even prevent particular programmes. Of course, political constraints have existed in the United Kingdom, and even Prime Minister Thatcher was occasionally very sensitive to them: privatizing welfare state provision was always delicately handled, and public spending in some areas even increased in real terms for political reasons. Yet the British Conservatives have not been confronted with the inherently costly or inhibiting, process of democratic transition when there is 'a primacy of politics' (Spain, Portugal, Greece) or of territorial reconstruction (Germany and even Belgium), or of persistently consensual modes of policy making – however eroded (the Netherlands, Germany, Denmark, Sweden).[54]

– *a willingness and capacity to restructure the policy networks* which were protective of the traditional system or to marginalise those who opposed reform (including not only the trades unions but also reluctant managers and even the head of the Civil Service!). Elsewhere, with one or two exceptions (Italy since late 1992, for example) an attempt has been made to avoid compulsion, and to negotiate the reform process with public-sector managers or unions: this is the case in France where union agreement has been necessary on certain issues, in Spain, Ireland, Belgium, Greece, Germany and Sweden, where the unions and managers have often been intimately involved in reform negotiations. In Spain, for instance, the 1988 reform package was discussed widely: between 1989 and 1991 over 1,500 people were consulted, and then a pilot scheme introduced, and an agreement to modernise the administration was signed in November 1991 between representatives of the four leading unions and the PSOE government. In France, the Rocard government, from September 1989, in pursuit of its reform ambitions decided on a vast programme of consultation. It organised 29 regional colloquia and a giant meeting in Paris in November 1990.

– *the lack of an effective political opposition* which was the case in the United Kingdom throughout the 1980s. However, this has not been the case in many other countries with Conservative governments. Thus, the Liberal Conservative government elected in 1982 in Denmark was forced to withdraw its plans to contract out a range of activities following effective opposition from the Social Democrats in Parliament backed by the public-sector unions.[55]

– *the ability to mobilise able insiders to push forward the reform programme*. Contrary to expectations, many civil servants have proved sensitive to the need for reform – and, in some cases, have even become the motor of the reform programmes (notably in Spain and France). However, in many countries (including Austria, Spain, Italy and Greece) these reformists (often technocrats) have encountered the indifference, apprehension or even hostility of their colleagues. Indeed, the traditional legal and bureaucratic culture remains entrenched in many administrations: there is frequently no one available for managing the kind of reform[56] which calls into question the operational ideology of the *Rechtsstaat*.[57]

– *the construction of a legitimizing discourse* which has taken a negative form (anti-big government, anti-remote and profligate bureaucrats, anti-state) or has been more positive in tone: privatizing and marketising in the name of individual choice; devolving authority to third-sector organisations in the name of strengthening civil society; introducing new technology in the name of modernisation, decentralising budgetary discretion to agencies in the name of efficiency. 'Efficiency' has frequently been invoked to push through specific reforms by most governments, whilst the Spanish and French Socialist governments have developed an ideology of modernisation to justify their programmes. Yet only the Norwegian and Danish Conservatives have adopted a British multi-pronged ideological strategy to attack the public sector and to legitimise their plans to reform it. Most European governments, through desire or prudence, have not attempted to pursue their limited, pragmatic and negotiated programmes in ideological terms.

Different programmes are, therefore, rooted in the differing intensity and timing of similar pressures, different pressures, ambitions, motives, constitutional, political and institutional capacity, constraints and will, and in the complex relationship between these factors. Complexity is heightened by the contingent nature of several of these factors. Each West European country has a unique blend of factors which explains persistent divergence in spite of clear evidence of convergence. In short, national contexts matter.

PUBLIC SECTOR REFORM: IMPACT, LIMITS, DILEMMAS, PARADOXES AND PROBLEMS

What picture emerges from this brief survey of the various public-sector reform programmes? The lack of systematic data, particularly on the implementation and impact of the various reform programmes, makes meaningful comparison very difficult. Yet several general trends are clearly discernible.

In the first place, public-sector reform is on the political agenda of every West European government, and the nature of reform programmes have broadened in scope in many countries and have been radicalised in nature in several. Arguably, as noted above, public sector reform is moving in some countries (such as Sweden and the United Kingdom) from the situation of being an '*ad hoc* activity' to one of being a generalised 'public policy'. Second, under the impact of convergent pressures many similar policies are being implemented – in spite of differences in the timing, pace and style of implementation. Such policies include attempts to peg the size of the public sector and the salaries of its officials, privatization in its various forms, greater transparency, the creation of new bodies, and the introduction of new technologies. Third, the enduring significance of different national contexts may be seen in the 'policy mix' adopted: the United Kingdom has been an active privatizer but a no less active centraliser; France has privatized but decentralised; Spain has decentralised radically but privatised little. New public management has affected some countries, notably the United Kingdom, but not others, such as Germany.

In general terms, the current situation of the public sector may be described in terms of the following contrived alliteration. Compared with the early 1980s, it is becoming:

– *more defined*, as national policy-makers (helped or hindered by the courts) seek the Holy Grail – the irreducible core of the state, and adjust the administration to the servicing of that core;

– *more diminished* in role and prestige, if not always in size (which, in spite of all reformist ambitions, remains obdurately stable and high);

– *more decremental* in many of its policy imperatives: automatic and reassuring incrementalism based on political and social accommodation has given way to greater budgetary prudence and discipline;

– *more divided* as the result of increased internal competition for resources;

– *more disaggregated* or fragmented as a consequence of decentralisation, deconcentration and diffusion;

– *more distant* from the citizen because implementation is being increasingly transferred to non-state agents;

– *more deregulated* in a whole variety of ways;

– *more denationalised*, as the result of globalisation and regionalisation;

– *more defensive and demoralised*, since it is the object of incessant criticism, being mistaken as the cause and not the symptom of the defects of the system it serves, and since it is the object of reform by politicians who are insensitive to the hidden long-term costs of collapsing morale.[58]

More importantly, the public sector appears to be more *disoriented*, or tension-ridden[59], with the apparent undermining of many of the remaining props of the traditional system. There props were: a public service rooted in the nation state; emphasis on size to ensure economies of scale, and on planning (hence the integration of purchasing and providing); extended hierarchical lines, with detailed rules to govern the levels of the hierarchy; application of the legal rule as the dominant operational mode, with services deemed efficient if they were provided, in uniform fashion, in accordance with the law; permanent and full-time officialdom – government service is a *career*; work organised according to general rules of an impersonal nature to guarantee equality (including salaries) amongst people of the same rank; a distinction between administration and policy-making, based on loyalty to political masters and the political neutrality of officials; a clear separation of the public and private domains; the anonymity of the public official; functional specialisation; a generalised ethos imbued with notions of 'the public interest', 'equity', 'fairness' and 'uniformity'.

Of course, this dismantlement of the traditional system should not be exaggerated. First, the traditional Weberian model was an ideal type (as Weber himself makes clear) and many of its characteristics in several countries were either fictional or totally absent. Yet, in other countries they remained important, and in most they provided a normative framework.[60] Second, as noted above, some governments (notably the German and the Belgian) even when confronted with great pressure have made no significant attempts to alter the internal functioning of their existing systems.[61] Third, past experiences teaches us to be sceptical about the impact of reform programmes of the public sector which has a long and distinguished record in burying the ambitions of politicians.[62] Constitutional and institutional rigidities as well as the lack of sustained political will frequently dilute the impact of reforms.[63] For instance, traditions of centralised decision-making, often centred on the Treasury or the sponsoring ministry hinders the pursuit of greater internal autonomy.[64] Thus, in the United Kingdom, 'new public managers' are supposed to develop an enterprise culture in the public services and to focus on outputs and the delivery of services – but within an input-dominated, cash-limited public expenditure system with a strong tradition of Treasury control. Moreover, they continue to be swamped with circulars and regulations, and rarely have the right to recruit, train, promote or fire the staff working for them.

More profoundly, we know very little about the impact of the various reform programmes on the culture of the public official.[65] Fragmentary evidence merely reinforces a natural scepticism: thus, in Britain and France powerful appeals for quality innovation, marketing and new participatory management do not appear to affect those high-ranking civil servants who make the appeals;[66] the spread of information technology to the public sector remains more limited than its champions would believe.[67] So, in spite of the changes and adaptations of the period since the early 1980s the traditional progressive public administration model remains intact in many of its essential features.

Nevertheless, the process of reform and adaptation has had its impact and has thrown up one central dilemma, several paradoxes, many contradictions and even more genuine problems.

The central dilemma for the reformers may be stated simply: effective reforms must generally attract the support of those affected, but many of those affected are allergic or hostile to reforms. Negotiation invariably entails modification and dilution whilst imposition runs the danger of demoralising and demotivating those involved in implementation.

The paradoxes are multiple. Thus, many of the reforms are inspired by private management (which is notoriously prone to fads) and by private business practices, which often leave a great deal to be desired. Indeed, large businesses naturally attempt to protect dominant positions, regulate competition and encourage protectionism. And they often do so by leaning on their respective governments. They also leech upon the public sector by asking it to provide a healthy, educated and trained workforce and a well-run public infrastructure.[68] The less charitable might also point out that imitating the private sector with its less than distinguished performance since the early 1980s is a paradox in itself. A second major paradox lies in the fact that state withdrawal in one direction may trigger increased state interventionism in another: privatization of public utilities in the United Kingdom has led to the creation of increasingly intrusive regulatory agencies; the retreat from universalism in order to cut costs has involved targeting and means-testing – both highly detailed forms of state interference. A third major paradox is that state withdrawal, through privatization, deregulation, decentralisation and functional devolution, requires sustained political will and activity by the state: legislative activism is one of the hallmarks of the self-effacing state.

The contradictions of the various reform programmes are no less numerous: the pursuit of administrative responsiveness may be costly in terms of economy and efficiency (though it may ensure greater effectiveness and equity . . .); greater transparency is unlikely to be ensured by fragmentation, devolution and increasing hybridisation; managerialism may clash with the objectives of open government and of participation; the drive for economy (less state and less budget) may conflict with effectiveness (improving performance sometimes requires budget expansion); evaluation designed to cut costs has the unpleasant side effect of identifying areas where costs have to rise; the devolution of authority to self-regulatory agencies is often accompanied by a policy of increasingly regulating previously self-regulated bodies (in financial services, for example).

Many of the problems encountered by the reformers are perhaps unavoidable: contract management erodes the responsibility and status of central departments and leaves their officials frustrated; cut-back management is a tension-ridden phenomenon; the multiplication of quasi-autonomous agencies and of sub-contracting agents heightens the already acute problem of politico-administrative coordination; membership of the European Union involves new and unavoidable regulations. Some of the problems, however, stem from rather simplistic notions of the nature of the public sector. For instance, performance-related pay may seem highly desirable as a method of motivating public-sector managers. Yet it has a demotivating effect upon those who do not receive it. Moreover, as has been frequently pointed out, it is difficult to assess performance when a great deal of work in the public sector is *collective* in nature, and when individuals rarely have one duty but a set of overlapping responsibilities.[69]

Evaluation in the public sector is an equally intrinsically difficult exercise, and it is not made easier by drawing misleading analogies with the private sector. Public-sector objectives are multiple, overlapping and frequently (often deliberately) nebulous,[70] and targets may pervert practices and indicators may distort or transform behaviour in unwelcome ways. All evaluation is not only factual or objective but value-laden, not only technical but also political.[71]

If performance-related pay and evaluation are riddled with problems, so, too, are certain forms of outsourcing, agencification and contract management. Thus, the outsourcing of computer services, for instance, has been criticised because policy and data-processing are closely related. The loss of immediately available data processing skills may be very damaging in the long term. Moreover, what effective redress exists if the private agent (chosen on the grounds of economy) proves inefficient, since the damage will have been done? Agencification – or automisation – which divorces policy-making elites from the implementing coal face is equally problematic – as the Danish and Swedish experiences demonstrate: policy-makers keep an eye on implementation whilst those who implement invariably make policy.[72]

Agencification also involves ticklish questions relating to the articulation of the agencies with central government as well as to their accountability. Contracting out – another facet of major reform programmes – is especially problematic. It often raises questions of *confidentiality* (should the British Inland Revenue go ahead with its plans to hand over tax codes and assessments to a private (possibly American) company?), of *accountability* (who is responsible when things go wrong?), of *legitimacy* (can a private security guard be invested with the same degree of trust as a police officer?) and of *control* and *coordination*.[73]

Indeed, there is a tendency in some countries towards the increased Balkanisation and privatization of the public domain, as the result of devolving authority to a diversified network of agencies, regulatory bodies, sub-contractors, third sector bodies, private companies. This network is bound together by a 'nexus of contracts' which has replaced integrated hierarchies. Exchange or bartered relationships are slowly replacing authoritative command structures. The tendency poses tricky legal questions, particularly in European countries nurtured on the myth of a single, unified administration which is juridically defined and enjoys a responsible personality.[74] However, in every country which is subject to this increasing process of policy obfuscation, or 'boundary-blurring' in which public and private interact in inextricable ways, significant practical, political and even constitutional issues are raised.[75]

Of no less importance is not only the possible demoralisation of groups of the public sector, but also, in some countries, the sapping of the public sector ethos rooted in a commitment to the public interest and in a set of 'standards of public conduct' – a point made forcibly by the House of Commons Public Accounts Committee in 1993. Such are the hidden – although increasingly visible – costs of insensitive reform.

RESHAPING THE APPARATUS OF THE STATE: SOME CONCLUDING REMARKS

There is nothing new about reforms or changes in the public sectors of Western Europe – whether imposed externally or as the result of internal adjustment to circumstances.[76] And the current wave of reform is by no means confined to Western Europe. Moreover, as we have seen, the intensity, timing and pace of reforms have varied across Western Europe. The variations may be explained by the nature of the public sector to be reformed, by the political commitment and durability of the reformers and the political opportunity structures in which they have found themselves. Several countries because of lack of need, lack of ambition, lack of means or lack of will have pursued very moderate, incremental and negotiated reform strategies. However, as noted, there are several aspects of the current reform programmes in several West European countries which appear to reflect a serious questioning of the bases of their traditional public-sector systems.

Observers have referred to the move towards 'the disinvesting state' (with privatization and deregulation), 'the frugal state' (with budgetary retrenchment and rigour), 'the strategic state' (with a withdrawal from 'low politics'), 'the enabling state' (which ensures provision rather than directly provides), 'the evaluative state' (with the multiplication of new bodies, mechanisms and criteria of evaluation), 'the regulatory state' (with the proliferation of new regulatory agencies), 'the hybridised state' (with the increasing interpenetration of the public and private spheres), and 'the supermarket state' ('a service provider – an epiphenomenon of technological, economic, demographic and physical forces outside the explicit control of any actors', based on the business corporation, and in which the key words are survival, flexibility, economy and efficiency).[77] Certainly, we see elements of all these moves – they are not mutually exclusive – but the mix varies from country to country. Furthermore, 'state withdrawal' in one direction tends to be compensated for, or neutralised by 'state expansion' in another.

The lesson of reform of a radical nature of the public sector – the mirror and motor of reform – tends to reveal the incoherencies, contradictions and hidden costs of such reform. It also underlines the limits to state redefinition in a minimalist and purely private, market-based direction. And it is not only because there are political or constitutional impediments. The problem lies at the very heart of the nature of the state. Markets may be useful in ensuring that producers are not dominant and that consumers have to be considered, and they may even, if allowed to function, ensure some degree of efficiency. Moreover, the state, with its emphasis on planning and its extended hierarchical structures, can be unresponsive and inefficient, but 'replacing hierarchies by markets' (to borrow Williamson's phrase) is fraught with difficulties.

The same may be said of extensively privatizing the state, and for much the same reason. The political context of the West European state is democracy, *Rechtsstaat*, with government making authorative decisions whilst managing overarching externalities, ensuring equity and accountability, and its organisational basis is rooted in impartiality, objectivity, regularity, predictability, legality and legitimacy.[78] The public sector, as the major instrument of the state, functions according to norms deriving from many – often conflicting – rationalities: political, legal, institutional, technical, social and economic, but a large part of its logic demands some form of Weberianism, with emphasis on uniformity, predictability impartiality, anonymity and juridification.

Whilst it is highly laudable to make government more business-like, it is highly problematic to make it more like business. The public sector has always had to juggle with many conflicting sets of values, including democracy, (hence accountability), equity (involving uniformity) and efficiency (minimising costs).[79] Too much current radical reform of the public sector is obsessed with efficiency, narrowly defined, and is based on a simplistic view of bureaucracy, a naive view of the market, an idealised view of the private sector, an insensitivity to the hidden costs of reform, an over-optimism about outcomes, and, perhaps more fundamentally, a misleading view of the state.

NOTES

1. V. Wright, 'Public Administration, Regulation, Deregulation and Reregulation' in Kjell A. Eliassen and Jan Kooiman, *Managing Public Organizations: Lessons from Contemporary European Experience* (London: Sage 1993), pp.252–3.
2. Sabino Cassese (ed.), *The European Administration* (Brussels: Int Inst. of Admin. Sciences (hereafter IIAS), 1987).
3 See, e.g., M. Keating and B. Jones, *Regions in the European Community* (Oxford: Clarendon Press, 1985).
4. See, e.g., Conseil Economique et Social, *La Modernisation de l'Administration* (Paris, 1989).
5. For a critique of these theories, see Peter Self, *Government by the Market? The Politics of Public Choice* (London: Macmillan Press, 1993).
6. Pierre Bouretz and Evelyne Pisier, *Le paradoxe du fonctionnaire* (Paris: Calman-Lévy, 1988).
7. See, e.g., Philip Cooper, 'Protecting the environment and its administrative implications', unpub. paper, annual congress of the IIAS, Vienna 1992.
8. Jean-Paul Baquiast, 'Administrative modernization and new technologies in France', *International Review of Administrative Sciences*, Vol.53 (1957) pp.171–82.
9. Calliope Spanou, *Fonctionnaires et Militants: étude des rapports entre l'administration et les nouveaux mouvements sociaux* (Paris: L'Harmatten, 1991); M. Barzelay, *Breaking Through Bureaucracy* (Berkeley, CA: Univ. of California Press, 1992).
10. See, e.g., Robert Lion, *L'Etat Passion* (Paris: Plon 1992).
11. David Osborne and Ted Gaebler, *Reinventing Government* (NY: Addison-Wesley, 1992).
12. Richard Murray and Claes Örtendahl, 'A Market-Oriented Administration in the Welfare State: Swedish Efforts to find a New Way', in United Nations, *Selected Studies on Major Administrative Reforms* (NY: UN, 1988), pp.52–3.
13. The literature on NPM is extensive. See, in particular, Andrew Hede, 'Trends in the Higher Civil Services of Anglo-American Systems', *Governance* 4/4 (Oct. 1991), pp.489–510.
14. See, e.g., Marie-Christine Kessler, 'Un paradoxe: les réformes administratives à l'étranger', unpub. paper, Annual Congress, IIAS, Vienna 1992.
15. On the issue of lesson-learning, see Franz-Xavier Kaufmann, Giandomenico Majone and Vincent Ostrom, *Guidance, Control and Evaluation within the Public Sector* (Berlin: De Gruyter, 1985).
16. C. Lesquesne, 'L'adaptation des ministères techniques à l'existence des Communautés européennes: le cas de l'administration française', *Revue Administrative*, 1988, pp.566–72; Charles Debbasch (ed.), Administrations Nationales et Intégration européenne (Paris: CNRS, 1987); IIAS, *The Administrative Implications of Regional Economic Integration: the case of the European Communities* (Brussels: IIAS, 1991); Claudio Franchini, Amministrazione Italiana e Amministrazione Communitaria, (Rome: Cedam, 1992); Sabino Cassese (ed.), *The European Administration* (Brussels: IIAS, 1980).
17. *Administration et nouvelles technologies de l'information: une necessaire adaptation du droit*, (Paris: Documentation Francaise, 1988); John A. Taylor and Howard Williams, 'Public Administration and the Information Policy', *Public Administration*, Vol.69, (Summer 1991), pp.171–90.
18. Jean-Paul Costa and Yves Jegouzo, *L'Administration Francaise face aux défis de la décentralisation* (Paris: Editions STH, 1988).

19. James G. March and Johan P. Olsen, *Rediscovering Institutions. The Organisational Basis of Politics* (NY: Free Press, 1989).
20. See further reading and Hans-Ulrich Derlien, 'Observations on the State of Comparative Administrations Research in Europe', *Governance* 5/3 (July 1992), pp.279–311.
21. Jonathan Smith and David Gould, *Civil Service Numbers* (London: European Policy Forum, 1993).
22. Andrew Dunsire and Christopher Hood, *Cutback Management in Public Bureaucracies* (Cambridge: CUP, 1989).
23. Vincent Wright (ed.), *Industrial Privatization in Western Europe* (London: Pinter Publishers, 1994).
24. Julian Le Grand and Ray Robinson (eds.), *Privatization and the Welfare State* (London: George Allen and Unwin, 1984); Ray Forrest and Alan Murie, *Selling the Welfare State: the Privatization of Public Housing* (London: Routledge, 1991); P. Taylor-Gooby and R. Lawson (eds.), *Markets and Managers: New Issues in the Delivery of Welfare* (Buckingham: Open UP, 1993).
25. Claude-Albert Colliard and Gérard Timsit, *Les autorités administratives indépendantes* (Paris: PUF, 1988); Jacques Chevallier, *Le autorità amministrative independenti* (Rome: Cappelli, 1986).
26. Wolfgang Streek and Philippe C. Schmitter (eds.), *Private Interest Government* (London: Sage, 1985); Helmut K. Anheier and Wolfgang Seibel (eds.), *The Third Sector. Comparative Studies of Nonprofit Organisations* (Berlin: De Gruyter, 1990); Tore Modeen and Allan Rosas (eds.), *Indirect Public Administration in Fourteen Countries* (Helsinki: Abo Akademis Förlag, 1988).
27. Donald Kettle, *Government by Proxy: Managing Federal Programmes* (Washington, DC: Congressional Quarterly Press, 1988).
28. Tore Modeen and Allan Rosas (eds.), *Indirect Public Administration in the Fields of Education and Pensions* (Helsinki: Abo Academy Press, 1990).
29. John J. Glynn, *Public Sector Financial Control and Accounting* (Oxford: Basil Blackwell, 1987); Henrik Nepper-Christensen, 'The Financial Management System of the Danish National Labour Inspection', *International Review of Administrative Sciences*, Vol.54 (1988), pp.233–46; Christian de Visscher, 'The modernization of budgetary techniques and financial control', *International Review of Administrative Sciences*, Vol.55 (1989), pp.323–64.
30. Eric Monnier, *Evaluations de l'action des pouvoirs publics* (Paris: Economica, 1992); Patrice Duran and Eric Monnier, 'Le développement de l'évaluation en France: nécessités techniques et exigences politiques', *Revue Française de Science Politique*', Vol.42 (1992), pp.235–61.
31. See, e.g., Howard Davies, *Fighting Leviathan: Building Social Markets That Work* (London: Social Market Foundation, 1992).
32. The best analysis of NPM is provided by C. Hood (note 43). See also the contribution of George Jones in Y. Mény and V. Wright, *La Riforma dell'amministrazione in Europa* (Bologna: Il Mulino, forthcoming); Spencer Zifcak, *New Managerialism: Administrative Reform in Whitehall and Canberra* (Buckingham: Open UP, 1993).
33. There is an extensive literature on *Next Steps*. See, e.g., 'Next Steps for the British Civil Service', *Governance* 3/2 (April 1990), pp.186–96; Patricia Greer, *Transforming Central Government. The Next Steps Initiative* (Buckingham: Open UP, 1994).
34. See, e.g., Abraham Vermeulen, 'Contract Management in the Netherlands', *International Review of Administrative Sciences*, Vol.54 (1988), pp.201–17.
35. *Financial Times*, 8 March 1994.
36. A. Guillen and E. Ramirez de Prado, 'Administracioñ por objetivos', *Documentacioñ Administrativa*, No.223 (1991), pp.139–204.
37. Florence Masa, *Gestion privée pour services publics*, (Paris: Inter Editions, 1990).
38. Nicole de Montricher, 'La fonction publique de carrière en France: problèmes et perspectives', *Revue Internationale des Sciences Administratives* 57/3 (1991), pp.433–4.

39. *Independent*, 23 Nov. 1993.
40. Céline Wiener (ed.), *L'évolution des rapports entre l'administration et les usagers* (Paris: Economica, 1991); OECD, *Administration as Service: the Public as Client*, (Paris: OECD, 1982).
41. J.R. Greenaway, 'Bureaucrats under pressure: the Thatcher Government and the Mandarin Elite', *Teaching Politics*, 13/1 (1984), pp.66–84; *Reflexiones para Modernicion* de la Administracion, Madrid, 1989.
42. Rune Premfors, 'The "Swedish Model" and Public Sector Reform', *West European Politics* 14/3 (July 1991), pp.88–9.
43. Christopher Hood, 'Reflections on the Variations in 1980s Public Management Reform', unpub. paper, LSE, Dec. 1991.
44. OECD, *Greece, Annual Report, 1991–1992* (Paris: OECD, 1992), p.59.
45. OECD, *Portugal: Annual Report, 1988–1989* (Paris: OECD, 1989), pp.52–3.
46. *La Repubblica* and *Il Messagero*, 16 Dec. 1993.
47. See, e.g., Miguel Beltran-Villalva, 'La administracion publica y los funcionarios', in Salvador Giner (ed.), *España: sociedad y politica* (Madrid: Espasa-Calpa, 1990), pp.342–8.
48. Jean Anastopoulos, 'Adapting the administration to the new economic situation: the case of Greece', *International Review of Administrative Sciences*, Vol.53 (1987), pp.35–48.
49. Hans-Ulrich Derlien, 'Historical legacy and recent developments in the German higher civil service', *International Review of Administrative Sciences*, Vol.57, 1991, pp.388–9; Klaus König, 'Administrative transformation: from a real-socialistic administration to a classical, European administration in Germany', unpub. paper, IIAS Annual Congress, Vienna 1992; Klaus Goetz, 'Rebuilding Public Administration in the New German Länder: a tale of differentiation', *West European Politics* 16/4 (Oct. 1993), pp.447–64.
50. George Vernardakis and Catheirne D. Papasthathopoulos, 'The Higher Civil Service in Greece', *International Review of Administrative Sciences*, Vol.55 (1989) pp.603–29.
51. Luc Rouban, 'La modernisation de l'Etat et la fin de la specificité française', *Revue Française de Sciences Politique* 40/4 (Aug. 1990), pp.521–45.
52. Walter J.M. Kickert, 'Administrative Reform in British, Dutch and Danish Civil Services', unpub. report, 1993, pp.9–10.
53. Premfors (note 42), pp.92–3.
54. See, e.g., U. Rosenthal and L.J. Roborgh, 'Administrative Trends in the Netherlands', in Mény and Wright (note 32).
55. Jorgen Gronnegard Christensen, 'Withdrawal of government: a critical survey of an administrative problem in its political context', *International Review of Administrative Sciences*, Vol.54 (1988) p.58.
56. Eduardo Zapico-Goñi, 'La modernisation de l'administration publique espagnole: un éclatement des réformes', *Revue Française d'Administration Publique*, Vol.66 (April–June 1993), pp.314–5.
57. Peter Gerlich, 'Deregulation in Austria', *European Journal of Political Research*, Vol.17 ((1989), pp.209–22.
58. B. Guy Peters, 'Morale in the public service: a comparative enquiry', *International Review of Administrative Sciences*, Vol.57 (1991), pp.421–40; Jean-Luc Bodiguel, 'Les fonctionnaires en période de décroissance: moral, motivation et image', *Politiques et Management Public* 6/7 (1989); Jean-Luc Bodiguel and Luc Rouban, *Le Fonctionnaire détrôné* (Paris: Presses de la FNSP, 1991); details of a leaked report from the Permanent Secretary of Social Security in *Independent on Sunday*, 20 June 1993 and one from Robin Butler, the Head of the Civil Service, in *Independent*, 21 Nov. 1993. Nicole de Montricher, 'The career public service in France: problems and prospects', *International Review of Administrative Sciences*, Vol.57 (1991), pp.373–84; details of a leaked report on the French higher civil service in *Le Figaro*, 14 Jan. 1993.
59. See Peter Aucoin, 'Administrative Reform in Public Management: Paradigms, Principles, Paradoxes and Pendulums', *Governance* 3/2 (April 1990), pp.115–37.

60. Christopher Hood, 'Public Administration: Lost an Empire, not yet found a role' in A. Leftwich, *New Developments in Political Science* (Aldershot: Gower, 1990).
61. Aymé François, 'Evolution et processus de modernisation de la fonction publique en Belgique', unpub. paper, IIAS Congress, Vienna 1992.
62. This is not only the case of the UK (where the reforms of the 1970s were short-lived in their impact). See, also, on the Netherlands, U. Rosenthal and L.J. Roborgh, 'Administrative Trends in the Netherlands', in Mény and Wright (note 32), p.25 (on the limited success of the first Lubbers cabinet). On the general issue see B. Guy Peters, 'Government Reorganisation: a theoretical analysis', *International Political Science Review* 13/2 (1992), pp.199–217.
63. Christensen (note 55), p.54; Zapico-Goñi (note 56).
64. Hanne Foss Hansen, 'Implementation of Modernisation. Paradoxes in the Public Control of Higher Educational Institutions – the case of Denmark', *Scandinavian Political Studies* 13/1 (1990), pp.37–56; Brian Edwards, 'The National Health Service: A Manager's Tale', Nuffield Provincial Hospitals Trust, 1993; P.M. Jackson, 'Management techniques in the UK public sector', *International Review of Administrative Sciences*, Vol.55 (1988), p.257.
65. For differing views on the British case, see Geoffrey K. Fry, 'The Thatcher Government, the Financial Management Initiative and the "New Civil Service", *Public Administration*, Vol.66 (Spring 1988), pp.1–20; Richard A. Chapman, 'The Changing Administrative Culture of the British Civil Service' in Colin Campbell and B. Guy Peters (eds.), *Organising Governance, Governing Organisations* (Pittsburg, PA: Univ. of Pittsburg Press, 1988); James B. Christoph, 'The Remaking of British Administrative Culture', *Administration and Society* 24/2 (Aug. 1992), pp.163–81.
66. Luc Rouban, 'The civil service and the policy of administrative reform in France', *International Review of Administrative Sciences*, Vol.55 (1989), pp.445–65; Patrick Gibert and Jean-Claude Thoenig, 'La gestion publique', *Politiques et Management Public* (March 1992).
67. See, e.g., Stefan Kuhlman, 'Informatization in Local Environmental Administration', in Ignace Th.N. Snellen *et al.* (ed.), *Expert Systems in Public Administration* (Amsterdam, NY, Oxford: Elsevier Science Publications, 1989).
68. Gerald Caiden, 'Comments', in Kenneth Kernaghan (ed.), *Social Change as a Source of Competing Values in Public Administration* (Brussels: IIAS, 1988), p.25.
69. Giuseppe Pennella, 'The management role and productivity increases in the Italian public administration: results of first application', *International Review of Administrative Sciences*, Vol.54 (1988), pp.219–31.
70. See Ray C. Rist (ed.), *Policy and Program Evaluation: Perspectives on Design and Utilization*, (Brussels: IIAS, 1990).
71. Mary Henkel, 'The New Evaluative State', *Public Administration* 69/1 (Spring 1991), pp.122–36.
72. Johan P. Olsen, 'Administrative Reform and Theories of Organisation', in Campbell and Peters (note 65) pp.249; Kickert (note 52), p.21; Lenart Gustafsson, 'Renewal of the Public Sector in Sweden', *Public Administration*, Vol.65 (Summer 1987), pp.179–81.
73. Abraham Vermeulen, 'Contract Management in the Netherlands', *International Review of Administrative Sciences*, Vol.54 (1988), pp.201–17.
74. Jacques Caillosse, 'La Modernisation de l'Etat: variations sur le modèle juridique d'administration', *AJDA*, No.11, 20 Nov. 1991, pp.755–64; Jean-Luc Bodiguel and Luc Rouban, 'La dysfonction publique ou la crise de corporatisme', *Revue Française de Science Politique* (Aug. 1987), pp.539–56; J. Chevallier, 'Un nouveau sens de l'Etat et du service public' in F. de Baecque and J.L. Quermonne (eds.), *Administration et Politique sous la Cinquième République* (Paris: Presses de la FNSP, 198?), p.164; Pierre Chambat, 'Service public et néolibéralisme', *Annales*, May–June 1990, pp.615–47; Luis Ortega, 'Le Reforma de la alta burocracia en España, *Sistema*, No.107 (March 1992), p.5.

75. See, e.g., Harold J. Sullivan, 'Privatization of Public Services: a growing threat to constitutional rights', *Public Administration Review*, Nov.–Dec. 1987, pp.464–6; the issue is also discussed in Christopher Hood and Gunmar Folke Schuppert (eds.), *Delivering Public Services in Europe* (London: Sage, 1988); Jan-Erik Lane, *The Public Sector: Concepts, Models and Approaches* (London: Sage, 1992).
76. F.F. Ridley, 'Administrative theory and administrative reform' in Gerald Caiden, *Strategies for Administrative Reform* (NY: Lexington Books, 1982), pp.1–14; B. Guy Peters, 'Government Reorganization: A Theoretical Analysis', *International Political Science Review* 13/2 (1992), pp.199–217.
77. Olsen (note 72) pp.233–54; B. Guy Peters, 'Government . . .', pp.199–217.
78. For a brief exploration of this issue, see P.C. Perry and H.G. Rainey, 'The public–private distinction in organisational theory', *Academy of Management Review*, No.13 (1988), pp.182–201. For a longer exposition, see the recent work of Peter Self, *Government by the Market? The Politics of Public Choice* (London: Macmillan Press, 1993). See also J. Chevalier and D. Loschak, 'Rationalité juridique et rationalité managériale dans l'administration française', *Revue Française d'Administration Publique*, No.24 (Oct.–Dec. 1992), pp.679–720.
79. Kenneth Kernaghan, 'Introduction', in *Social Change as a Source of Competing Values in Public Administration*, (Brussels: IIAS, 1988), p.8.

FURTHER READING

Administrative reform has generated an extensive literature. Apart from the works cited in the footnotes of this contribution, see, for the comparative data, the annual report of the OECD, *Public Management Developments* (Paris: OECD); United Nations, *Selected Studies on Major Reforms* (NY: UN 1988); the annual *Annuaire Européen d'Administration Publique* (one of the best sources); Sabino Cassese and Claudio Franchini (eds.), *Tendenze Recenti della Riforma amministrativa in Europa* (Bologna: Il Mulino, 1989); L.J. Roborg, R.R. Stough, Th. Toonen (eds.), *Public Infrastructure Redefined* (Leiden: Groen, 1988); Gerald E. Caiden (ed.), *Administrative Reform Comes of Age* (Berlin: De Gruyter, 1991); Joan Corkery (ed.), *The Implications for Public Administration of the Changing Role of the State* (Brussels: IIAS, 1991); special issue of the *International Review of Administrative Science*, Vol.57 (1991), edited by Kenneth Kernaghan; Gary Warmsley *et al.* (eds.), *Refounding Public Administration* (London: Sage 1990); Yves Mény and Vincent Wright (eds.), *La Riforma dell'amministrazione in Europa*, Bologna, Il Mulino (forthcoming).

Italian reforms have been well studied in the numerous books published within the framework of the *Progetto Finalizatta* directed by Sabino Cassese. For a very useful brief overview see the special issue of the *Revue Française d'Administration Publique* on 'L'Administration Italienne Aujourd'hui', Vol.67 (July–Sept. 1993).

On Spain, see Luis Ortega, 'La Reforma de la alta burocracia en España', *Sistema*, 107 (March 1992); Eduardo Zapico-Goñi, 'La modernisation de l'administration publique espagnole: un éclatement des réformes', *Revue Française d'Administration Publique*, Vol.66 (April–June 1993), pp.309–17; *La modernizacion de la administracion del Estado: planes de formacion del Instituto Nacionale de Administracion publica* (Madrid: Ministerio para las administraciones publicas, 1991).

On France, see the 'Chroniques' which appear in the *Revue Française d'Administration Publique*; *L'Année Administrative*, published by the Institut Français d'Administration Publique; Jean-Luc Bodiguel and Luc Rouban, 'Civil Service policies since 1981: crisis in administrative model or inertia in policies', *International Review of Administrative Sciences*, Vol.54 (1988), pp.177–99; Luc Rouban, 'La modernisation de l'Etat et la fin de la spécificité française', *Revue Française de Science Politique* 40/4 (Aug. 1990), pp.521–45; same author, 'Fonction publique et politique de modernisation', *International Review of Administrative Sciences* 55/3 (1989), pp.533–55.

On Belgium, see Aymé François, 'The modernisation of administration in Belgium', *International Review of Administrative Science*, Vol.53 (1989), pp.299–343.

On the Netherlands, A.J.G-M. Berkke, 'Changing Functions and Roles of the Dutch Civil Service', unpub. paper, 1992 IIAS Congress, Vienna.

On Sweden, see Rune Premfors, 'The "Swedish Model" and Public Sector Reform', *West European Politics* 14/3 (July 1991), pp.83–95.

The country which has attracted most attention is the United Kingdom. See Howard Elcock, *Change and Decay: Public Administration in the 1990s* (London: Longman, 1991); David Farnham and Sylvia Hortonb (eds.), *Managing the New Public Services* (London: Macmillan Press 1993); Geoffrey K. Fry, *The Changing Civil Service* (London: George Allen and Unwin, 1985); *Future Shape of Reform in Whitehall* (London: RIPA, 1988); Anthony Harrison and John Gretton, *Reshaping Central Government* (Oxford: Transaction Books, 1987); Les Metcalfe and Sue Richards, *Improving Public Management* (London: Sage, 1990); Christopher Pollitt, *Managerialism and the Public Services: The Anglo-American Experience* (Oxford: Basil Blackwell 1990); James Radcliffe, *The Reorganisation of British Central Government* (Aldershot: Dartmouth, 1991); Ian Taylor and George Popham (eds.), *An Introduction to Public Sector Management* (London: Unwin Hyman 1989); Owen E. Hughes, *Public Management and Administration* (London: Macmillan, 1994).

STATISTICAL ANNEX

TABLE 1: SIZE OF THE GOVERNMENT SECTOR, 1989
(in terms of employment)

	Total population (1 000)	Labour Force, percentage of total population	Total Employment, percentage of labour force	Civilian Employment, percentage of total employment	Government Employment, percentage of total employment
	(1)	(2)	(3)	(4)	(5)
AUSTRALIA	16 833	49.3	93.9	99.1	15.6
AUSTRIA	7 624	45.3	96.9	..	21.1
BELGIUM	9 938	41.7	90.7	97.6	..
CANADA	26 248	51.7	92.5	99.4	20.3
DENMARK	5 132	56.1	91.9	98.7	29.8
FINLAND	4 964	52.0	96.6	98.6	20.6
FRANCE	56 160	43.3	90.6	97.5	22.8
GERMANY	61 990	48.0	93.2	98.1	15.4
GREECE	10 033	39.5	92.5	..	10.4
ICELAND	253	56.1	98.6	..	16.8
IRELAND	3 515	36.8	84.4	98.8	17.9
ITALY	57 525	42.2	88.2	97.4	17.4
JAPAN	123 120	50.9	97.7	..	8.1
LUXEMBOURG	378	48.7	98.9	99.5	..
NETHERLANDS	14 849	45.2	91.7	98.5	15.1
NEW ZEALAND	3 343	47.1	92.9	..	..
NORWAY	4 227	51.0	95.1	98.3	30.8
PORTUGAL	10 337	45.2	95.0	98.5	14.1
SPAIN	38 888	39.0	83.1	97.3	14.3
SWEDEN	8 493	53.3	98.7	..	31.5
SWITZERLAND	6 723	52.6	99.5	..	10.6
TURKEY	55 255	34.7	90.0	97.1	9.1
UNITED KINGDOM	57 236	49.8	93.9	98.8	19.5
UNITED STATES	248 762	50.5	94.8	98.6	15.1
YUGOSLAVIA	..	..	..	..	..

Sources: (1) to (4): OECD Labour Force Statistics (OSIRIS Database, segment LFSTG), March 1991. (5) OECD Analytical Database (segment EOY), March 1991.

TABLE 2: SIZE OF THE GOVERNMENT SECTOR, 1988–89
(in terms of expenditure)

	GDP per Capita (in $US, current prices, current exchange rates)		Current Government Disbursements, percentage of GDP	
	1988	1989	1988	1989
AUSTRALIA	14.937	16.774	34.2	..
AUSTRIA	16.684	16.590	47.0	..
BELGIUM	15.275	15.393	44.1	..
CANADA	18.738	20.783	40.1	39.6
DENMARK	21.299	20.685	58.6	57.4
FINLAND	21.342	23.261	40.0	39.9
FRANCE	17.101	17.061	46.8	46.5
GERMANY	19.557	19.182	43.8	44.6
GREECE	5.286	5.399	34.0	31.8
ICELAND	23.680	20.516	35.4	36.6
IRELAND	9.250	9.644	..	..
ITALY	14.484	15.051	39.6	41.1
JAPAN	23.235	22.895	34.3	0.0
LUXEMBOURG	17.989	18.564	..	..
NETHERLANDS	15.405	15.064	52.4	50.1
NEW ZEALAND	12.756	12.484	..	..
NORWAY	21.251	21.503	55.1	..
PORTUGAL	4.046	4.386	..	..
SPAIN	8.877	9.772	..	..
SWEDEN	21.551	22.303	61.9	..
SWITZERLAND	27.492	26.350	35.0	34.1
TURKEY	1.313	1.431	..	..
UNITED KINGDOM	14.612	14.633	40.2	39.7
UNITED STATES	19.525	20.630	31.6	..
YUGOSLAVIA	..	..	..	..

Sources: OECD Labour Force Statistics and National Accounts (OSIRIS Database, segments LFSTG, INCOUT and GDP-DOLL), March 1991.

TABLE 3: TRENDS IN GOVERNMENT SOCIAL EXPENDITURE, 1980–88

(percentage of final consumption expenditure/GDP*)

	Total Final Consumption Expenditure		Education		Health		Social Security and Welfare	
	1980	1988	1980	1988	1980	1988	1980	1988
AUSTRALIA	17.8	16.7	4.5	3.8	3.1	3.1	0.5	0.7
AUSTRIA	18.0	18.5	3.9	..	4.4	..	3.3	..
BELGIUM	18.3	15.8	7.0	5.9	..	..	1.3	1.2
CANADA	..	..	..	..	..	..	..	..
DENMARK	..	..	..	..	..	..	..	..
FINLAND	18.1	20.1	4.9	5.1	3.9	4.4	2.3	3.2
FRANCE	..	..	..	..	..	..	..	..
GERMANY	20.1	19.6	4.1	3.7	5.9	6.1	1.9	2.1
GREECE	16.4	20.2	2.2	2.9	1.7	2.3	0.2	0.3
ICELAND	16.4	18.6	3.6	3.9	5.4	7.0	0.8	1.2
IRELAND	..	..	..	..	..	..	..	..
ITALY	14.7	17.0	4.2	4.8	3.0	3.3	0.6	0.7
JAPAN	10.0	9.5	3.7	3.8	0.4	0.4	0.5	0.6
LUXEMBOURG	..	..	..	..	..	..	..	..
NETHERLANDS	17.9	15.8	6.3	4.9	..	..	0.7	0.8
NEW ZEALAND	..	..	..	..	..	..	..	..
NORWAY	18.8	21.0	5.1	5.4	4.1	4.9	1.6	2.1
PORTUGAL	14.5	..	3.4	..	2.6	..	0.9	..
SPAIN	..	..	..	..	..	..	..	..
SWEDEN	29.1	26.0	5.9	..	7.3	..	4.8	..
SWITZERLAND	..	..	..	..	..	..	..	..
TURKEY	..	..	..	..	..	..	..	..
UNITED KINGDOM	21.2	19.6	4.3	3.8	4.7	4.6	1.4	1.4
UNITED STATES	17.6	18.4	4.6	4.5	1.0	0.9	0.6	0.6
YUGOSLAVIA	..	..	..	..	..	..	..	..

Source: OECD National Accounts (OSIRIS Database, segments GDP and GOVE), March 1991.

TABLE 4: TRENDS IN GOVERNMENT TAX INCOME, 1980–88

(percentage of GDP)

	Total Taxes		On Income and Profits		Social Security Contributions		On goods and and services	
	1980	1988	1980	1988	1980	1988	1980	1988
AUSTRALIA	28.6	30.8	16.0	17.4	..	..	8.9	8.6
AUSTRIA	41.2	41.9	11.0	10.8	12.7	13.7	13.0	13.4
BELGIUM	43.5	45.1	17.8	17.5	13.2	15.2	11.4	11.2
CANADA	31.6	34.0	14.7	15.7	3.3	4.5	10.3	10.2
DENMARK	45.5	52.1	25.0	30.5	0.8	1.2	17.0	17.8
FINLAND	33.0	37.9	16.2	19.1	3.1	3.1	12.8	14.3
FRANCE	41.7	44.4	7.6	7.7	17.8	19.2	12.7	13.1
GERMANY	38.0	37.4	13.3	12.8	13.1	14.0	10.3	9.4
GREECE	29.4	35.9	5.7	6.4	9.7	11.7	12.1	16.3
ICELAND	30.5	31.7	7.8	8.4	0.7	0.8	18.3	18.1
IRELAND	34.0	41.5	12.4	16.0	4.9	5.8	14.9	17.4
ITALY	30.2	37.1	9.4	13.2	11.5	12.4	8.0	10.4
JAPAN	25.5	31.3	11.7	14.8	7.4	9.1	4.2	3.9
LUXEMBOURG	40.9	42.8	17.7	17.8	12.0	10.9	8.6	10.8
NETHERLANDS	45.8	48.2	15.1	13.4	17.4	20.4	11.6	12.5
NEW ZEALAND	33.1	37.9	23.1	22.7	..	..	7.4	12.0
NORWAY	47.1	46.9	19.4	15.7	9.9	12.0	16.7	17.6
PORTUGAL	28.7	34.6	5.7	7.7	8.5	9.3	12.9	16.6
SPAIN	24.1	32.8	6.3	9.7	11.7	11.7	5.0	10.0
SWEDEN	49.1	55.3	21.3	24.3	14.1	13.9	11.8	13.4
SWITZERLAND	30.8	32.5	12.7	13.2	9.5	10.4	6.3	6.1
TURKEY	21.7	22.9	11.2	7.8	3.0	3.4	5.6	7.3
UNITED KINGDOM	35.4	37.3	13.5	14.0	5.9	6.9	10.3	11.6
UNITED STATES	29.5	29.8	13.9	12.8	7.7	8.8	4.9	5.0
YUGOSLAVIA	..	..	..	..	..	..	..	0.0

Source: OECD Revenue Statistics (OSIRIS Database, segment TAXREV), March 1991.

TABLE 5: TRENDS IN GOVERNMENT EMPLOYMENT, 1980–1990
(percentage of total employment)

	1980	1985	1988	1989	1990
AUSTRALIA	16.0	17.5	16.5	15.6	15.6
AUSTRIA	17.6	19.4	20.9	21.1	20.8
BELGIUM	18.7	20.2	..	..	..
CANADA	19.4	20.8	20.3	20.3	20.6
DENMARK	28.3	29.7	29.4	29.8	29.9
FINLAND	17.2	19.2	20.6	20.6	20.9
FRANCE	20.0	22.7	22.9	22.8	22.6
GERMANY	14.6	15.6	15.5	15.4	15.2
GREECE	8.9	9.9	10.1	10.4	10.2
ICELAND	15.7	16.5	16.9	16.8	17.3
IRELAND	16.4	18.8	18.4	17.9	17.2
ITALY	15.7	16.8	17.3	17.4	17.2
JAPAN	8.8	8.7	8.3	8.1	7.9
LUXEMBOURG	..	..	..	..	..
NETHERLANDS	14.8	16.0	15.4	15.1	14.9
NEW ZEALAND	17.2	14.9	..	..	..
NORWAY	25.3	29.2	29.3	30.8	32.0
PORTUGAL	10.7	13.2	14.1	14.1	14.3
SPAIN	10.5	13.4	14.1	14.3	14.5
SWEDEN	30.7	32.9	31.8	31.5	31.8
SWITZERLAND	10.1	10.3	10.5	10.6	10.6
TURKEY	10.5	9.1	9.1	9.1	9.3
UNITED KINGDOM	21.3	21.7	20.7	19.5	19.1
UNITED STATES	16.4	15.3	15.1	15.1	15.5
YUGOSLAVIA	..	..	..	..	..

Source: OECD Analytical Database (segment EOY), March 1991.

TABLE 6: TRENDS IN GOVERNMENT CURRENT DISBURSEMENTS, 1976–89
(percentage of GDP)

	1976	1980	1985	1986	1987	1988	1989
AUSTRALIA	29.8	30.7	34.1	35.2	35.0	34.2	..
AUSTRIA	42.4	46.4	48.5	48.2	47.9	47.0	..
BELGIUM	40.1	42.7	45.9	45.1	45.4	44.1	..
CANADA	35.8	36.2	38.7	39.5	40.0	40.1	39.6
DENMARK	46.9	52.2	56.5	58.3	58.8	58.6	57.4
FINLAND	41.0	35.8	40.5	41.8	39.7	40.0	39.9
FRANCE	41.8	44.5	47.6	46.9	47.4	46.8	46.5
GERMANY	44.0	44.7	45.6	44.9	44.4	43.8	44.6
GREECE	29.5	30.5	34.6	35.6	36.5	34.0	31.8
ICELAND	33.0	33.3	32.5	32.1	32.1	35.4	36.6
IRELAND	37.9	38.8	43.6	43.5	43.7	..	..
ITALY	..	33.0	38.0	39.0	39.2	39.6	41.1
JAPAN	23.6	27.6	31.2	31.5	33.4	34.3	0.0
LUXEMBOURG	50.2	53.3	55.9	52.9	..	..	..
NETHERLANDS	49.5	52.8	54.3	53.0	53.6	52.4	50.1
NEW ZEALAND	..	..	..	..	..	..	..
NORWAY	49.8	53.2	55.1	54.7	55.2	55.1	..
PORTUGAL	..	31.4	35.9	37.6	..	..	..
SPAIN	..	29.7	34.5	35.0	..	..	..
SWEDEN	..	56.3	59.5	60.4	62.2	61.9	..
SWITZERLAND	33.9	32.8	34.4	35.0	34.5	35.0	34.1
TURKEY	..	..	..	..	..	..	..
UNITED KINGDOM	39.7	39.9	42.2	41.2	40.6	40.2	39.7
UNITED STATES	29.5	30.8	31.3	31.4	..	31.6	..
YUGOSLAVIA	..	..	..	..	..	..	..

Sources: OECD National Accounts (OSIRIS Database, segments GDP and INCOUT), March 1991.

The New Role of the State in Telecommunications: An International Comparison

EDGAR GRANDE

The role of the state in telecommunications has changed significantly in the last decade. The old PTT model, characterised by a public administration with exclusive rights, has been replaced by a new institutional arrangement in most advanced industrial countries. The direct provision of services by the state has been cut back and commercialised, and public monopolies have given way to private activities. This retreat of the state, however, is only one side of the coin. Based on comparative empirical evidence on telecommunications policies in Western Europe, it is argued that the state also plays a key role within the new institutional arrangements which have evolved in this sector.

For most of the time since its beginnings in the nineteenth century, telecommunications has been considered a part of the public infrastructure that should be provided or at least guaranteed by the state. In historical and international comparison, it has been one of the economic sectors with the highest level of state ownership and activity. There are only a few sectors in which the state played such a dominant role, such as transportation (railways, air traffic), energy supply (electricity, gas) and postal services (often closely linked to telecommunications). And in economic theory, the telecommunications sector has been treated as an exceptional case where public activity is not only legitimate, but even necessary.[1]

Recently, however, a remarkable redefinition of public functions in the telecommunications sector and a far-reaching reform of their organisation has begun in most advanced industrial countries. Be they incremental (as in the United States), radical (as in Great Britain) or moderate (as in most West European countries), efforts to restructure the 'old' model of state organisation, regulation and intervention can be observed almost everywhere. The necessity to design a new institutional arrangement of public and private functions in this sector is no longer controversial; the sometimes fierce disputes of the 1980s are almost over. However, the exact shape of this arrangement and the 'new' role of the state in telecommunications remain unsettled. Has the state retreated from telecommunications? Has this sector simply been left to private actors and commercial calculations, or is there a 'new' role for the state in telecommunications?

This essay argues that within the new institutional arrangements which have evolved in telecommunications, the state also plays a key role. Comparative empirical evidence suggests that the reforms of organisation, ownership and regulation have not led to a complete loss but to a *change of functions*. Far from becoming superfluous, the state has taken on a host of new functions as it has retreated from old domains and activities. This development has been greatly underestimated by advocates of radical 'deregulation' and 'privatisation'.

Telecommunications policies in Western Europe can serve to demonstrate this argument. Following a brief sketch of the 'old' role of the state in telecommunications, a cursory survey of the reforms that have taken place in Western Europe in the 1980s will be given. Then, the sector-specific technological background of these changes will be described and, finally, the 'new' role of the state in the new institutional arrangements in telecommunications will be analysed.

THE 'OLD' ROLE OF THE STATE IN TELECOMMUNICATIONS

The 'old' model of telecommunications is characterised by both an *intensive* and an *extensive* politicisation of functions. In its ideal-type form, telecommunications was organised and managed as a public *administration* with a *universal service obligation* whose activities were protected from private competition by a far-reaching *legal monopoly*. The explicit (often legally codified) functions of these administrations – to build, maintain and operate the public telecommunications systems – comprise the domain of *intensive politicisation* in telecommunications.

Empirically, of course, the *institutional forms*, that is, the organisational structures and regulatory practices used to carry out these functions, varied considerably.[2] The most frequent organisational form to be found in advanced industrial countries was the public PTT administration. In the early 1970s, telecommunications in 17 of the 24 Organization for Economic Co-operation and Development (OECD) countries was organised as a public administration. Alternative institutional solutions included regulated private companies (as in the United States and Canada) or a coexistence of private companies and public administrations (as in Finland).

Regardless of this organisational diversity, we can observe a high degree of public involvement in the telecommunications sector everywhere at that time. The public telecommunications monopoly encompassed not only the operation of telecommunications networks and the supply of the entire range of telecommunications services, but also the licensing, distribution and maintenance of all the terminal equipment necessary to use these services.

However, this institutional presence was only one part of the politicisation of telecommunications. The state's legal rights and administrative capacities allowed interventions into the telecommunications sector in many ways and for various reasons: tariffs were always treated as 'political prices' and manipulated for reasons of social, fiscal, macroeconomic or regional policy; the procurement of telecommunications equipment was guided by industrial policy goals; the modernisation of networks was sometimes motivated by mass-media policy; the design of technical systems and equipment took national security interests into account. These aspects, to mention only some of the most important, were part of the *extensive politicisation* of the telecommunications sector.

These political goals were not consistently and equally relevant over time, and they were not equally important; however, telecommunications was always *politically over-determined*. As a consequence, telecommunications policy was usually a complex 'ecology of games'.[3] Apart from their genuine functions, the telecommunications administrations (and private network operators) had to meet a multitude of (sometimes conflicting) public demands, and they were expected to balance them internally in their day-to-day business. Of course, the PTT's efficiency was hampered by such requests – but the legitimacy of their public status was safeguarded.

DEREGULATION, LIBERALISATION AND PRIVATISATION: THE TRANSFORMATION OF TELECOMMUNICATIONS IN WESTERN EUROPE

The institutional structures of the entire telecommunications sector have been under enormous pressure to change, especially since the beginning of the 1980s. With varying levels of intensity and radicalness and at different rates of speed, several countries have realised reforms of the 'old' model concerning both the status and the internal organisation of telecommunications administrations and public network operators and the regulation of the telecommunications markets. Frequently discussed under the notions of 'deregulation', 'liberalisation' and 'privatisation', these efforts indicate a significant 'retreat of the state' from its former role. Public debate, however, has been characterised by considerable conceptual confusion and rash conclusions. To arrive at a more adequate assessment of institutional reforms in telecommunications, we must separate various aspects of the complex changes taking place, distinguishing particularly between:

- *Organisational reforms*, namely, changes in the status and/or the structure of existing organisations in telecommunications, the creation of new organisations, the break-up or the abolition of existing ones. Well-known examples of such organisational reforms are the organisational separation of posts and telecommunications administrations, the transformation of public administrations into public corporations, the 'divestiture' of AT&T in the US, and the establishment of new regulatory bodies such as the Office of Telecommunications (Oftel) in Great Britain.
- *Deregulation*, that is, the relaxation or abrogation of existing laws, statutes, rules and regulations by means of which the state tried to influence the activities of private actors. Given the intensive regulation of the telecommunications sector, its 'deregulation' affects a variety of activities, such as licensing, standardisation, access conditions, procurement instructions, fixing of tariffs etc.
- *Liberalisation*, that is, the lifting of existing barriers to market entry. Here, 'liberalisation' primarily means the relaxation or repeal of the legal monopolies in telecommunications. Even though 'liberalisation' in telecommunications is an aspect of the general 'deregulation', the terms are not synonymous and, as we shall see, should not be confused.
- *Privatisation*, that is, changes in the legal form of public administrations or corporations (from public to private law status) and/or the selling of shares of publicly owned corporations. Examples of a 'privatisation' in telecommunications were the selling of shares of the public network operators in Japan (NTT) and Great Britain (British Telecom). In contrast to the public debate, 'privatisation' in our context is deliberately defined very narrowly, which allows us to pay attention to the complicated interrelation between 'liberalisation' and 'privatisation' and between 'deregulation' and 'privatisation' in telecommunications.

Each of these various reforms aims at a change of basic features of the 'old' PTT model. Taken together, they lead to a completely 'new' model of telecommunications characterised by private corporations providing optimal supply for rationally calculating citizens within unregulated markets. According to this new model, the state's only function is to organise its own retreat and to watch private activities as a judge.

The feasibility and the opportunities of this 'new' model were first shown in the *United States*.[4] There, the entire organisation and regulation of the telecommunications sector has been transformed fundamentally in an incremental process which began in the 1950s. Competition was introduced into the three main sectors of the telecommunications market: the supply of apparatus, the provision of services, and the running of public networks themselves (with the exception of local networks). The scope of existing regulations was reduced, and the dominant network operator (AT&T) was reorganised according to the requirements of the new competitive environment.

Compared to the developments in the US, the West European countries were remarkably resistant to such a 'deregulation' and 'liberalisation' of their telecommunications sectors. It is true that repeated attempts were made to reorganise the public network operators in order to improve their – quite often unsatisfactory – performance and to enable them to seize the commercial opportunities of technological change. And some telecommunications administrations tried to make more flexible use of their monopolies and to allow private supply in niches of minor significance. By and large, however, the West European countries adhered to the 'old' PTT model well into the 1980s.

The first West European country to aim at a full-scale retreat of the state from telecommunications was *Great Britain*.[5] During the fundamental reorientation of British economic and industrial policy after 1979, telecommunications were used as a test case to demonstrate the feasibility – both technically and politically – of Mrs Thatcher's free-market programme. Within only a few years, the Thatcher government enforced a far-reaching redefinition of the state's role in telecommunications. In 1981 it passed its first 'Telecommunications Act', which not only provided the legal basis for the organisational separation of telecommunications (now British Telecom) from the old Post Office, but also empowered the government to liberalise the existing telecommunications monopoly. The government used this power to liberalise the connection of terminal equipment in 1981;[6] in February 1982 Mercury was licensed to build and operate a second public telecommunications network and to compete with British Telecom;[7] and in October 1982 a general license was put into force which permits the supply of private telecommunications services (especially value-added services) with the exception of the simple resale of leased lines. In 1984 the 'British Telecommunications Act' was passed, which empowered the government to privatise British Telecom and established an independent regulatory body for the telecommunications sector, the Office of Telecommunications (Oftel), following the US model.

By selling 50.2 per cent of its shares of British Telecom in November 1984, the Thatcher government implemented the first privatisation of a former PTT administration in an advanced industrial country. Thus, within only four years, the PTT model in telecommunications was dismantled almost entirely. After a period of consolidation in the second half of the 1980s, the government decided to remove most of the remaining restrictions to competition. The simple resale of leased lines was permitted in 1989; in March 1991 the government announced that it would license further network operators. In addition, it started to sell the rest of its shares of British Telecom.

The developments in the US and in Great Britain (as well as in Japan) have served as a background for attempts to discuss and to reform the existing public monopolies and organisations in various West European countries.[8] In Italy, the '*Commissione Morganti*' presented a report proposing institutional reforms of the telecommunications sector in 1984; in the following year, the '*Steenbergen Commission*' made its recommendations in the Netherlands; in 1987, the '*Wise Men Commission*' in Belgium and the '*Witte Commission*' in West Germany presented their report.[9] Some of these efforts were in vain (as in Italy), some of them were followed by toilsome legislative measures. They were all intensified by initiatives of the *Commission of the European Community*, which successfully established itself as a key actor in the field of telecommunications policy in the mid-1980s. In its view, the harmonisation and liberalisation of telecommunications markets were decisive steps towards the full completion of a Common Market in Europe.[10]

In its *Green Paper* 'On the Development of the Common Market for Telecommunications Services and Equipment' of June 1987,[11] the European Commission presented far-reaching proposals concerning the reform of the institutional and regulatory structures in telecommunications. The Commission accepted the existing monopolies for networks and a few basic services, especially the basic telephone service, which should facilitate the building of a modern, efficient European telecommunications infrastructure. It did, however, recommend a liberalisation of monopolies for terminal equipment and the rest of telecommunications services, especially value-added services. Furthermore, it saw a need for a separation of the state's regulatory functions from its remaining business functions and a closer link between tariff structures and cost structures. The Green Paper was the basis for several directives and recommendations of the Commission in the following years.[12] For our

TABLE 1

THE LEVEL OF COMPETITION IN WEST EUROPEAN TELECOMMUNICATIONS MARKETS IN 1991

	Infrastructure		Services				Terminal equipment			
	Public switched network	Leased lines	Telephone service	Mobile communications, Satellites	Text and data	Value-added services	Main telephone	Modems	Private switches	Data and fax terminals
Austria	Monopoly	Monopoly	Monopoly	Monopoly	Monopoly	Monopoly	Monopoly	Competition	Competition	Competition
Belgium	Monopoly	Monopoly	Monopoly	Monopoly	Monopoly	Monopoly	Monopoly	Monopoly	Partial Competition	Competition
Denmark	Monopoly	Competition	Monopoly	Partial Competition	Monopoly	Competition	Competition	Competition	Competition	Competition
Finland	Monopoly	Competition	Monopoly	Partial Competition	Monopoly	Competition	Competition	Competition	Competition	Competition
France	Monopoly	Monopoly	Monopoly	Partial Competition	Monopoly	Competition	Competition	Competition	Competition	Competition
Germany	Monopoly	Competition	Monopoly	Partial Competition	Competition	Competition	Competition	Competition	Competition	Competition
Greece	Monopoly	Monopoly	Monopoly	Monopoly	Monopoly	Monopoly	Monopoly	Competition	Competition	Competition
Iceland	Monopoly	Competition	Monopoly	Monopoly	Monopoly	Competition	Competition	Competition	Competition	Competition
Ireland	Monopoly	Monopoly	Monopoly	Monopoly	Monopoly	Partial Competition	Monopoly	Competition	Competition	Competition
Italy	Monopoly	Monopoly	Monopoly	Monopoly	Monopoly	Monopoly	Competition	Competition	Competition	Competition
Luxembourg	Monopoly	Monopoly	Monopoly	Monopoly	Monopoly	Monopoly	Competition	Competition	Competition	Competition
Netherlands	Monopoly	Competition	Monopoly	Monopoly	Monopoly	Competition	Competition	Competition	Competition	Competition
Norway	Monopoly	Monopoly	Monopoly	Partial Competition	Monopoly	Competition	Competition	Competition	Competition	Competition
Portugal	Monopoly	Monopoly	Monopoly	Monopoly	Monopoly	Monopoly	Monopoly	Partial Competition	Competition	Competition
Spain	Monopoly	Monopoly	Monopoly	Monopoly	Monopoly	Partial Competition	Monopoly	Competition	Competition	Competition
Sweden	Monopoly	Competition	Monopoly	Partial Competition	Competition	Competition	Competition	Competition	Competition	Competition
Switzerland	Monopoly	Competition	Monopoly	Monopoly	Competition	Competition	Competition	Competition	Competition	Competition
United Kingdom	Partial Competition	Competition	Partial Competition	Partial Competition	Partial Competition	Competition	Competition	Competition	Competition	Competition

Legend: Monopoly; Partial Competition; Competition

Source: Thomas Schnöring, *Entwicklungstrends auf den europäischen Telekommunikationsmärkten*, Diskussionsbeiträge Nr. 102 (Bad Honnef: WIK, 1992)

analysis, the two most important directives enacted by the Commission were those liberalising the terminal equipment market[13] and telecommunications services.[14]

A brief survey of the degree of the liberalisation of telecommunications markets in Western Europe at the beginning of the 1990s shows that the Commission's efforts have not been futile (see Table 1). The differences between the various countries are still considerable if we compare, say, Britain with Belgium and Spain. The breakdown of the telecommunications monopolies is becoming quite apparent, however. This is most obvious in the field of terminal equipment, which by now has been almost completely liberalised, and in the area of value-added services. Britain with its radical reforms set aside, the public telecommunications monopoly in Western Europe is restricted more and more to the terrestrial network and basic telephone service. And according to the Commission's plans, these markets should be liberalised by the end of the 1990s, too.

TABLE 2

THE STATUS OF MAJOR TELECOMMUNICATIONS NETWORK OPERATORS IN WESTERN EUROPE (1992)

Country	Corporatisation	Privatisation	Public shares
	of main operator / year		per cent
Austria	No	No	[2]
Belgium	1991	No	100
Denmark	1990	1992	51
Finland	1987	No	100
France	1990	No	100
Germany	No	[3,4]	100
Greece	1942	No	100
Ireland	1984	No	100
Italy[1]	Yes		60,4
Luxembourg	No	No	[2]
Netherlands	1989	[4]	100
Norway	1990	No	100
Spain	1924	1924	35
Sweden	1993	[4]	100
Switzerland	1992	No	100
United Kingdom	1981	1984/91	22

[1] SIP
[2] Reform in preparation
[3] Corporatisation under discussion
[4] Privatisation under discussion

Source: OECD, *Communications Outlook 1993* (Paris: OECD, 1993), pp. 12–15, 145–148

Moreover, both the organisational structures and the ownership of public network operators have changed considerably (see Table 2). In 1992 only four OECD member countries – Austria, Iceland, Luxemburg and West Germany – were still organising their public network operators in form of a public administration. In 11 countries the public network operator has the status of a public company. In nine countries these network operators are companies under private law, only three of which are completely owned by the state (in Australia, the Netherlands and Sweden) and two of which are the objects of privatisation plans. By the end of 1992 a full-scale privatisation of telecommunications, however, had only taken place in one OECD country, New Zealand. In all the other cases, the state has kept at least a minor part of the shares.

Whatever arrangement the various countries have found, their new institutional structures in telecommunications all tend to reduce the 'old' role of the state significantly. Public services and exclusive rights have, partly or completely, been abandoned; private actors and competition have started to dominate the scene. And even in the cases in which the state has not given up its position, its activities have become commercialised; they have lost their official character and administrative rigidity and are oriented 'closer to the market'.

TECHNOLOGICAL INNOVATIONS AND PRESSURES FOR CHANGE

The recent experiences in the telecommunications sector are often used as an example to demonstrate the possibility and the necessity of an almost complete 'de-nationalisation' of advanced industrial economies. It is argued that gas and electricity, railways and airlines, even prisons would benefit from the 'rules of the market' in the same way as the telecommunications sector has. Generalisations from this case, however, should be made with care. The state's retreat from telecommunications has been based on *particular, sector-specific conditions*.[15] 'Privatisation' in this case has not only been a matter of political will and skill. More importantly, some penetrating technological innovations have profoundly changed the political economy of telecommunications, thus eroding the preconditions of the old PTT model.

The stability and efficiency of the old institutional arrangements were based on at least two premises: (i) *technically*, on a stable and clear-cut separation of public and private functions, and (ii) *economically*, on a clear and limited use of telecommunications systems (which, for a long time, were mono-functional). The 'microelectronic revolution' in information and communication technologies has invalidated both premises in every main sector of telecommunications (networks, services and terminal equipment). The much-cited 'convergence of telecommunications and data processing'[16] is only one aspect, albeit an important one, of a much more comprehensive and complex process of technological transformations.

First of all, we can observe a rapid *diversification* and *specialisation* in the field of telecommunications *networks*. Existing terrestrial networks have been supplemented by numerous special networks meeting specific user demands, for example, data transmission at various speeds and with varying capacities. Furthermore, non-terrestrial transmission facilities (satellite services, mobile communications) have entered into competition with terrestrial switched networks. The digitisation of switching and optical fibres for transmission have also offered new opportunities to integrate the variety of specific networks into new *integrated services networks* (ISDN, IBC). And the computerisation of switching has changed the functionality of telecommunications networks. Modern networks equipped with digital switches and advanced software have become 'intelligent', that is, they can do much more than simply connect two subscribers.

Based on these network innovations, a multitude of *new services and applications* have emerged. In addition to conventional services (telephone, telex), new 'basic' services (such as data transmission) and so-called 'value-added' or 'enhanced' services (such as information and mailbox services) are being offered. As a consequence of this 'revolution in services', the distinctions (i) between (public) telecommunications and (private) data processing, (ii) between 'basic' and 'enhanced' telecommunications services, and (iii) between (individual) telecommunications and (mass) communications and broadcasting have been blurred in the last two decades.

Finally, progress in microelectronics has led to more 'intelligent', multi-functional *terminal equipment*. Conventional apparatuses have many new features, and functions once distributed among several devices now are integrated into one. As a consequence, the boundary lines between telecommunications equipment and equipment for data processing, office communications and private entertainment (e.g., TV sets) have become vague.

As a consequence of all these developments, the telecommunications infrastructure, once relatively standardised and homogeneous, 'has become a heterogeneous and complex system of publicly and privately operated components'.[17] In this new environment, the premises of the 'old' model of public activity have lost their footing. First, the boundaries between public and private functions have become fragile and permeable. Existing regulations have been threatening to restrict private applications, and new suppliers have been eager to compete with public network operators and established equipment suppliers. Second, new applications of telecommunications have spread exponentially within only a few years, increasing the demands on the flexibility and innovativeness of (public) network operators. And it is this new 'variousness of situations' (Wilhelm von Humboldt) which is said to overstrain an (inflexible) public administration.

These *new and specific* conditions – the *permeability of boundaries* and the *variousness of applications* – have both facilitated and necessitated a political redefinition of public functions in telecommunications. This implies, on the one hand, that any attempt to restore the 'old' PTT model in telecommunications must fail. It means, on the other hand, that the latest experiences in telecommunications cannot be taken as a model for a more *general* retreat of the state from other sectors of the economy.

THE NEW ROLE OF THE STATE IN TELECOMMUNICATIONS

Although the state has lost ground in telecommunications, it did not vanish; nor is its new function limited to the creation of 'favourable market conditions'. The reality of liberalisation, deregulation and privatisation in Western Europe has revealed a surprising presence of the state – in a new role, but with undiminished vitality. I suggest that, rather than being expiring residuals of the state's former role, these activities indicate new, permanent functions within the new institutional arrangement in the telecommunications sector. Three areas, at least, have displayed an *increase* of public activity: (i) the enforcement of economic efficiency, (ii) the maintenance of social efficiency, and (iii) the protection of privacy.

New Public Functions I: Enforcing Economic Efficiency

The rhethoric on 'deregulation', whether political or academic, often suggests that a liberalisation and privatisation of public activities will put an end to the nightmare of regulatory problems. The 'disciplines of the market' are expected to replace government control effectively. Official statements and commission reports, not to mention the articles of neoliberal economists and journalists, never tire of this argument, but they ignore that the state's regulatory function in telecommunications has not ended with its retreat from the provision of services; in fact, this function has increased in importance. The experience of liberalisation since the 1980s has shown that the 'disciplines of the market' are not strong enough to enforce economic efficiency – that is, fair and equal competition, free consumer choice and a high quality of services – in the telecommunications sector. To be effective, they have to be supported by government control and intervention. In this perspective, liberalising monopolies and allowing market entry are only first steps on the way to effective competition.

In the ideal worlds of economics textbooks, it may be true that under conditions of intensive, equal and unrestricted competition public regulation is not necessary. Reality is different, however, especially in telecommunications. After liberalisation, the public network operators, whether in public or private ownership, have held onto their dominant market position, which gives them considerable control over the activities of their competitors and their competitive conditions. This is most evident in the sectors of the telecommunications market where competition is said to be most beneficial: networks and new services. Effective market entry of new network operators and service suppliers depends (at least for some time) on the connection to and the use of the existing public network. By defining interconnection conditions and by determining access charges, the former monopolist is in a position to control the supply conditions and revenues of its new competitors directly. Hence, at least in the short term, the intensification of competition cannot serve as a substitute for the public control of the competitive behaviour of the dominant network operator. For this reason, in every country that has liberalised its telecommunications sector there is still public regulation, although the regulatory functions have frequently been underestimated and their institutionalisation insufficient.

Great Britain, the model of a radical reform in telecommunications, is no exception. Even there, the state's retreat from telecommunications, announced emphatically by the Thatcher government, has turned out to be illusionary. This is indicated not only by the long list of conditions included in British Telecom's licence, but also by the host of functions to be executed by the new regulatory body – with a small staff and little (legal) authority. And in spite of the government's 'free-market rhetoric', the British telecommunications markets are still highly *administrated markets*, in which 'the scale and effectiveness of competition ultimately remain a matter of political will'.[18] The extensive regulation of British Telecom's tariffs, one of the most contested issues in previous years, is a clear indication of the state's 'new' role in British telecommunications. However, neither public regulators nor private competitors have managed to break up the market power of British Telecom yet.[19] Not without reason, the British government has decided to intensify both competition *and* regulation in spring 1991.[20] In Britain as in the US,[21] it has become apparent that beyond simply meaning 'deregulation', the liberalisation of telecommunications markets represents a *dynamic process whose success depends on permanent public regulation and intervention*.[22] By establishing a new institutional arrangement in telecommunications, the state has not completed its mission – its job has just begun.

In West Germany, too, the brief history of liberalisation in telecommunications has shown that the government's aim to manage with as few regulatory interventions as possible is difficult to attain.[23] The new competitive environment created by the government has brought about a multitude of problems and raised many conflicts. On the one hand, the government wanted to introduce 'fair competition' between the *DBP Telekom* and new service suppliers; on the other hand, however, competition was not to jeopardise the remaining monopolies of the public network operator.[24] Pursuing both aims simultaneously has turned out to be difficult. After the new telecommunications law had been in force for less than a year, the Minister of Posts and Telecommunications,

Christian Schwarz-Schilling, had to admit that 'the deregulation of the telecommunications sector has resulted in an increase of regulatory functions'.[25]

New Public Functions II: Maintaining Social Efficiency

The enforcement of 'fair' competition has not been the only reason for state interventions into the liberalised telecommunications markets. In spite of all the optimism about the *economic* benefits of liberalisation and privatisation, skepticism prevailed regarding their *social* consequences. According to the logic of neoliberal economics, any decision in favour of unrestricted competition implies that social goals such as distributional equality and universal services will either be realised by market forces – or they will have to be abandoned.[26] Neither alternative has been acceptable and practicable thus far. The universal principles and social policy goals embedded in modern welfare states have been insuperable *political* limits to any deregulation of telecommunications. The state still has to guarantee an equal and universal supply of (basic) telecommunications services, whether profitable or not, and it must safeguard the quality of these services. The Western European countries have chosen different ways of achieving these goals, including regulatory obligations and, in cases in which the state is still liable for services, restraints of competition.

Britain is the model for the first solution in Western Europe. Contrary to Thatcherite rhethoric, British Telecom was not released from its social obligations after its privatisation and the liberalisation of the British telecommunications markets. On the contrary, these obligations were explicitly confirmed in the British Telecommunications Act and in British Telecom's licence. The licence contains a long list of conditions designated to assure that British Telecom will continue to fulfill its social obligations in its capacity as a private company, too.[27] For example, British Telecom is obliged:

- to provide a universal telecommunications service (condition 1);
- to provide a service in rural areas (condition 2);
- to provide emergency call services (conditions 6 and 7);
- to provide public call box services (condition 11);
- to supply and connect apparatus for the disabled (condition 31);
- to provide special telephones for the hearing impaired (condition 32).

These provisions clearly mirror the public fears that a private company committed only to its profitability will not supply such services in adequate quality and volume. And at the same time, they indicate the extent of the 'new' role of the state in this field. Doubts about the social efficiency of private companies in telecommunications are not unfounded, if we consider the growing complaints about the quality of services after British Telecom's privatisation.[28] Partly due to public pressure and regulatory interventions, British Telecom's performance has clearly improved in the last few years, however.

West Germany can serve as a model for the solution chosen by most of the West European countries and by the EC Commission. While advocating competition in principle, the federal government claims a 'particular public responsibility' in the field of telecommunications.[29] This includes a universal supply with a basic telecommunications infrastructure, equality of tariffs, tariff reductions for disabled persons and regionally disadvantaged areas, etc. The basic instrument to reach these goals is the exclusion of competition from key markets: the terrestrial network and the basic telephone service. Moreover, the public network operator, the *DBP Telekom*, has service obligations for 'mandatory services' (*Pflichtleistungen*) which are not defined precisely in the new telecommunications law. In our context, it is not only interesting to see that the state has kept a considerable part of its old functions in this model; it is even more important to notice that the *mixture* of old functions and new competitive conditions has given rise to a multitude of new regulatory functions.

The new category of 'mandatory services' (*Pflichtleistungen*) introduced in the West German telecommunications law illuminates the tightrope walk between economic and social goals required by this new institutional arrangement. If the scope and quality of these mandatory services are defined extensively, the public network operator is burdened with a serious competitive disadvantage; if they are defined narrowly in order to assure 'fair' competition, the social goals are threatened. The regulatory work resulting from this dilemma is enormous. The regulatory body, namely, the Ministry of Posts and Telecommunications, has to decide case by case, and, moreover, its decisions cannot be based on general principles and criteria alone but have to take (technical) details into consideration as well.

In both cases, it has become apparent that the state has to play an active role in order to maintain the social efficiency of the new institutional arrangements in telecommunications. As long as Western societies have not been persuaded that 'telecoms have stopped being a social service',[30] public supplies, regulations, controls, and interventions will be of central importance even in a liberalised and privatised telecommunications sector.

New Public Functions III: Protection of Privacy

The public regulations discussed so far serve to extend and improve the use of modern telecommunications facilities. The function of a third category of regulations is to restrict the negative external factors resulting from the wealth of technical opportunities for information processing and communication which have emerged in recent years. Especially the protection of privacy, while it is not a new problem in telecommunications, has taken on a new quality in the face of the rapid modernisation of telecommunications networks.[31] Most important in our context is the host of new *regulatory* problems presented by the need to protect privacy in the 'information society'.

The realisation of an 'information society', that is, the planning and introduction of new telecommunications networks and services, has been guided by a rather simple and – at least for engineers – fascinating technical vision: the free and unrestricted flow of information. Everyone should be able to communicate with everyone else at any time by means of modern communication technology. Hence, technical barriers to a free flow of information have been removed; networks now have 'open' interfaces which facilitate their integration, the unrestricted supply of services and the flexible use of terminal equipment. Such an 'open' network has, without doubt, a multitude of benefits, both private and public. However, it has negative consequences as well. Most importantly, the separation of public communication and privacy, one of the cornerstones of modern civil society, has been eroded. In an 'open' telecommunications system, privacy consists of two distinguishable but related aspects:[32]

- The protection against intrusion by unwanted information, that is, the control of information *inflows*.
- The ability to control information about oneself and one's activities, that is, the control of information *outflows*.

Since technical barriers have fallen away, and privacy is still valued, it has become the state's function to establish *regulatory* barriers to information flows between the individual and society at large.

First of all, the protection of privacy requires an adaption of existing legislation to the new problems, for example the enactment or revision of data protection laws, which are either inexistent or ineffective in most West European countries. In the early 1990s five out of twelve EC Member States still had no national law on data protection: Belgium, Greece, Italy, Portugal and Spain.[33] The large discrepancies among the EC Member States concerning privacy and data protection and the 'regulatory gap' in some of them have stimulated activities by the

European Commission in this field. In summer 1990 the Commission proposed a package of measures relating to data protection, among them a Directive 'concerning the protection of personal data and privacy in the context of public digital communications networks, in particular the integrated services digital network (ISDN) and public digital mobile networks'.[34] Recognising that the effective protection of personal data and privacy is an essential precondition for social acceptance of the new digital networks and services, the Commission seeks to guarantee telecommunications users in all member states a basic level of protection.

However, changes here and there in the legal framework will not be sufficient. Experiences in the US, the country with the most extensive and differentiated supply of new telecommunications services, have shown that 'almost every new service has raised new types of privacy issues and concerns'.[35] These problems have resulted in numerous court decisions and legal measures on federal and state level to regulate and control the collection and storage of, and the access to, individual data.[36]

These difficulties are not peculiar to the US, although the way they have been dealt with there has been shaped by American legal traditions. In Western Europe, privacy issues have also been debated both on a European and a national level, due partly to the introduction of the Integrated Services Digital Network (ISDN), for example.[37] Key issues in this debate have been the central storage of connection data by the network operator, itemised billing and automatic call identification. In each of these cases, there have been severe conflicts between the operational requirements and commercial interests of the network operator and the data protection norms and privacy concerns of the user. As these conflicts show, commercial interests and legal norms cannot be harmonised easily, but have to be balanced by public regulation.

CONCLUSION: FROM THE POSITIVE TO THE REGULATORY STATE

The role of the state in telecommunications has changed significantly in the last decade. The old PTT model, characterised by a public administration with exclusive rights, has been replaced by a new institutional arrangement. The direct provision of services has been cut back and commercialised, and the state has given way to private activities. In addition, public interventions into the telecommunications sector, namely, its extensive politicisation, have been significantly reduced and made more transparent. This retreat of the state, however, is only one side of the coin. The other side is a surprising number and variety of *new* public activities: laws and regulations, obligations and controls, interventions and sanctions. Existing institutions took on new functions, and new organisations were established to make sure that (old and new) *public* demands would be met by *private* actors.

Quite obviously, the state has not retreated from telecommunications; there is still an intensive politicisation of this sector. What we have observed is its mutation from the 'positive state' of the old PTT model to a 'regulatory state'.[38] The state's new regulatory functions must not be confused with the creation and protection of a general (legal) framework for private activities. As we have seen in recent years, the state has to regulate case by case and in great detail. The 'variousness of situations' which characterises advanced telecommunications demands a *multitude of interventions*.

This new role of the state has usually been neglected or underestimated in the debates on a 'deregulation' or 'privatization' of telecommunications. The experiences of the telecommunications reforms in Western Europe, as well as in the US and Japan, have shown, however, that there is no easy way out for state. No matter which new model has been chosen, any reform of the old PTT model in the telecommunications sector has turned out to be a complex and protracted process. The success of this transformation process depends on a thoughtful redefinition of state functions – and not on the state's retreat. Moreover, there are clear indications that the 'new' role of the state is not a transitional phenomenon, but will have to be played for some time. As long as competition is not 'fair', supply of telecommunications services is expected to be 'just', and privacy has to be protected, a complete retreat of the state from telecommunications is a romantic, and sometimes dangerous, illusion.

NOTES

1. See, e.g., William S. Sharkey, *The Theory of Natural Monopoly* (Cambridge: CUP, 1982).
2. For comparative surveys of organisational structures and regulatory practices in telecommunications see Robert A. Bruce, Jeffrey P. Cunard and Marc D. Director, *From Telecommunications to Electronic Services: A Global Spectrum of Definitions, Boundary Lines and Structures* (London: Butterworth, 1986); OECD, *The Telecommunications Industry: The Challenges of Structural Change* (Paris: OECD, 1987); James Foreman-Peck and Jürgen Müller (eds.), *European Telecommunication Organizations* (Baden-Baden: Nomos, 1988); Volker Schneider, 'The Governance of Large Technical Systems: The Case of Telecommunications', in Todd La Porte (ed.) *Social Responses to Large Technical Systems: Control or Anticipation* (Dordrecht:

Kluwer, 1991), pp.19–42; Eli Noam, *Telecommunications in Europe* (Oxford: OUP, 1992).

3. William H. Dutton, 'The ecology of games in telecommunications policy', in Harvey M. Sapolsky *et al.* (eds.), *The Telecommunications Revolution* (London: Routledge, 1992), pp.65–88; see also Edgar Grande and Volker Schneider, 'Reformstrategien und staatliche Handlungskapazitäten: Eine vergleichende Analyse institutionellen Wandels in der Telekommunikation in Westeuropa', *Politische Vierteljahresschrift*, Vol. 32(1991), pp.452–78.
4. See Gerald W. Brock, *The Telecommunications Industry: The Dynamics of Market Structure* (Cambridge, MA: Harvard UP, 1981); Günter Knieps, Entstaatlichung im Telekommunikationsbereich (Tübingen: J.C.B. Mohr, 1985); Jill Hills, *Deregulating Telecoms: Competition and Control in the United States, Japan and Britain* (London: Pinter, 1986); Jeremy Tunstall, *Communications Deregulation: The Unleashing of America's Communications Industry* (Oxford: Basil Blackwell, 1986); Peter Temin, *The Fall of the Bell System: A Study in Prices and Politics* (Cambridge: CUP, 1987); Robert W. Crandall, *After the Breakup: US Telecommunications in a More Competitive Era* (Washington, DC: Brookings, 1991).
5. See Arnulf Heuermann and Karl-Heinz Neumann, *Die Liberalisierung des britischen Telekommunikationsmarktes* (Berlin: Springer, 1985); Hills (note 4); Jeremy Moon, J.J. Richardson and Paul Smart, 'The privatisation of British Telecom: a case study of the extended process of legislation', *European Journal of Political Research*, Vol.14 (1986), pp.339–55; Edgar Grande, *Vom Monopol zum Wettbewerb? Die neokonservative Reform der Telekommunikation in Großbritannien und der Bundesrepublik Deutschland* (Wiesbaden: Deutscher Universitätsverlag, 1989).
6. To protect the national equipment industry, the monopoly for the main residential telephones was kept for a transitional period of three years until the end of 1984.
7. In 1983 the government decided to restrict competition to two public network operators for seven years, thus creating a temporary duopoly.
8. See, e.g., Grande and Schneider (note 5).
9. Referring to US experiences, the West German Monopoly Commission had made a futile attempt to demand a liberalisation of telecommunications monopolies as early as 1981.
10. See Herbert Ungerer and Nicholas P. Costello, *Telecommunications in Europe* (Luxembourg: Office for Official Publications of the EC, 1988).
11. Commission of the European Communities, *Green Paper on the Development of the Common Market for Telecommunications services and equipment* (Brussels: COM(87)290, 30 June 1987).
12. A complete account of the Commission's activities is given in Commission of the European Communities, *Status Report on EC Telecommunications Policy* (Brussels: DG XIII/50-EN(92), 1992); for a summary see Hans-Peter Gebhardt, 'Telekommunikationspolitik in Europa', in Edgar Grande *et al.* (eds.), *Perspektiven der Telekommunikationspolitik* (Opladen: Westdeutscher Verlag, 1991), pp.238–48.
13. O.J. No. L131/73, 27 May 1988.
14. O.J. No. L192/10, 24 July 1990.
15. And the results of the reforms, if they can be identified already, are debatable. At least in the short term the benefits of the new 'market laws' are not distributed evenly. News about new services, more flexibility and choice, especially with respect to services and terminal equipment, contrasts strikingly with complaints about the lower quality of some services and higher tariffs, especially for private households. Some of these complaints might be exaggerated – as well as the high hopes for the 'free market' have been, as we shall see later.
16. Simon Nora and Alain Minc, *L'informatisation de la societé* (Paris: Ed. du Seuil, 1978); OECD, *Convergence between Communications Technologies: Case studies from North America and Western Europe* (Paris: OECD, 1992).
17. Robin Mansell, 'Rethinking the telecommunications infrastructure: The new "black box"', *Research Policy*, Vol.19 (1990), p.504.

18. Jonathan H. Solomon, 'Telecommunications evolution in the UK', *Telecommunications Policy*, Vol.10 (1986), p.192.
19. All in all, British Telecom's competitor Mercury has seized a share of about 5 per cent of the British market.
20. See Department of Trade and Industry, *Competition and Choice: Telecommunications Policy for the 1990s* (London: HMSO [Cmnd. 1461], 1991); Roger Pye *et al.*, 'Competition and choice in telecommunications. The Duopoly Review consultative document', *Telecommunications Policy*, Vol.15 (1991), pp.10–14; David Gillick, 'Telecommunications policy in the UK. Myths and Reality', *Telecommunications Policy*, Vol.15 (1991), pp.3–9.
21. See Tunstall (note 4); Robert W. Crandall, 'Entry, Divestiture and the Continuation of Economic Regulation in the United States Telecommunication Sector', in Giandomenico Majone (ed.), *Deregulation and Re-regulation? Regulatory Reform in Europe and the United States* (London: Pinter, 1990), pp.59–71.
22. Even in the US, the result of the market liberalisation in the 1970s is not a completely 'deregulated' telecommunications market, but 'regulated competition' (Crandell, note 21, p.70).
23. See Bundesregierung, 'Die Reform des Post- und Fernmeldewesens in der Bundesrepublik Deutschland. Konzeption der Bundesregierung zur Neuordnung des Telekommunikationsmarktes.' *Deutscher Bundestag*, 11. Wahlperiode, Drucksache 11/2855(1988), p.39.
24. See Bundesregierung, p.28.
25. *Handelsblatt*, 17 May 1990, p.17; translation by author.
26. According to neoliberal economists, in a 'free economy', 'there is one and only one social responsibility of business – to use its resources and engage in activities designed to increase its profits so long as it stays within the rules of the game, which is to say, engages in open and free competition, without deception or fraud'. Hence, '(f)ew trends could so thoroughly undermine the very foundations of our free society as the acceptance by corporate officials of a social responsibility other than to make as much money for their stockholders as possible' (Milton Friedman, *Capitalism and Freedom* [Chicago: Univ. of Chicago Press, 1962], p.133).
27. Monopoly and Mergers Commission, *British Telecommunications PLC and Mitel Corporation. A report on the proposed merger* (London: HMSO [Cmnd. 9715], 1986), pp.85–8.
28. See Clemens Arzt, Knud Bach and Klaus W. Schüler, *Telekommunikationspolitik in Großbritannien. Auswirkungen von Liberalisierung und Privatisierung* (Cologne: Bund Verlag, 1990), pp.178–90.
29. See Bundesregierung (note 23), p.34.
30. *Economist*, 17 Oct. 1987, p.6.
31. For a recent summary of the complex social issues raised by new technological developments in telecommunications see William H. Dutton, 'The social impact of emerging telephone service', *Telecommunications Policy*, Vol.16 (1992), pp.377–87.
32. See Eli Noam, *Privacy in Telecommunications Services* (NY: State of NY Public Services Commission, 1989), p.6.
33. Portugal and Spain, however, made constitutional amendments to improve the protection of privacy.
34. O.J. No. C277, 11 May 1990.
35. Noam (note 32), p. 13.
36. Ibid., pp.25–39, for a summary.
37. Herbert Kubicek and Peter Berger, *Was bringt uns die Telekommunikation? ISDN – 66 kritische Fragen* (Frankfurt a.M.: Campus, 1990); Herbert Kubicek, 'Telekommunikationspolitik und die Folgen für Privatsphäre und Arbeitswelt', in Edgar Grande *et al.* (eds.), Perspektiven der Telekommunikationspolitik (Opladen: Westdeutscher Verlag, 1991), pp.178–97.
38. The distinction between the 'positive' and the 'regulatory' state has been borrowed from Harold Seidman and Robert Gilmour, *Politics, Position and Power. From the*

Positive to the Regulatory State (Oxford: OUP, 1986, 4th ed.). In their view, the rise of the 'regulatory state' is the very essence of a fundamental change in the way the state conducts its business: 'providing services without producing them' (ibid., p.119).

FURTHER READING

Eli Noam's *Telecommunications in Europe* (Oxford: Oxford University Press, 1992) includes a comprehensive analysis of the rise and beginning fall of the telecommunications monopolies in Europe. It covers a wide range of subjects and most, even very small, countries. *European Telecommunication Organisations*, edited by James Foreman-Peck and Jürgen Müller (Baden-Baden: Nomos, 1988), can be read in addition for a more detailed description of the organisation and regulatory structures of telecommunications in ten West European countries. For a comparison with telecommunications policies in the United States and Japan see especially Jill Hills' *Deregulating Telecoms: Competition and Control in the United States, Japan and Britain* (London: Frances Pinter, 1986). *Telecommunications in Europe* by Herbert Ungerer and Nicholas P. Costello (Luxembourg: Office for Official Publications of the EC, 1988) should be consulted by those interested in the goals and activities of the EC Commission in telecommunications policy. In addition to these books, *Telecommunications Policy* is the most valuable journal for those students who want to be informed about recent developments in the field.

The State and the Financial Services Revolution: A Comparative Analysis

MICHAEL MORAN

The creation of a single European market in financial services is a small part of a bigger story: the financial services revolution in the leading financial centres of the advanced capitalist world. A revolution usually pictured in the language of deregulation is in reality something very different: a series of seismic changes in regulatory structures caused by the combined ambitions of corporate actors and national governments. Regulation is driven both by struggles for competitive advantage and by the pressures of democratic politics. The result is a regulatory system which is highly unstable.

THE EUROPEAN REVOLUTION IN FINANCIAL SERVICES

The creation of a single market in financial services is central to the attempt to create a single market in the European Union (EU). In financial services the achievement is already impressive. In many important industries – securities, banking, insurance – the EU has devised, or is on the verge of devising, a 'passport' for financial services firms. The concept of a passport is central to the creation of single market. The operation of the passport principle means that authorisation of an enterprise to conduct a business activity in one member state will automatically confer a right to conduct that activity in all other member states of the Union.

Financial corporations are institutionally complex forms, and their destructive potential far exceeds that of private citizens. Thus the creation of the legal and institutional conditions for the exercise of the passport principle in corporate activity is considerably more complex than any agreement to issue passports to individual citizens. Table 1 illustrates the point. It summarises the main steps in the long road to the creation of a single market in banking and securities. Behind these regulatory innovations lies a history of intense struggle between competitive actors in markets, national governments and institutional interests in Brussels. Part of the story of the European financial

TABLE 1

LANDMARKS IN THE CREATION OF A SINGLE EUROPEAN MARKET

DIRECTIVE	REGULATED INDUSTRY	SUBSTANCE
First Banking Coordination Directive, 1977	Banking	Compulsory authorisation of all credit institutions; compulsory monitoring of solvency and liquidity
Admissions Directive, 1979	Securities	Harmonises conditions for admission to stock exchange listing
Listing Particulars Directive, 1980	Securities	Prescribes information to be offered on listing or offer of sale
Interim Reports Directive, 1982	Securities	Requires all companies listed on EC stock exchange to publish twice yearly accounts.
Consolidated Supervision Directives, 1983, extended 1993	Banking	Regulates supervisory arrangements between parents and subsidiaries
Bank Accounts Directive, 1986	Banking	Sets minimum standards for financial reporting
Disclosure of Major Shareholdings Directive, 1988	Securities	Obliges disclosure of holdings above prescribed thresholds
Branch Accounts Directive, 1989	Banking	Liberalises rules for publication of accounts by separate branches
Prospectuses Directive, 1989	Securities	Regulates contents of issue prospectuses
Second Banking Coordination Directive, 1989	Banking	Creates a banking passport: authorisation by home state allows EC wide operation
Insider Dealing Directive, 1989	Securities	Obliges member states to make insider dealing illegal by 1992
Own Funds Directive, 1993	Banking	Defines what is to count as capital for prudential requirements
Solvency Ratio Directive, 1993	Banking	Establishes framework for minimum capital requirements
Large Exposures Directive, effective 1994	Banking	Harmonises rules for exposure to individual borrowers or groups of connected clients
Investment Services Directive, effective 1996	Securities	Provides a passport for full range of securities services: home state authorisation confers entitlement to EU-wide activity
Capital Adequacy Directive, effective 1996	Securities	Sets minimum capital requirements for investment businesses

Source: Data drawn from 'The EC single market and financial services', *Bank of England Quarterly Bulletin* 33/1 (1993), pp.93–7

services revolution will have to be a history of those struggles. Yet there is an oddity about this story. Important as is the financial services revolution at the level of the EU, it remains a sideshow. It only makes sense in the context of a wider revolution in the financial markets of the advanced capitalist world. What is more, the engines of financial change have been to a substantial extent non-European; and where change has been driven by European forces those forces have been national in character, and have been shaped by the struggles for competitive advantage between national actors. In short, making sense of the politics of financial change in Europe is not primarily a matter of making sense of Europe at all; it involves understanding the world financial services revolution which reached its climax in the 1980s.

These considerations shape the present study, which begins with the wider revolution, and then moves into European backwaters like Frankfurt and Paris.

THE STATE AND THE FINANCIAL SERVICES REVOLUTION

The financial services revolution was one of the most intensely studied events of the 1980s. Nor is this surprising. During the decade a dramatic set of changes came over the financial markets of the leading capitalist nations. These changes both altered business practices and – perhaps as important – altered public perceptions of the nature of the markets. Banking, insurance, stockbroking and accountancy, occupations once by-words for dullness and respectability, became invested with a seedy glamour. The glamour was reflected in the increasing way artists turned to financial markets for their subjects – as witness films like *Wall Street*, plays like Caryl Churchill's *Serious Money* and bestselling novels like Tom Wolfe's *The Bonfire of the Vanities*.[1]

By the second half of the decade the seediness seemed more noticeable than the glamour, as the business practices of Wall Street and the City of London were transferred from the financial pages to the front pages, and from banking parlours to police cells. In the trial and conviction of the disgraced financier, Ivan Boesky, and in the long hunting down of the culprits in the Guinness Affair, Wall Street and the City experienced their greatest financial scandals for over half a century. Nor was this long persecution of financiers confined to the Anglo-Saxon world. In Japan, the 'Recruit' scandal embroiled both politicians and securities markets in Japan's biggest postwar political scandal. Across Europe, trading practices once thought routine – notably insider dealing – became the object of prosecution.

In the minds of many critics the seediness and the glamour were connected. According to this view the scandals revealed at the end of the 1980s are the direct consequence of the financial services revolution. More competition meant more corruption. The argument put here is that these views are wrong. Far from declining, ethical standards in the major world financial markets probably rose in the 1980s. The scandals happened not because standards of behaviour fell, but because expectations rose. These expectations rose because of an aspect of the financial services revolution which is too commonly ignored: it was not only an economic revolution, but also a political revolution. By the latter I mean that it involved a drastic change in the relations between markets and states. There occurred a new and dramatically altered regulatory settlement in the markets. This regulatory settlement greatly increased the influence of the state. In all the cases that interest us – the leading international centres of New York, Tokyo and London, the continental European centres like Frankfurt and Paris – the states in question were democratic, after a fashion. In other words, the expanded jurisdiction of the state exposed the markets to the demands and pressures of democratic political life. In this exposure lies the increased vulnerability to scandal.

Of course not all states were affected in the same degree and at the same time. States are both promoters of economic change and players attempting to secure their own institutional interests in the face of change. The most active promoters of change were non-continental European, leaving state actors like Germany and France with the problem of responding to revolutionary events originating elsewhere. States become players in part because they regulate competitive struggles between corporate actors. Yet states cannot afford to be olympian regulators of competition. In financial services they also pursue their own institutional interests. One of the most important of these is the defence, and if possible advancement, of their national financial capitals as international financial centres. The competition between centres for world prominence is a powerful force shaping state behaviour. Consider the case of the United Kingdom. The regulatory strategies of the British state since the 1950s have meant that London has remained a leading international banking centre. That in turn has had major consequences for the economy of south east England. At the height of the financial services boom at the end of the 1980s, for instance, 22 per cent of total employment in the Greater London area was in financial and allied services.[2] The buoyant economy of south-east England was in turn a foundation of the Thatcherite coalition which dominated British politics during the 1980s. London's leading edge was particularly valuable to key institutions in the state structure, notably the central bank.

The Bank of England was the major promoter of regulatory change in the 1980s. It promoted change in the interests of defending London's leading position, and with good reason. London's status as a major financial capital allows the Bank to play a leading role in the international community of central bankers. How else could the central bank of a declining industrial power with a weak currency hope to play a leading role on the world stage? Thus, a state with a major international centre has acquired a resource which, in its capacity to enhance the prestige of state actors, is as valuable as a competitive edge in a leading manufacturing industry or the possession of nuclear weapons.

Occupying a leading place internationally has become more important with the development of transnational networks of institutions supervising financial institutions. The Basel Committee on Banking Supervision, and the International Organisation of Securities Commissions (IOSCO) provide institutional bases for these networks among the leading capitalist states. Taking a leading part in these organisations is a great source of job satisfaction for individual regulators, and a source of prestige for national regulatory institutions. The control of a major financial centre guarantees an important role. (The Bank of England, for instance, has been the leading figure in the Basel Committee since it was established in 1975.)

The argument anticipated here has two important implications. First, the financial services revolution cannot be understood as a functional change produced by the structural interests of key actors in the markets. On the contrary, it has in many important ways damaged the interests of those actors, notably the interests of key corporate actors. Second, the scandals so far are not likely to be the end of the story. Democratic politics creates a thirst for scandals and exposures. This thirst has to be slaked, irrespective of the actual operation of markets. There will be more Boesky and Guinness affairs, because the financial services revolution has produced a new relationship between the state and the financial markets of the advanced capitalist world; an important part of the story of the revolution involves the diffusion of the culture of scandal beyond Anglo-American circles to other arenas.

In what follows, the argument begins with reference to three countries: the United Kingdom, the United States and Japan. The reason for this concentration is simple: these countries contain the financial markets that really matter. America has the largest financial system in the world, and was the heartland of the financial services revolution. London contains the world's biggest international banking markets, and is a key centre in the chain linking New York and Tokyo. Japan in turn is the great new power in banking and securities, and it is competition for Japanese markets which is driving the latest stages of the financial services revolution.

MESO-CORPORATISM AND THE MYTH OF DEREGULATION

Any analysis of change needs to start with a description of the past; in short, with an account of the traditional relationship between states and financial markets in these three countries. Obviously the particular arrangements were the result of individual national peculiarities, but there is nevertheless a striking common pattern in the nature of the regulatory settlement. This pattern is best summed up, after Middlemas, as a *bias to meso-corporatism*.[3] At the meso-sectoral level the state commonly franchised or delegated the task of regulation to private or to quasi-public bodies. The most striking examples of this are provided by the securities industry, where stock exchanges had usually managed to appropriate regulatory tasks.

Middlemas's image of a 'bias' exactly catches the arrangements. There existed a tendency for regulation to drift in the direction of meso-corporatism, in precisely the way the wood in bowls has a built in bias causing it to drift in a particular direction. And just as the bias in a wood can be corrected, so the bias to meso-corporatism was modified, or accentuated, by the particular national setting in which markets operated. The form of modification can be analysed along three dimensions.

The first is *codification*. Systems of meso-corporatism differ in the extent to which the substantive rules and regulatory procedures are codified – spelt out in an explicit way. Codification was limited in the United Kingdom, extensive in the United States – and had a tendency to grow everywhere. The second dimension is *institutionalisation*. Some meso-corporatist arrangements were more formally organised than others: in the main institutionalisation was higher in the securities industry than in banking. Finally, there is the dimension of *juridification* – the extent to which the powers and procedures of meso-corporatist institutions are embodied in statute. Banking was more juridified than was the securities industry.

The bias to meso-corporatism in the regulation of financial markets reflected well established features of systems that unite democratic institutions with private enterprise. In such systems the owners of property simultaneously face great dangers and enjoy special privileges. The dangers come from democracy – from the possibility that democratic majorities in institutions like assemblies will combine to control, and perhaps even expropriate, private wealth. The privilege comes from the resources which control of property brings – wealth, information, control over production and investment in the economy.[4] Meso-corporatism exploited these privileges to protect the markets against democratic dangers. It was secured in turn by three factors. First, ideology: doctrines of 'self-regulation' asserted that markets could only function efficiently, and be regulated effectively, when they were controlled by those with practical experience of doing business. (I have elsewhere explored the way doctrines of *Selbstverwaltung* were used to mystify the constitutional position of stock exchanges in the German system, thus insulating them from democratic control.[5]) Second, the markets themselves controlled most of the expertise actually needed to do the job of regulation. Finally, there were the brutal realities of regulatory implementation: states did not have the resources, and did not have the will to acquire the resources, needed to carry out the detailed task of policing financial markets.

Acknowledging the bias to meso-corporatism is crucial to understanding the political character of the financial services revolution. That revolution is usually described as an exercise in 'deregulation'. It is true that many restrictions on competition have been abolished in recent years. However, as a description of the changing character of the meso-corporatist system it is misleading. During the financial services revolution corporatism in the financial markets was not dismantled. On the contrary it was strengthened. In the major financial centres meso-corporatism is now, by comparison with the mid-1970s, more *codified, institutionalised and juridified*. There are more rules, and they are more elaborately worked out; formal organisation is more important; and statute and the courts have grown immeasurably in significance. It is this change in the character of corporatism which also explains the growing salience of scandals in the markets.

EXPLAINING THE TRANSFORMATION OF MESO-CORPORATISM: SOME UNCONVINCING ACCOUNTS

There exists a popular explanation for this transformation of corporatism, an explanation which provided the starting point for the present analysis. This suggests that we are witnessing a turning of the regulatory cycle. According to this view, the financial services revolution deregulated trading, displaced traditional elites and brought to prominence new social groups whose behaviour was unscrupulous. In turn this led to abuses, the revelation of those abuses, the call for action to deal with scandal, and the reconstruction of a more closely controlled corporatist system.

This thesis is falsified by the evidence. Were it true, then codification, institutionalisation and juridification should have come some time after the deregulation of trading practices. Yet the changed organisation of meso-corporatism *accompanied* the deregulatory moment. In New York, the unfixing of commissions on the New York Stock Exchange – the act which is generally agreed to have originated the economic revolution – came in 1975. That same year also saw the passage of Securities Amendments Acts which reconstructed meso-corporatism in a more formal and hierarchical way. The deregulation of London's trading practices happened in the period 1983–86, the very same period covering the preparation and passage of the Financial Services Act, which reorganised British meso-corporatism. In Japan the deregulation of the later 1980s exactly coincided with a campaign against the 'abuse' of insider trading and legislation to control it more tightly. In France, the 'little big bang' was simultaneously a reform of regulatory structures and of trading practices. In Germany, as we shall see later, the reforms intended to break up the old regionally based stock exchange system have accompanied the tightening of trading rules and the revelation of 'scandals' over trading practices.[6]

A more plausible, but still unconvincing, account starts with the similarities between leading financial centres. In all, corporatism is being changed in similar ways. And in all similar structural conditions prevail: trading practices are converging, the markets are being dominated by similar multinational corporations – and in some cases exactly the same corporations are prominent. Is it not reasonable to suggest, therefore, that we are witnessing the adjustment of regulatory systems to the interests of the most privileged participants in the markets – the big multinationals?

This account founders on two obstacles. The first arises from the general character of capitalist interests. It has been a truism since Marx that capitalists form a 'hostile brotherhood', partly united by their enemies but divided by the competitive character of markets. Even the most casual acquaintance with a trade association soon reveals the hostility of the brotherhood towards each other. The giant firms in the financial markets, and the trade associations, are divided in this way. It is sometimes assumed that the growth of the giant firm solves this problem of capitalist solidarity. But the giant firm more often than not simply internalises these tensions. As Hawley noted in his study of the Euromarkets

> The organizational complexity of . . . interests results from the diversified, multinational, hence multimarket transnational form . . . . what a single market institution could once define as inter-

> ests located in one market or a few markets become increasingly internalised within a bureaucratic form . . . transnational enterprises are intentionally structured around bureaucratic units with competing (and often cross-cutting) claims, making 'interests' opaque.[7]

The second obstacle to a structural account lies in the impact of the new corporatism on the interests of firms. The newly codified, institutionalised and juridified meso-corporatism has been highly damaging to the interests of the biggest firms in the financial markets. It has imposed on them complex and expensive systems of rules, and obliged them to bureaucratise their internal regulatory systems in order to meet external standards. More generally, by insisting on open and responsible regulation it has helped create the very scandals which are so damaging to the business community.

In short, the regulatory changes embodied in the financial services revolution are not controlled by the business community and cannot be understood as a functional response to its needs. Understanding the puzzle of what is happening ought to begin by analysing how the revolution happened – which involves looking at its origins in the United States.

EXPLAINING THE AMERICAN FINANCIAL REVOLUTION

The financial services revolution is an American creation, in two senses: it originated in the United States; and its features are being copied elsewhere. The twofold significance means that we in turn have to explain two aspects of the revolution: why it happened in the United States; and why it is being diffused to other countries.

Three features lie at the heart of the changes that came over the United States, especially after the mid-1970s: the role of the American state; the vulnerability of meso-corporatism to capitalist competition and to democratic politics; and the altered attitudes to business power in America at the moment when meso-corporatism in financial services plunged into crisis.

First consider the altered role of the state in financial regulation. When the modern American system of regulation was created in the 1930s the state was a relatively weak institution in the financial markets. After the Wall Street crash, and the abuses which the aftermath of that crash revealed, there was a widespread democratic demand for reform. This reform was accomplished by creating a system of meso-corporatist control in which state institutions were weak. This weakness was due to the reasons summarised earlier: state agencies had little experience of regulation; the markets already employed most of the people who could do the job of regulation; and there was a hegemonic ideology of self regulation which decreed that the task was most likely to be done best by the practitioners in the markets – in other words, by the business community itself. Yet in the generation after the introduction of these reforms the state became 'stronger'. The history of the Securities and Exchange Commission illustrates the alteration. At its foundation it was necessarily the prisoner of Wall Street; indeed its first chairman, the notorious Joseph Kennedy, had been one of the main beneficiaries of the age of rascality during the 1920s. However, in the succeeding decades the Commission acquired relative autonomy from the markets: it became a prestigious and successful actor in the bureaucratic politics of Washington; it built up a core of able and committed staff; and it became itself a major source – perhaps *the* major source – of information and expertise about the financial markets.[8]

In the 1960s the growing strength of the state in financial regulation coincided with a major structural crisis in the markets. Meso-corporatist arrangements are always in tension with the dynamic character of a capitalist economy. The point of meso-corporatism is to create a privileged, enclosed group of interests. On the other hand, the dynamic of market competition is constantly creating new, challenging interests and undermining old ones. Meso-corporatist institutions are thus constantly faced with the problem of whether to suppress or to incorporate the new interests created by market competition. That problem was faced by the New York Stock Exchange in the 1960s, when ambitious entrepreneurs tried to break its 'cartel' which mandated minimum commissions in securities brokerage. The Exchange responded by attempting exclusion and suppression rather than incorporation.

Yet meso-corporatism is not only menaced by capitalism; it is also endangered by pluralist democracy. Because meso-corporatism operated in democratic America, rather than in Franco's Spain or Mussolini's Italy, the excluded interests could openly contest their exclusion. This is precisely what they did: they sued in the courts, appealed to the Justice Department, lobbied in the Securities and Exchange Commission and took their case into Congress. The early 1970s saw a wholesale politicisation of financial regulation; notably, there took place extended congressional investigations of the industry where all the contesting parties fought their case in the public arena.

This politicisation links to the third factor explaining the American revolution. The changes climaxed in the late 1960s and early 1970s – precisely the time, as Vogel has demonstrated, when there was a high level of hostility to the business community among the public at large and among key sections of the intelligentsia.[9] This hostility was partly chronic – based on the development, Schumpeter fashion, of a sceptical and hostile intelligentsia – and was partly a transient product of the scandal-mongering culture created in the Watergate era. (Indeed, some bits of the regulatory community in financial services were victims of the Watergate scandal.) In short, politicisation occurred at a moment when democratic politics was driven by suspicion of business and a conviction that it needed tight control.

These factors explain why the moment when trading practices were deregulated in the mid-1970s was also the moment when meso-corporatism was reconstructed along more codified, institutionalised and juridified lines. The interaction of growing state capacity, politicisation and hostility to business fuelled both sets of changes. Once this politicisation had occurred, however, it could not be reversed. The changes of the mid-1970s made the financial markets both more open to scrutiny, and a suitable subject for scandal. That is why the age of the financial services revolution was also the age of scandal in the American financial system.

Yet if this account makes sense of America it does not make sense of the two other leaders in the financial services revolution, the United Kingdom and Japan. Both are democracies, though admittedly pretty peculiar democracies. By comparison with the United States their political systems are secretive and hierarchical. How did American patterns become diffused to more democratically backward countries?

EXPLAINING DIFFUSION

Britain was a leader in the 'Americanisation' of regulatory systems, and is the easier case to explain. Three influences were at work.

The first of these concerns, not financial regulation, but the more general character of the British state. In the history of the international system since the emergence of the United States to a position of dominance, Britain has been distinctive in its closeness to American power. British society, for historical and linguistic reasons, is uniquely Americanised. The elite of the British state has tried to carve out a post-imperial role for itself as the junior partner of America. The state which conducts the business of financial regulation in the United Kingdom is thus uniquely receptive to American patterns and practices.

In the financial sector this has been reinforced by a second factor, the postwar Americanisation of the City of London. The revival of the City as a great financial centre from the 1950s was accomplished by attracting to London numerous American firms, many escaping a more restrictive regulatory regime at home. London became a laboratory for American financial innovation. Even now, London's importance rests on the role it has carved out for itself in an American-dominated international financial system. More immediately still, structural change in London has involved the penetration of City institutions by American, or American controlled, institutions.

The third influence is more direct. It can be summarised as copying. When the Financial Services Act – the crucial piece of regulatory reform introduced in Britain in recent years – was being formulated, the planners had a ready model on the other side of the Atlantic. The years of preparation saw a stream of British visitors examining American arrangements. And while copying was never slavish, the broad outlines of American meso-corporatism are reproduced in the British system, notably in the creation of a Securities and Investments Board and in the establishment of a subordinate set of self-regulatory organisations.

The diffusion of American influences to Japan is harder to understand, for two reasons. The first of these is analytical. In recent attempts to characterise states according to their 'strength' – their ability to act strategically in shaping their economic environment – the Japanese state emerges as a 'strong' state, while America is usually pictured as a 'weak' state. This ought to suggest to us that the initiative in shaping the financial services revolution would lie with the Japanese – an interpretation which indeed is sometimes offered in journalistic accounts of events.[10] Yet the actual sequence is at variance with this: it was the 'weak' American state which bullied the 'strong' Japanese into reform, as we will shortly see.

The dominance of the United States in the regulatory process is also hard to understand because of the recent pattern of competition in the world financial services industry. The 1980s saw the emergence of Japan as a financial superpower, just as the preceding decades saw her emergence as an industrial superpower. She became the leading funder of the chronically indebted American state; her financial institutions emerged to challenge American banks and securities firms in world markets; and her domestic financial markets promised a veritable Eldorado to firms hunting profit. Regulatory standards in business life tend to be shaped by the strongest economic actors. One might wonder, therefore, why there occurred 'Americanisation' rather than 'Japanification' of regulatory arrangements.

Once again an answer starts with reconstructing the sequence of change. Japan was a laggard in deregulating trading practices – indeed, for all the reforms of recent years she remains so. Although there were some reforms in the later 1970s, chiefly in the markets for public debt, the significant changes only came after the mid-1980s. Moreover, they came as the direct result of American pressure, notably from a coalition embracing the American Treasury and big American banks and securities firms. The crucial moments were twofold: an agreement to proceed on negotiations to open up Japanese markets to foreign competition made in late 1983; and the report of a joint committee of American and Japanese officials (the Yen-Dollar Working Group) which resulted in the Yen-Dollar Agreement in May 1984. The latter not only established a programme of financial liberalisation, but also set up a joint American-Japanese committee to oversee the development of that programme. This agreement showed America in the saddle. It was the product of ferocious pressure, notably from the hard driving Donald Regan, President Ronald Reagan's Treasury secretary. In the words of a leading American commentator, it gave the United States a unique say in the process of regulatory change in Japan: 'Pressure from one country to another to liberalise its markets is common in trade policy, but never before has one country so pressed another to integrate its financial markets with the rest of the world.'[11]

It is this process of integration which explains the growing Americanisation of financial regulation in Japan. Three key factors are at work: American structural power in the international system; American policy priorities; and the symmetry between the needs of key parts of the American state and economic interests in Japan.

The first concerns the power structures of the international system into which the Japanese are integrating. For all the advances made by Japanese firms in world markets, structural power in the system is, as Susan Strange has convincingly demonstrated, still American dominated.[12] One of Strange's structures – the knowledge structure – is peculiarly American dominated within the sphere of financial regulation. The finest theoretical and empirical work on regulation is done by American scholars. The most important sources of practitioner knowledge are in American firms – in the big law corporations, the securities firms and the banks. And among public institutions the dominant organisations in the world regulatory community are agencies like the SEC. In regulatory debates Americans are in the intellectual driving seat.

Second, the opening of the Japanese markets begun by the Yen-Dollar Agreement was governed by American policy priorities. There existed within the United States a coalition uniting parts of the core of the American state, notably that part in the Treasury, and parts of the core of the financial community, especially the biggest securities and banking firms. Both were convinced that, whatever comparative advantage the Japanese enjoyed in manufacturing, American firms had a comparative advantage in financial services. The opening of Japanese markets to foreign competition was designed to allow the advantaged Americans to enter the Eldorado of the Japanese financial system. On the Japanese side, as Gilpin has convincingly argued, the policy priority was to avoid the growth of protectionist sentiments in the United States, and the possible closure of American markets.[13] This fear was brutally exploited by Donald Regan when he pressed the Japanese into the position which led to the Yen-Dollar agreement:

> Your markets are not open to our financial institutions. Your markets are not open to the capital for the rest of the world to enjoy as is the United states market, and the message that I'm giving to your Ministry of Finance, to others, is not a new message. It's a message that I've been delivering for three years now, and people have been saying to me: Patience, Patience. I'm about to run out of patience. I've had this now for three-and-a-half years. How much more patience do you want? My response is : action, action, action, that's what I want now. I'm through with patience.[14]

Third, the urgency of this appeal was intensified by a particular need of the American state, and especially of that part of the state which Donald Regan controlled. The fiscal heart of Reaganism was a huge budget deficit. Funding that budget depended on Japanese willingness to buy treasury debt. The American state and key parts of the Japanese financial services industry were therefore chained together in the common task of Americanising the Japanese system, in order to preserve Japanese access to American markets.

EXPORTING THE FINANCIAL SERVICES REVOLUTION: PROBLEMS AND CONSEQUENCES

The heart of the struggles over the shape of financial services regulation can be found in the great financial centres of the United States, Japan and the United Kingdom, but ripples from the storm are also disturbing the other European systems. Some of the consequences, and some of the problems, are illustrated by the case of the most powerful European financial system, that of the Federal Republic of Germany.[15] Structural forces have already begun to break up established interest formations. The insurance industry, for instance, is divided over how to respond to the perceived competitive challenge from the price aggressive British in the Single European Market, and over how to respond to the challenge from banks attempting to market insurance instruments. The division is polarising around a defence of established principles – notably *Spartentrennung*, the segregation between markets – and a response which embraces competition and liberalisation.

However, the heart of the debate about how to cope with the financial services revolution lies in the securities industry, because it is here that the problem of securing the position of *Finanzplatz Deutschland* is most acute. The organisation of securities exchanges has for over a decade been a central issue in German financial regulation. After the banking collapses of the mid-1970s the leading world financial centres turned to 'securitisation' (the denomination of assets and liabilities as instruments tradeable on securities markets). This encouraged the expansion in the United States and Britain of existing exchanges, and stimulated the development of new markets trading newly invented instruments, like financial futures.

The dominant German system of universal banking left German securities exchanges with an unimportant role. In pre-unification Germany there were eight exchanges, and while Frankfurt and Düsseldorf commanded most business, the system was fragmented and parochial. Each exchange enjoyed considerable powers of self regulation, under the oversight of the respective *Land* government. Some of the securities traded on the most rapidly growing and innovative Anglo-American markets – notably financial futures – were until recently prohibited by law in Germany. The organisation of trading on the exchanges, their administrative resources and their use of technology have all placed them well behind the Anglo-American institutions. This backwardness was also reflected in the organisation of investor protection. While the United States and the United Kingdom extended their legal controls over insider dealing in the 1970s and 1980s, German markets were until recently indifferent to the practice.

By the late 1980s an intense struggle was under way over the fate of the system. On one side were ranged interests with a metropolitan outlook, sensitive to the wider world financial services revolution, and anxious to secure for *Finanzplatz Deutschland* a leading place in the revolutionary new world. They encompassed the biggest commercial banks, the Frankfurt Stock Exchange, the government of Hesse (which has the oversight responsibility for the Frankfurt Exchange) and the biggest financial services firms established in Germany, which were anxious to integrate their operations worldwide. As this list shows, this was a 'Frankfurt' coalition, because it was recognised that if *Finanzplatz Deutschland* was to achieve world status, it would have to do so by creating for Frankfurt a position akin to that enjoyed by capitals like

London and Paris in their respective financial systems. On the other side stood the threatened small exchanges and their institutional patrons, like the *Land* governments who carried weight in the federal politics of Bonn.

In this struggle, those resisting modernisation have had the weight of federal institutions on their side, as well as powerfully engrained cultural suspicions of financial innovation. Nevertheless, the modernisers have made considerable progress, aided by two factors. Both reflect the inexorable pressure of external events. The first is the threat of losing business – and in some instances the actual loss of business – to innovative foreign markets. A particularly traumatic event was the decision in 1985 of the Deutsche Bank to move its international banking operations to London. In September 1988 the London International Financial Futures Exchange (LIFFE) began trading a contract in German federal government long bonds. The contract proved immensely popular because, in the absence of a financial futures market, it offered institutions their first opportunity to hedge risk in this important securities market.[16]

More threatening still was the second external development, the rise of Paris as an international financial centre.[17] London's role as one the Big Three, alongside New York and Tokyo, is acknowledged to be special, but this still leaves available the position of leading continental European financial centre. The rise of Paris as a centre for trading futures and options is thus especially challenging. Markets like these are obligatory for any financial centre that aspires to world status, because the largest financial institutions now demand a full palette of instruments offering hedges against exchange rate and interest rate risk. The inroads made by London, and the rise of Paris, are therefore not just a threat to the German securities exchanges; they threaten the whole future of Frankfurt as a major financial centre. The urgency of the challenge and the determination of the Frankfurt-dominated metropolitan elite to meet it, is shown by the blunt words of the Bundesbank President in June 1989. In a lecture widely reproduced in the newspapers of the financial elite he warned: 'We are in a backward condition and our backwardness threatens to become greater because the tempo (of change) elsewhere is higher.' He advocated a reformed stock exchange structure centralised in Frankfurt and went on to criticise the very constitutional basis of the regulatory system. In conditions where Frankfurt was the Federal Republic's obvious international financial centre, he noted, questions of exchange structure were no longer 'bundesrepublikanisch-föderativ'; they were international, turning on the relations between Frankfurt and other foreign centres. He also expressed scepticism about another principle of exchange government,

Selbstverwaltung. The arrangements for the new German futures market (see below) he remarked, would be a serious test of the capacity of the system to achieve reform: 'It remains to be demonstrated that the existing system of self-regulation can in future keep pace with other countries which will be efficiently and tightly directed from the centre. I think here above all of Paris.'[18]

This envious glance at French centralisation shows that the process of regulatory change, even when it involves the abolition of regulatory restrictions, by no means involves a retreat by the state. The President's remarks convey a desire to exercise more state control over the stock exchanges in order to meet international competitive challenges (a lesson already demonstrated by London and Paris.)

The intensity of international competitive challenges helps explain a major subsequent development in securities regulation: the amendment to the Stock Exchange Law which came into effect in August 1989. The amendment is the most important piece of reform since the Nazi measures of 1934, perhaps the most important since the original stock exchange legislation of 1896. The chief purpose of the new measure was to allow the establishment of German financial futures exchange (DTB). This began operating at the end of 1990, trading options contracts in 14 leading German shares, a futures contract in government bonds and a futures contract on the newly created DAX (German Stock Index.)

The DTB is, by German standards, an extraordinary innovation: it is a fully computerised marketplace in which participants are linked electronically rather than trading on an exchange floor; although based in Frankfurt and under the supervision of the state of Hesse, it breaks with the regional exchange principle because it is a Germany-wide exchange.

It is also in a political sense a breakthrough, because it represents a clear victory for the reforming coalition that for many years tried, without notable success, to break the power of the regional exchanges and their allies in the state governments. The intensification of the reformers' campaign, and their success in creating the new futures exchange, has been connected to international pressures. The same is true of another major set of changes, concerning the regulation of insider trading. In this case the German system is being pressed in the direction of what was earlier called codification and juridification. There has been an incremental growth in the scope and detail of the non-statutory rules operated by individual exchanges. In 1988, for instance, Düsseldorf widened the range of individuals covered by its insider-dealing rules (to include journalists and large shareholders) and created a system for publicly identifying those firms which declined to commit themselves to its voluntary code.[19] In 1989 the adoption of a new directive on insider dealing by the EC finance ministers in effect juridified German insider dealing regulation for the first time.

Since the landmark changes introduced in 1989 the reformers have pressed home their advantage. At the start of 1993 a centralised, all German stock exchange was finally introduced in Frankfurt, with the old regional exchanges relegated to the role of catering for small firms and grooming newcomers for entry to the national exchange. Continuing advances have also been made in the development of electronic trading.[20] At the same time, in an almost exact replication of the cycle of events in London and New York the moment of reform in trading practices is coinciding with scandal and with radical regulatory reform. The latest victim of an insider dealing scandal is the formerly respected trade union leader Franz Steinkühler. Under proposals likely to be enacted in 1994 a new Federal regulatory body will be created. This marks an attempt to break with the principles of *Selbstverwaltung* and decentralised administration.

Even now, however, the break may not be decisive, for the *Länder* have managed to defend their institutional interests by retaining some authority in the new system. One of the major responsibilities of the new body will be to enforce an unprecedentedly strict regime controlling insider trading. A practice which was until lately part of the culture of the markets will thus soon attract a prison sentence of up to five years. The reason has been candidly explained by the Bundesbank, one of the major agents of reform. Developing Frankfurt as a major rival to centres like London demands an interventionist regulatory regime to ensure that investors have confidence in the honesty and stability of the markets.[21] How successfully Germany can recoup lost ground is uncertain: by February 1992, for instance, the German financial futures exchange (DTB) still had only 28 per cent of the total turnover in long term Bund futures contracts on the DTB and on its London rival, LIFFE.[22]

The experience of the German exchanges in recent years shows how inadequate is 'deregulation' as a summary of what has been going on in financial markets. In essence we see an attempt – often frustrated by the structure of German federalism – to mobilise state power to counteract the threat posed by the wider international financial services revolution.

STATES AND FINANCIAL REVOLUTIONS

This account of the political face of the financial services revolution shows how inadequate is any merely economic interpretation of that revolution. It is economic accounts which have produced the misleading depiction of the process as 'deregulation'. The depiction is, precisely, misleading rather than wrong. It is certainly true that in some spheres deregulation has indeed happened. Many barriers to price competition, to market entry, to changes in ownership, have been abolished in recent years. Yet at the heart of any theory of regulation must be an account of the role of the state, the most important actor in the design of regulatory systems. Economic accounts of the financial services revolution largely ignore the state or, in the simple image of deregulation, suggest that the story of the last few years is one of state retreat.

The reality is otherwise. The state has not retreated. In the systems of regulation that preceded the financial services revolution the state had a limited role. In the major capitalist nations the state has been a democratic institution during the postwar years, and in some, like the United States and the United Kingdom, democratic influences had an even longer historical pedigree. The democratic character of states has posed a danger to the privileged business interests operating in financial markets. Meso-corporatism allowed these privileged interests to use state power to support regulation while erecting barriers against democratic control.

The financial services revolution in the most democratic of the three states, the USA, blew this all apart. Meso-corporatism in America became more codified, institutionalised and juridified – and more scandal ridden as a consequence. The overwhelming power of the United States diffused the new meso-corporatism to the other main competitor nations. The financial services revolution thus cannot be understood without putting the state at the heart of the analysis. It was the subordinate role of the state which was the chief mark of the old meso-corporatism. It was the more active role of the state which was the mark of the new system. And it was the relations between states in the international system which governed the diffusion of the new arrangements. Nor is there much to be gained by focusing on the financial services revolution as a European phenomenon. To do so is to view the changes through a distorting glass in which marginal events on the continent of Europe are grotesquely magnified. The story is a world story, and one dominated by the Anglo-Saxon world and Japan.

NOTES

This contribution was originally given to the conference 'The Comeback of the State?' organised at the University of Vienna, 7 May 1993. I am grateful for the helpful comments I received on that earlier draft.

1. Caryl Churchill, *Serious Money* (London: Methuen, 1987); Tom Wolfe, *The Bonfire of the Vanities* (London: Picador, 1988).
2. 'London as an international financial centre', *Bank of England Quarterly Bulletin* 29/4 (1989), pp.516–28 (at 517). The figure is for 1989.
3. K. Middlemas, *Politics in Industrial Society* (London: Deutsch, 1979). Some would call the pattern described here private interest government. I use corporatism because it contains the essence of a corporatist arrangement – the attribution of public functions to private bodies.
4. Charles Lindblom, *Politics and Markets* (NY: Basic Books, 1977).
5. Michael Moran, 'A state of inaction: the state and stock exchange reform in the Federal Republic of Germany' in Simon Bulmer (ed.), *The Changing Agenda of West German Politics* (Aldershot: Gower, 1989), pp.110–27.
6. Explored in Michael Moran, 'Regulatory change in German financial markets' in Kenneth Dyson (ed.), *The Politics of German Regulation* (Aldershot: Dartmouth, 1992), pp.137–57.
7. James P. Hawley, 'Protecting capital from itself: US attempts to regulate the Eurocurrency system', *International Organisation* 38/1 (1984) pp.131–65.
8. I rely heavily on the monumental scholarly history of the SEC by Joel Seligman, *The Transformation of Wall Street: A History of the Securities and Exchange Commission and Modern Corporate Finance* (Boston: Houghton Mifflin, 1982).
9. David Vogel, *National Styles of Regulation* (Ithaca, NY: Cornell UP, 1986).
10. Richard W. Wright and Gunter A. Pauli, *The Second Wave: Japan's Global Assault on Financial Services* (London: Waterloo, 1987).
11. C. Fred Bergsten, 'Preface' to Jeffrey A. Frankel, *The Yen-Dollar Agreement: Liberalising Japanese Capital Markets* (Cambridge: MIT Press, 1984).
12. Susan Strange, *States and Markets* (London: Pinter, 1988).
13. Robert Gilpin, *The Political Economy of International Relations* (Princeton, NJ: Princeton UP, 1987).
14. Extract from a speech to Japanese businessmen in March 1984, reprinted in Frankel, *The Yen-Dollar Agreement* (note 11), pp.71–2.
15. This section draws on parts of Moran (note 6).
16. H. Benke, 'Terminhandel mit Bundesanleihen – London', *Die Bank*, 10 (Oct. 1988).
17. P. Cerny, 'The "little big bang" in Paris', *European Journal of Political Research* 17/2 (Feb. 1989) pp.169–72 describes the background to the French reforms.
18. K. Pöhl, 'Frankfurt im Konkurrenzkamp der Finanzplätze', *Frankfurter Allgemeine Zeitung*, 24 June 1989.
19. G. Schubert, 'In die Enge Getrieben', *Wirtschaftswoche*, 29 April 1988.
20. K. Westrick, 'Finanzplatz Deutschland slowly taking shape', *International Financial Law Review* Vol. 1 (1992), pp.30–33.
21. 'Financial centre Germany: underlying conditions and recent developments', *Monthly Report of the Deutsche Bundesbank* 44/4 (1992), pp.23–31.
22. Ibid, p.28.

FURTHER READING

Susan Strange's *States and Markets* (London: Pinter, 1988) has in the few years since its publication achieved the status of a classic. It is about, though not only about, the exercise of financial power between states. My own study, *The Politics of the Financial Services Revolution* (London: Macmillan, 1991) examines several country case studies of the financial services revolution. Philip Cerny, 'The "little big bang" in Paris', *European Journal of Political Research* 17/2 (1989), pp.169–72 is a highly sophisticated analysis of how one backward state has responded to the financial services revolution. S. Woolcock, M. Hodges and K. Schreiber, *Britain, Germany and 1992* (London: Pinter, 1991) contains a discussion of the impact of the single market on some parts of the financial services industries.

Doing Less by Doing More: British Government 1979–1993

JEREMY RICHARDSON

Britain has developed a long tradition of close co-operation between government and interest groups, with the consequent erosion of the distinction between 'public' and 'private'. However, the election of Mrs Thatcher's Conservative Government in 1979 saw a determined challenge, both to established groups and to the established 'policy style'. A new, more active and impositional style of government was attempted, with few institutions and organisations escaping scrutiny. The new approach was characterised by a desire to introduce new rules of the game in many policy areas, a determination to change organisational cultures in both the public and the private sectors, and a wish to change resource allocation mechanisms. Far from introducing a retreat of the state, this new policy style has seen a more interventionist and centralised state in operation. The system may have gyroscopic tendencies, however, in that a gradual return to more familiar state/society relations may be taking place.

GOVERNMENT, THE STATE, AND THE PUBLIC INTEREST

In trying to analyse the so-called retreat of the state in Britain the first problem is that Britain has no clear conception of the state. Usually, we refer to 'the government' rather than to the state, or even use the terms interchangeably. Similarly, it is difficult to distinguish between the national and the public interest and the interest of the state. As Dowding suggests,

> Where one person would describe public order as in the national or the public interest another may describe it as in the interests of the state. Whilst these different claims obviously have different normative implications there is no obvious empirical difference. The claim that the state brings its own unique interests is not always unempirical, but in order to recognize a disjunction between the interests of the state and the members of society we need some means of recognizing the state interest.[1]

Dowding's method of doing so is to suggest that we need to look at the beliefs and desires of state actors – civil servants and politicians – to understand state interests. In fact this is rather useful in terms of the purposes of this study as much of what has happened in British politics post-1979 can be explained in terms of the beliefs of a particular set of politicians and particularly in terms of the beliefs of Mrs Thatcher, as Prime Minister. Thus, 'retreat of the state' is best understood in terms of what Dowding suggests is 'state actor autonomy' or 'state actor interests'.[2] However, the concept of the 'public interest', though equally difficult, also has some potential for our analysis. Thus, the new regulatory agencies appear to be developing some independent notion of the public interest as a guide to their own actions. As Brian Barry has suggested, 'public interest' can have at least two very different meanings.

> One is that the public interest points to a fairly clearly definable range of considerations in support of a policy and if it is a very popular concept at the moment all this shows is that (for better or worse) these considerations are highly valued by many people at the moment. This is my own view. The other is that politicians and civil servants find it a handy smoke-screen to cover their decisions, which are actually designed to conciliate the most effectively deployed interest.[3]

Barry's observation is also helpful. It points to the cause of the increasingly bitter conflict between some regulatees and their regulators in the post-privatisation environment. At least some of the regulatees had grown used to Barry's second view of the public interest, whereas the new regulators are beginning to articulate views (and exhibit behaviour) which appear to reflect some considerations – such as the need for genuine competition and attention to consumer interests – which have become quite popular ('highly valued') *as a result* of privatisation.

An added complication is that the post-1979 history of state withdrawal contains an important paradox – namely that, in practice, governmental intervention has increased quite considerably. Two contrasting perceptions have developed following this burst of 'intervention'. From the perspective of those groups now affected by increased governmental intervention at the sectoral level – for example, teachers, doctors, lawyers, university lecturers, water companies – the 'state' is now considerably more intrusive. From the government's perspective, this increased intervention is a temporary phase. The philosophy behind the intervention is that it is generally designed to facilitate the operation of market forces, so that ultimately there can be a general withdrawal of government. It is the governmental equivalent of forcing people to be free. Rather restrictive and inflexible arrangements (often self-regulation) have been replaced by what the government sees as a more loosely organised arrangements and a competitive and more efficient sets of rules. A further complication is that there are many examples of the continuation of governmental or state interventions and regulations and of new regulatory regimes being introduced in response to political or practical problems. Thus, the British case is exceedingly complex and full of contradictory trends and developments.

POLICY PROCESSES AND POLICY OUTPUTS

Before considering in detail Britain's experience in attempting to reduce the role of the state, it is important to outline some essential features of the United Kingdom (UK) policy process and the nature of state/society relations prior to the 1980s. That decade saw a major change in the aspirations and behaviour of governments. In making these changes, the Conservatives were challenging deeply entrenched policy-making procedures and were attempting to introduce a new set of values which would determine the scope of governmental, or state, action. This process was accompanied by a rhetorical commitment to 'rolling back the state' and a commitment to the introduction of market forces in what used to be considered legitimate areas of public activity.

Policy-Making Traditions: Public/Private Symbiosis

Britain has a long tradition of democratic institutions and an equally long tradition of a well organised, highly mobilised, interest group system. Over time these two sets of institutions – public and private – have developed a very close and often symbiotic relationship. Although 'the state' is not a term which is commonly used in Britain, it is true to say that in practice a clear distinction between state activity and private activity has not been easy to identify. Britain has also exhibited a high level of traditional state intervention. For example, it was often thought to have a 'model' national health service dedicated to providing universal free medical care; it (until recently) had a rather high proportion of its basic industries and utilities in public ownership; and private industry had become used to a significant degree of state subsidy and regulation. In a more subtle way, governments have been adept at 'ear stroking' private organisations, in addition to using the carrot and the stick.

A concomitant to the responsiveness of private organisations to various forms of state intervention and steering has been that most private organisations have experienced few problems in gaining access to the policy process at all levels. In practice, very few organised interests have been refused access to policy makers; there have been very strong tendencies to incorporate groups into the permanent machinery of policy-making; and groups have generally been able to gather effective advance intelligence of possible policy change. Thus it is difficult to reconcile the notion of a closed and secret world of power with the argument of observers such as Mancur Olson, that Britain's long decline has much to do with strong 'distributional coalitions' preventing much needed policy change.[4]

Traditionally, power has been shared between government and *organised* society. We have elsewhere argued that Britain had seen a degree of 'franchising' of public policy and that the processes by which public policies were formulated and implemented were largely about the private management of public business.[5] Moreover, many policy sectors had become much more difficult to manage because of the overcrowding caused by more and more groups becoming more and more active in the policy process.[6] The myth of secrecy and impenetrability is largely founded on the distinction between the levels of information and openness in the general public domain, and the levels of information and openness with the many specialised 'policy communities'[7] which are a primary characteristic of the policy-making process.

This interpenetration of public and private goes back to at least the Victorian period, but reached a particular level of intensity after World War II with some suggestions (incorrect!) that Britain had developed its own system of corporatism. Thus, by 1979 and the election of Mrs Thatcher's reforming government, Britain presented two very different images to the outside world. The popular image was of a secret but deeply *adversarial* system of politics – of strong and secretive government with major shifts in policy caused by changes in government after general elections. The reality was that parties were relatively unimportant influences on policy, and that changes of government did not usually make a major difference in policy terms.[8] As we argued prior to Mrs Thatcher's election, there was considerable emphasis on bargaining.[9]

Do We Know Whether the State has Retreated? The Logic of Intervention.

One of the many problems in discussing the retreat of the state is that we have no means of *measuring* the role of the state in modern societies. Big state budgets and big state bureaucracies are by no means the only way to affect the ways in which society behaves. For example *regulation* has become a central and cheap policy instrument of the modern state. This presents enormous problems to researchers in deciding whether there has been a rolling back of the state or, put more colloquially, whether government is getting off the people's backs. Not only is the task difficult in terms of quantitative measures, it is difficult conceptually – for example do we have more or less government when the government *imposes* new rules of competition, or *imposes* the contracting out of services, or confers new statutory *rights* on the consumers of utilities? This may sometimes be presented by central policy-makers as 'less' government, yet from the bottom up it may seem like tighter state regulation of activities which were hitherto unregulated or were at most self-regulated. 'Less government' may be seen as 'more government', depending upon where one sits! In general the Conservative government's 'logic of intervention' has been that governments must intervene in order to allow market forces to function properly. For example, in 1993 the government was in the process of introducing a bill to reform leasehold of properties. The objective was to grant 750,000 leaseholders the right to purchase their properties from reluctant landlords, that is, the government decided to intervene in order to create new 'market' rights.

Our argument is that in the short run at least, British government has been considerably *more* 'intrusive' when viewed from the bottom up. This increase in state activity has been conducted, however, in the name of the retreat of the state – or in terminology more familiar in Britain, in the name of less government. In practice, since 1979, we have witnessed a new state dynamic in very many policy areas which were hitherto stable and to a considerable degree self-regulating.

The Role of the State and Recognition of Reform Deficits

Critics of both left and right have pointed to a failure of *government* as one of the main causes of Britain's economic decline. Those on the left have argued that government has either intervened too little, too late, or has intervened in the wrong way. Those on the right have argued that the very fact of increased intervention is itself one of the main causes of the decline and that market forces should be re-introduced. This author would argue that there is a link between the *style* of decision-making and the nature of policy *outputs*. If a system of decision-making places great emphasis on the accommodation of key (often producer) interests and places great emphasis on achieving *agreed* solutions, then particular kinds of policy outputs are likely to emerge.

It took the severe affects of the world depression after the 1974 oil crisis to expose the true extent of Britain's reform deficit in many policy areas. By the late 1970s, as the Labour Prime Minister Jim Callaghan put it, the party was over! By then, Britain had begun to realise that what had hitherto been a rather civilised management of decline was about to become decidedly less civilised, unless a backlog of reform was tackled. Had the severe economic crisis arisen in a different decade, when quite different policy fashions were current, governmental responses might have been quite different. We could have seen a burst of traditional governmental intervention in the economy. As it happens, Britain (and Mrs Thatcher) were as much the victim of the new fashion for the retreat of the state as were many, if not most, other Western democracies.[10] Thus, we need to remind ourselves that it is something of a myth that the idea of the retreat of the state was invented by Mrs Thatcher and her supporters, and that what has become known as 'Thatcherism' was a British invention. Restraining or reducing public expenditure, controlling the money supply, de-regulation, privatisation and marketisation, are familiar policy initiatives worldwide, irrespective of party or country.

DOING LESS BY DOING MORE?

Post-1979, two broad categories of governmental response can be identified. First, there was a definite shift in the *policy style* of government. There was a conscious attempt to move from a consensual to an *impositional* style of governing. To a lesser degree there was also an attempt to move to a more *anticipatory* approach to problem solving. The former is best illustrated by the Prime Minister's public pronouncement of her own distaste for the postwar traditions of policy-making described above. Thus, to Mrs Thatcher, the politics of compromise was the politics of 'fudging' issues – by which she meant that many if not most issues could not be resolved by agreement. Solutions had to be imposed on recalcitrant interests. In this simple diagnosis lay the origins of the conflictual politics that emerged post-1979 (most notably, of course, between the Conservative government and the coalminers in 1985, but also in the health service, local government, and education). This conflict became a key element in external perceptions of Britain post-1979. If the British experiment in rolling back the state is unique it is in the willingness of its government to withstand the high decibels of protest (or whingeing as Mrs Thatcher would describe it, no doubt) when the Olsonian distributional coalitions were challenged, one after the other. This was reflected in a shift in policy style (captured in the French saying of 'if you want to drain the swamp, don't consult the frogs'). The government's willingness to risk the electoral consequences of mass unemployment was perhaps the clearest example of this new style in operation.

Evidence of a more *anticipatory* approach to problem solving is less reliable, but it can be argued that the Conservative governments, post-1979, have had some long-term strategy of changing the nature of British society, both in terms of the role of government itself and in terms of the underlying values and the structure of the economy. The long-term strategy is, paradoxically, somewhat more visible post-Thatcher, under the apparently more consensual style of Prime Minister John Major. Thus the drive towards a wholly privatised economy is continuing, even in those areas (coal, rail, postal systems and policing) where Mrs Thatcher was noticeably cautious. There is also a strong desire to create a labour market as untrammelled by 'social regulation' as possible, even at the cost of serious disputes with Britain's European Union partners. There also appears to be a willingness to address some rather difficult long-term questions of welfare funding. The difference, under Majorism, is that there is clearly a greater willingness to consult (even in the run-up to the budget) and to return to a more consensual style of policy delivery. In terms of policy style we are seeing a reversion to the more traditional, pre-1979, approach to the *process* of making and implementing public policies.

'Handbagging' Society as a Form of State Retreat?

The greatest paradox in these shifts in style and purpose is that Britain has witnessed a massive increase in direct state intervention in many aspects of its society. It was a sexist remark that Mrs Thatcher could not look at a British institution without hitting it with her handbag (and it gave rise to a new verb 'to handbag'!) but it does capture the spirit of the decade – namely that virtually no aspect of society should remain *untouched* by government. On the contrary, most aspects of society were, ultimately, to be put under the governmental microscope, destabilised, and then reformed. This is not to suggest that there was always (or often) a clear plan or a clear policy outcome in mind. More usually the government had a general notion that all was not well, that change was necessary – that there was a reform deficit. However, it had only a rudimentary idea of what might be achieved. The new policy style is aptly described by Wistow who quotes a newspaper report as follows:

> Mr Willets, the closest of the 'outsiders' to the NHS review, said he asked a senior civil servant what he would do to the NHS if he were Minister. The reply was 'I'd leave it entirely alone because it is too politically dangerous or I'd destabilise it and see what happened.'[11]

If there is a primary characteristic of this broadly-based reform process it is the desire on the part of the post-1979 governments to introduce new 'rules of the game' for many policy areas. The aim was also to change organisational cultures in both the public and private sectors, and to ensure that resources were allocated according to new (usually market) principles. As the existing rules of the game were generally 'peace treaties' agreed in the past after long and difficult negotiations, there was considerable resistance to these major disturbances. Moreover, strong pressures emerged to re-stabilise policy environments. Thus, after initial destabilisation and conflict, there would follow a more familiar phase of consultation and even negotiation between government and groups, in order to allow the interests to have their say (and real influence) on the detailed points of implementation.[12] So glad were the interests to be back in the policy process, that they often found themselves actively helping the government to make new policies work, despite their earlier opposition.

The really significant change, post-1979, was, therefore, not so much *less* government as the emergence of *strong* government. Government became a more self-confident institution willing to act against what it saw as vested interests. Faced with this new style of governing, groups had little practical option but to re-enter the policy process on the government's own terms. Whilst in earlier decades governments may have seemed weak actors – certainly not particularly strong when compared with the big economic and professional interest groups – by the mid-1980s the balance of power had shifted decidedly in favour of government in terms of setting the agenda and initiating policy change.[13] Most examples of reform ended up in detailed negotiations between government and groups (e.g., in the health service), but the negotiations were based upon the government's own proposals.

Sectoral Destabilisation

The essential characteristic of the 'governments must govern' approach (in order to enforce an ultimate reduction in the role of the state) was for the government to attempt to introduce new sets of 'rules' in each main policy area. These new rules were designed to achieve two objectives. First, the relationship between the government and the sector as a whole was to be changed. Second, the relationship between actors within the sectors was to be changed, usually by the introduction of market forces. In terms of the former, the principle was not applied consistently. Thus, privatisation policy was based on the principle that the state had failed in its attempt to produce an effective industrial policy and so should withdraw in favour of 'the market'. Yet in other policy areas, for example, local government, the government imposed tough new central controls , particularly in financial matters. (The end result of this trend has been to produce one of the weakest forms of local government in Western Europe.) Occasionally, sectors have become so destabilised that policy disasters have occurred. For example, the introduction of the Community Charge (or Poll Tax as it became known) from the late 1980s saw one of the biggest policy failures of postwar British government.

In education, the picture is also one of increasing centralisation of policy, with a more disintegrated and marketised form of implementation. A national curriculum and educational testing have been introduced in schools in an attempt to improve standards via central direction. However, schools are now able to 'opt out' of the local government system, becoming independent trusts with rather more favourable state funding arrangements and with a more direct relationship with central government. The opting out procedure has, moreover, provided the potential for a shift in the power relationships within the sector by allowing greater opportunities for parental influence – believed by the government to favour more 'traditional' forms of education. By insisting on the publication of exam results the government has also introduced a degree of 'marketisation' in that it expects parents to choose those schools with the 'best' performance, thus gradually shifting resources to those schools. The end-point of this complex set of policy changes in education is, therefore, likely to be a more 'atomised' school system, directly funded by central rather than local government. It will also introduce a degree of competition, in some kind of market for education, with resources following pupils. A more direct relationship between schools and the central government has opened up opportunities for much greater central control.

In higher education, too the state has become much more intrusive. The traditional 'arms length' relationship between the state and the universities, operated via the buffer of the (then) University Grants Committee (UGC) had begun to change prior to 1979. The arrival of a Conservative government in 1979 heralded a whole series of changes, particularly to funding arrangements. On the one hand the Government has placed greater emphasis on research performance via a research ranking exercise which has rewarded those universities judged to be excellent in research and has penalised those who are not. On the other hand, it has begun to emphasise the importance of teaching with at least the threat of differential funding should the new teaching 'audits' show marked differences in performance. These two major changes, externally imposed, have again been accompanied by a significant degree of marketisation. Thus, on the research front, a gradual shift is underway moving research funding from a block grant system towards the Research Councils, forcing universities and individual academics to compete for research funding. On the teaching side, student fees have become a more important element in the funding of universities and polytechnics so that a greater proportion of funding follows student demand. Finally, the longstanding distinction between universities and polytechnics has been abolished, and the two funding councils have merged. Pay settlements, too, have been partially linked to performance evaluation, within very tight controls over general pay increases under what amounts to a strict pay policy for public sector workers. Also, higher education has been pressurised to become more 'relevant' to the needs of industry. In a tight budgetary situation, higher education institutions have also been very susceptible to rather more subtle forms of steering. Basically they have responded positively to any proposal which provided funding opportunities.

A similar situation has been created in the health sector – with even more controversy. The reform thrust in this sector has been focused on resource allocation mechanisms. A clear impositional policy style has been evident in the introduction of the so-called internal market into the health service. This has been a complete break with the tradition of the service since 1945, as a new principle has been introduced – the separation of providers and purchasers. This has been the clearest example of government challenging the power of producers over service provision. In both education and health, policies had traditionally been formulated from within the 'worlds' of education and health. This has now been subject to a very determined challenge by government. In the health sector, health authorities now purchase healthcare from hospitals (which, as with schools, have the right to opt out in order to become self-governing trusts) and resources follow patients. As in education, these major policy changes have been accompanied by shifts in the distribution of power *within the sector*, as well as the imposition of new rules from outside. Thus, General Practitioners (and possibly patients) have been given greater powers in relation to hospitals and hospital consultants, in those cases where GPs have become budget holders. Both the opting out of hospitals and the choice of budget-holding status have increased considerably – despite initial strong opposition from the medical profession – because the government has been able to construct a set of rules which increase the incentive to follow its policy preferences. Liberalisation has, again, been accompanied by an increase in the government's capacity to 'steer' previously self-regulating sectors.

It is in the field of employment law and labour relations that the state has been able to redefine the rules without making significant concessions to the affected interests. Reflecting both the unpopularity of unions as institutions and the very depressed economic climate for a significant proportion of the post-1979 period, Britain has seen successive waves of governmental intervention to change the laws under which labour relations are conducted. Thus, the state has certainly not withdrawn or retreated in this policy area either – it has introduced quite massive rule changes designed to weaken unions and to re-balance the power relations between labour and capital. Large areas of industrial relations now operate within a framework of law, where previously arrangements were largely the affair of the participants. For example, whatever the merits of pre-strike ballots, postal ballots for union officials, the barring of secondary picketing etc., they can hardly be presented as a *retreat* of the state. Actors in the labour market now operate under radically different rules of the game, set by the state and not by the parties themselves.

It is in the labour market that we can find the clearest example of the state genuinely *withering*, however – namely that aspect of labour market affairs relating to 'social regulation'. Indeed, the core of the dispute between Britain and her EU partners is the government's opposition to what it sees as excessive state intervention to impose new social conditions on employers. Britain has gradually weakened its social regulations – such as minimum wages, redundancy protection, pension and maternity rights – to a level which is generally considered to be the lowest in the EU. Where regulations existed before, they have been removed or relaxed considerably, allowing market forces to operate much more freely. Legal protections previously afforded to certain categories of workers by the state have been removed. The government's problem is that it is proving difficult to resist the trend of EU legislation (e.g., on health and safety) which is in the opposite direction.

Another area where retreat is more evident is in the field of industrial support. There has indeed been a major reduction in both the level of state financial support for industry and in the range of interventionist schemes. (However, in those schemes which do remain, e.g., in the field of anti-unemployment measures, the degree of state regulation associated with state funding has actually increased, albeit under the guise of decentralisation.) In the early years of the Conservative governments, it proved impossible to reduce state subsidies to ailing industries at anything near the rate envisaged in 1979. In particular, the problems of the state owned industries were so great that it was impossible for the government to withdraw subsidies rapidly. Indeed, in some cases the government had to *increase* subsidies in order to fund the restructuring processes deemed necessary to prepare the industries for privatisation.

It was only after this restructuring process (which was certainly a further increase in state intervention) that the state has been able to markedly reduce both its direct funding and its direct steering capacity.

Yet, even here, there have been notable exceptions. The major exception – the increase in regulation post-privatisation – is discussed below, but the government has found it necessary to both retain the nuclear energy industry in public ownership and to subsidise it heavily, notwithstanding its determination to end the feather-bedding of industry. Similarly, the acceleration of the run-down of the coal industry (partly caused by the effects of electricity privatization) has necessitated a good deal of state subsidies and arm twisting in order to get the policy accepted by its own backbenchers. And in the high technology sector, which in the early Conservative years saw a proliferation of state intervention and subsidies, followed by a major withdrawal, EC intervention has been a convenient substitute. More lately, the more interventionist role of the Department of Trade and Industry under the President of the Board of Trade Michael Heseltine – and the return of sponsorship – has been reflected in policy towards the aerospace industry. A ten-year strategy has been announced, in response to pressure from the industry itself and from the House of Commons Select Committee on Trade and Industry.

Privatisation and Deregulation

Privatisation and deregulation present the most complicated case, in terms of assessing whether or not the state has retreated. In one very obvious sense, there has, indeed, been a major retreat of the state. Very little of British industry remains in public ownership and by the late 1990s virtually no industry of significance (other than the unsaleable nuclear industry) will remain in public ownership. When contrasted with the programme of state ownership enacted in 1945–51, this is a massive lessening of the role of the state. Equally, deregulation and liberalisation are, on the face of it, a retreat of the state in favour of market forces. Closer examination of the post-privatisation and post 'deregulation' situation reveals a much more complex picture, however.

This complexity has a fairly simple cause – namely that society is unwilling to accept the full consequences of either completely unregulated markets or of private monopolies. Financial markets provide a perfect example. As Moran argues, there is no doubt that there has been a retreat of the state in the face of competitive struggles and innovations in markets. But he goes on

> While the state has withdrawn from some areas of control, it has advanced in others. In particular states, the totality of state control may have increased rather than diminished. The most dramatic case is that of Britain where, *after almost two decades of 'deregulation', the state is a more pervasive presence then ever in financial markets. In recent years, many financial markets in Britain have for the first time been subject to regulation backed by the power of the statute book.*[14]

This pattern has been repeated in nearly all cases of so-called deregulation of industries and services and again in the many cases of privatisation for which Britain has become known. In privatisation, particularly, the government has had to resolve two major conflicts of policy goals.[15] For privatisation to be successful, the industries to be privatised had to be attractive to investors. The lower the risk to investors, the more attractive the share offers would be. In each case, key decision points were reached and on each occasion the 'floatation test' was applied. What effect would the various options have on the likelihood of a successful floatation? The overriding policy goal was that the shares had to be taken up in full. In practice this set severe constraints on the introduction of competition into the privatised industries and on the possible break-up of the big corporations into smaller units.

Equally, it was politically impossible to have totally unregulated private monopolies and so new regulatory regimes have been introduced. For example, the water industry now has some eight different regulators (principally OFWAT – the price regulator, NRA the environmental regulator, and the DWI – the drinking water quality regulator). Each privatised industry now has a new regulatory regime with new policy actors – the regulators. The new regulatory agencies are rather more inclined to act on behalf of what continental Europeans would regard as 'the state' than were government departments previously. Thus, not only do the industries have regulators, where few if any existed before, but the regulators have quite different values and modes of behaviour to those of traditional mainline departmental civil servants. Of primary importance is that they are independent of government and it is much more difficult for the industries to exercise the kinds of influence possible when dealing with their 'sponsoring' department in the past.

Then, despite the industries' complaints about 'excessive' political interference, the industries proved to be very powerful and successful lobbies. In so far as state regulation was exercised, it was done so via a rather symbiotic and private relationship between the departments and the public corporations. The relationship with regulators is now much more open to public scrutiny and pressure and is certainly not symbiotic. Rather it is openly conflictual and adversarial, with little or no sign of regulatory capture by the regulated industries. Of more significance, in terms of the thrust of this essay, the regulators appear to have their own independent conceptions of what is in the state's interest, and this takes in broader considerations than would have been usual under the previous 'regulatory' regimes.

REGULATORY CREEP AND THE EMERGENCE OF A CONCEPT OF THE STATE?

As Veljanovski notes, Britain now has three main types of regulatory watchdog – economic, quality, and competition.[16] In exercising these functions, the regulators are exhibiting a fairly common trend – to increase the scope and impact of regulation of their industries. Thus, if privatization was meant to free industry from controls and from governmental 'interference' it has not been achieved.[17] Relatively free from political direction and very conscious of being in a goldfish bowl of public scrutiny, the regulators have begun to change the original rather favourable regulatory bargain struck by the industries and their investors.[18] In exercising their considerable powers, the regulators have taken on board much broader policy (or even 'public interest') considerations than would have been the case under earlier regimes. For example, OFWAT is increasingly concerned with the distributional effects, in terms of welfare, of tougher water environmental laws and has drawn attention to the impact of these improvements on the increased burden on poor families. To some degree, the regulator is, therefore, beginning to 'represent' *unorganised* interests as part of its general brief to guard the public interest. Similarly, the electricity regulator, OFER, has caused much controversy (and difficulty for the government) in allowing the rapid development of gas-powered electricity generation, in the broader public interest, and despite the obvious consequences for the politically sensitive coal industry.

Perhaps the greatest paradox in Britain's attempt to secure a major retreat of the state is that, for the first time, Britain is developing a system of public administration which has a basic notion of 'the state' (or at least of a general public interest). This burgeoning development is disorientating both government and the powerful producer groups, long used to the British conception of 'the state' as 'the government'. The somewhat philosophical change on the part of this group of public administrators (some of whom, such as the Director of OFWAT are ex-civil servants) has yet to be understood by regulatees, used to a quite different system of state 'steering'. It is no wonder that one observer has complained that it is time to have a major review of the regulatory system as '. . . unaccountable to anyone, regulators pursue their own agenda, leaving regulated companies, shareholders and customers to play a costly guessing game.'[19] Indeed it is now being argued that the regulators themselves need regulating and that Britain needs a new system of checks and balances on the regulators.[20]

The regulators would no doubt reject this charge and would point to their own statutory obligations. In practice, they are aware of popular notions of the public interest and are aware that privatisation itself actually increased consumer *expectations*. What might have been acceptable under public ownership, is now unacceptable from privatised companies (especially where they are monopolies) run by managers who are in receipt of private sector remuneration packages.[21] Regulators are as aware of public pressure and expectations as are elected politicians and are aware that these expectations in practice help to redefine the public interest. The regulatory bargain is being changed because the 'definition' of the public interest has changed. There are now so many examples of 'regulatory creep' that it is fair to begin to characterise post-Thatcherite Britain as the regulatory state. Just as Mrs Thatcher's attempts to reduce the number of 'quangos' have been largely reversed, then so deregulation has really meant reregulation.

Yet the government can claim that a major effort is being made genuinely to reduce the total regulatory burden in industry. The government has been extremely conscious of the costs to industry – particularly small business – of regulatory creep. Since the mid-1980s it has been implementing a compliance cost exercise which has been re-enforced as part of the current Deregulation Initiative (see below), following the introduction of compulsory compliance cost assessments for all government departments. In 1991 the Department of Trade and Industry published *Cutting Red Tape for Business* which reported on progress since the original deregulation initiative was launched in 1985. One difficulty in reporting the achievements is that many of the regulations which have been either removed or changed appear singularly esoteric and are therefore easy to ridicule. (For example following a 1988 review, compulsory dips for sheep scab control were reduced from two per year to one! Unspectacular, but it apparently saved over £5 million to those concerned). John Major has given the Initiative new backing. There are currently seven Deregulation Task Forces, set up to advise ministers on policies for the repeal or simplification of existing regulations and enforcement methods, so as to minimise the costs on business.

Work on the Initiative is also steered and supported by the Advisory Panel on Deregulation, a group of business people representing a wide range of business interests. The President of the Board of Trade, Michael Heseltine, also has his own deregulation adviser – Lord Sainsbury, the President of J. Sainsbury plc, one of Britain's leading food retailers. Interestingly, the Task Forces are almost exclusively comprised of business people, with no trade union or consumer representation. (This is, however, not the case with the seven *separate* Task Forces set up by the Health and Safety Executive, which do include trade unionists, reflecting the HSE's tripartite structure). Yet, as we suggest below, there are often practical and, especially, *political* constraints on removing 'red tape'. Not only is there often considerable adverse media reaction, and the usual opposition from consumer groups and trade unions, but there can also be dissension amongst the producer groups who are assumed to benefit from less red tape. One firm's red tape is another firm's profit!

So, how can we make sense of these apparently contradictory trends? On the one hand we have unambiguous examples of the retreat of the state – in such areas the abolition of Wages Councils for the low paid, the gradual withdrawal of state subsidies to industry, and the government's efforts to reduce red tape via the Deregulation Initiative. On the other hand, we see a significant increase in the amount of regulation of industry, notwithstanding privatisation, and a major increase in state intervention in health, education and the professions. Can it be that in the modern state the political culture is, ultimately, incapable of sustaining a major and permanent withdrawal of the state? If this is so, then the debate is more likely to be about the most appropriate form of state intervention rather than whether there should be state intervention at all. Rather than discussing the retreat of the state, one should perhaps be discussing changing the relationship between state and society.

CONCLUSION: THE SHIFT FROM GOVERNMENT TO GOVERNANCE, AND THE LOGIC OF INTERVENTION

The really significant areas of change have been in the governance (rather than *government*) of many policy areas. This shift from government to *governance* is difficult to describe in specific terms. It is a move from conventional direct governmental action or 'interference', to a more complex system of rule-making and implementation, with new sets of formal and informal rules and new sets of actors and relationships.

For example, in the case of the water, telecommunications, electricity and gas industries, Britain has over a period of years moved from a quite straightforward model of governmental steering and control (the Morrisonian public corporation/sponsoring department model) to a more complex set of institutions, ownership and relationships. Paradoxically, these older forms of state intervention and 'control' may prove to have been weaker than the new more diffuse system of power. The new policy communities and networks[22] are still seeking a new stability. Hence, it is difficult to be absolutely confident in our characterisation of the new role of the state. A process has been started, the outcome of which is difficult to predict. What is clear is that these changes have been initiated and to a considerable degree controlled by the government. Changes in formal and informal rules, resource allocation mechanisms, and a degree of marketisation have been overriding characteristics of a more impositional (and therefore in one sense more interventionist) policy style by the government in most policy sectors.

Yet there are signs that there may be some gyroscopic tendencies at work in terms of state/society relations. We make this suggestion for two reasons. First, it has proved necessary to re-integrate groups in order to secure successful policy implementation. What we elsewhere termed 'the logic of negotiation'[23] has not been completely ignored in practice. Thus, in the end, the doctors could be won over only by the government agreeing to bargain with them over the form and resourcing of implementation. The teachers managed to force significant concessions on the testing of pupils in primary schools and on the content of the national curriculum and (possibly) on the publication of examination 'league tables'. If the role of the state has changed, the state has not escaped the need to incorporate interest groups in the policy process, particularly at the implementation stage. In policy formulation, there has often been a break in traditional state/groups relations, but this has not broken the integrated nature of the majority of public and private decision-making activity. Second (and more significantly), the benefits (to the government) of the new rules of the game have been 'front-loaded' and only now are the costs emerging. The costs are largely related to marketisation in varying degrees. The unacceptable face of state withdrawal has been met with new forms of state intervention.

Quite simply, the government is coming to realise that unregulated markets produce costs and externalities which are politically, socially, and economically unacceptable. For example, in April 1993, it was reported that one of the effects of water privatisation was that there had been an increase in cases of diseases caused by lack of access to pure water. It was alleged that this was directly related to the new policy of the privatised water companies of discontinuing the supply of water to those customers who could not or would not pay their water bills. As one Sunday newspaper dramatised it 'Hepatitis and dysentery, diseases of Victorian slums, are spreading in Britain's inner cities as a direct result of privatised water companies disconnecting supplies' (*The Observer*, 11 April 1993). Whilst water may have become more of a commodity than a service in the eyes of policy makers, to citizens it remains a public utility to be available to all.

The consequences of a collapse in the housing market produced effects that were bad for the economy and for individuals, and politically damaging to the government. This led to various schemes both to stimulate the housing market and to reduce the number of housing repossessions by building societies. The many cases of problems with the quality of services provided by private suppliers under the contracting out provisions led to more and better performance targets and closer monitoring of the actual delivery of the contracted out services. In a sense, because of the controversial nature of privatization, deregulation, and contracting out, even more efforts were required from the state to ensure that the new systems worked and were not seen to be patently against the public interest. Citizens had to be reassured that the change in the organisation, funding, and ownership of services did not mean a change, other than for the better, at the point of delivery. Service provision might be reduced or withdrawn for the unorganised sections of society, but for the vast majority of citizens having recourse to vociferous and well organised groups, significant constraints are placed on reducing the role of the state. Policy and organisational change, though not easy, has proved less difficult than changing deeply-held values in the citizenry regarding the role of the state in welfare, for example.

Finally, it should not be assumed that the government can rely on the automatic support of producer interests who might be thought to benefit from a reduced role for the state. Indeed, they sometimes form new pressure groups designed to press for increased state intervention. For example in June 1993, 11 leading companies launched a lobby group to campaign for the government to create a national childcare policy, in support of efforts which private companies are already making. The group – Employers for Childcare – published a policy statement which pointed out that in other European states, publicly-funded childcare provision was the norm. Consequently, 'The Government needs to develop a strategy to enable more parents of children from 0 to 14 to participate in the labour market.' In a more surprising move, business interests have also backed demands for greater governmental regulation in order to tackle global warming and have attacked the government for rejecting tougher curbs on emissions.

Generally, however, the present administration's style – in contrast to some aspects of Mrs Thatcher's – is to place emphasis on *increased* consultation and collaboration with industry, particularly in relation to Europe. In its own review of the implementation and enforcement of EC law in the UK, it recommended the setting up of 'consultative colleges', once key business interests had been identified following news of new EU initiatives. This was to create what is termed a more 'collegiate style of consultation'.[24] Interestingly, the report went on to distinguish between 'inner circle' consultation with the initial members of the consultative college and 'outer circle' consultations with a wider range of groups. The whole tenor of the report was of the need to bring government and business into closer liaison.

One further factor, ultimately the most important factor of all perhaps, needs to be mentioned – namely Britain's membership of the European Union. Whilst we have argued that extreme caution is needed in accepting the conventional wisdom that Britain has witnessed a real retreat of the state since 1979, we have so far neglected the impact of the neo-state to which Britain belongs – the EU. A significant proportion of the increasing regulatory burden is, of course, European legislation of various types. (Water regulation is a good example). In many cases, the British government has little or no choice but to implement EU regulations. As regulation is a major resource for the EU in its drive towards European integration, it seems unlikely that any one member country will be able to achieve a major reduction in the role of the state without a corresponding reduction in Union-wide activity.

NOTES

I would like to thank Laura Cram and Keith Dowding for commenting on earlier drafts.

1. Keith M. Dowding, *Rational Choice and Political Power* (Aldershot: Edward Elgar, 1991), p.124.
2. I am grateful to Keith Dowding for making these suggestions, following his reading of an earlier draft.
3. Brian Barry, 'The Public Interest', in Anthony Quinton (ed.), *Political Philosophy* (London: 1967), p.112.
4. Mancur Olson, *The Rise and Decline of Nations* (New Haven: Yale UP, 1982).
5. J. J. Richardson and A. G. Jordan, *Governing Under Pressure: The Policy Process in a Post-Parliamentary Democracy* (Oxford: Martin Robertson, 1979).
6. A. G. Jordan and J. J. Richardson, *British Politics and the Policy Process* (London: Unwin Hyman, 1987).
7. See Richardson and Jordan, *Governing Under Pressure* (note 5), A. G. Jordan and J. J. Richardson, 'The British Policy Style or the Logic of Negotiation?' in J. Richardson

(ed.), *Policy Styles in Western Europe* (Hemel Hempstead, Allen and Unwin, 1982), pp.80–110, and R. A. W. Rhodes and D. Marsh, 'New Directions in the Study of Policy Networks', *European Journal of Political Research* 19/1 (Jan. 1992), pp.1–25.
8. Richard Rose, *Do Parties Make a Difference?* 2nd ed. (London: Macmillan, 1984).
9. Richardson and Jordan, *Governing Under Pressure* (note 5).
10. Peter Gerlich, Erik Damgaard and Jeremy Richardson (eds.), *The Politics of Economic Crisis: Lessons from Western Europe* (Avebury: Gower, 1989).
11. G. Witstow, 'The National Health Service' in D. Marsh and R. A. W. Rhodes (eds.), *Implementing Thatcherite Policies: Audit of an Era* (Buckingham: Open UP, 1982).
12. Jeremy Moon and J. J. Richardson, 'Policy-making with a difference? The technical and vocational education initiative', *Public Administration*, No. 62/1 (1984) pp.23–33.
13. Jeremy J. Richardson, 'Interest Group Behaviour in Britain: Continuity and Change' in idem (ed.), *Pressure Groups* (Oxford: OUP, 1993), pp.86–99.
14. Michael Moran, 'Financial Markets' in James Simmie, and Roger King (eds.), *The State in Action: Public Policy and Politics* (London: Pinter, 1990). See also his contribution to this work.
15. Jeremy J. Richardson, 'Pratique des Privatisations en Grande-Bretagne' in Vincent Wright (ed.), *Les Privatisations en Europe* (Arles: Actes Sud, 1993).
16. C. Veljanovski, 'The Regulation Game' in idem, *Regulators and the Market* (London: IEA, 1991).
17. William Maloney and Jeremy J. Richardson, 'Post-Privatisation Regulation in Britain', *Politics* 12/2 (1992), pp.9–14.
18. Veljanovski, 'The Regulation Game' (note 16), pp. 9–10.
19. Dieter Helm, 'Rewrite the Rules for Regulation', *Financial Times*, 7 April 1993.
20. Cento Veljanovski, *The Need for A Regulatory Charter* (London: European Policy Forum, 1993).
21. Jeremy J. Richardson, 'Public Utilities Management' in Kjell A. Eliassen, Jan Kooiman and Jan Erik Lane (eds.), *Managing Public Organisations: Lessons from Contemporary Experience* (London: Sage, 1993).
22. Jeremy J. Richardson, William A. Maloney and Wolfgang Rüdig, 'The dynamics of policy change: lobbying and water privatization', *Public Administration* 70/2 (1992), pp.157–75.
23. Grant Jordan and Jeremy Richardson, 'The British Policy Style or the Logic of Negotiation', pp.80–110.
24. DTI Report, p.5.

FURTHER READING

David Judge, *The Parliamentary State* (London: Sage 1993).
D. Marsh and R.A.W. Rhodes, *Implementing Thatcherism* (Milton Keynes: Open UP, 1992).
C. Graham and T. Prosser, *Privatizing Public Enterprises* (Oxford: Clarendon Press, 1991).
Andrew Gamble, *Britain in Decline*, 3rd ed. (Houndmills: Macmillan, 1990).

Book Reviews

Party Policy and Government Coalitions. Edited by M.J. LAVER and IAN BUDGE. London and New York: The Macmillan Press/St. Martin's Press, 1992. Pp. 448, tables, figures, biblio, index. £50 (hardback); £20 (paperback); ISBN 0–333–55617–8 and 0–312–07979–6.

The politics of coalition government is a topic to which many political science books and articles have now been devoted. Ever since the early 1960s the process of coalition formation has been analysed on the basis of various approaches: rational choice models (mainly game theoretical) led the way, and were criticised, and extended. This development was partly based on cross-national analysis on the one hand, and on case-oriented evidence on the other. Without going into detail one could argue that the study of coalition government has now reached a state of affairs in which there is *communis opinio* on the fact that pure 'office seeking' models are empirically insufficient and that both the institutional context and 'policy seeking' aspects must be taken into account in order to fit theory with the facts of the formation of coalition government. Lijphart for instance, states that 'the theories based on the parties' policy preferences perform best' (1984, p.52).

However, at the same time the policy dimension within coalition studies (e.g., de Swaan, Grofman, etc.) remained underdeveloped. Either this dimension was statically formulated, or was empirically weakly founded, or was based on the characteristics of the country under review. Not so in this volume edited by Ian Budge and Michael Laver. Both are well known comparativists and well versed in the study of the politics of coalition government (see Laver/Schofield, 1990; Budge/Keman, 1990) and are thus in a position to avoid the above-mentioned shortcomings.

In this book Laver and Budge have taken it upon themselves to direct an empirical analysis of the impact of different parties' policy preferences on coalition formation in various West European countries (i.e., those in Scandinavia, the Benelux countries, France, Germany, Italy, Ireland and Israel). In addition they have examined the extent to which these policy preferences were represented in the government's policy programmes (i.e., the pay offs for a policy-seeking actor). This is the important contribution of this volume to the comparative analysis of coalition theory. And particularly interesting is the research design applied and the results that are reported.

The research design is quite straightforward: on the basis of content analytical data derived from electoral programmes (see Budge *et al.*, 1987) a unidimensional (defined a priori as left v. right) and a multidimensional scale (consisting of the 20 categories making up the unidimensional one) were developed and have been constructed for each country under review *over time* (i.e., the postwar period). This procedure is of great importance: the policy dimension is not only empirically founded but has also a dynamic quality. Second, *a policy driven* 'model' of coalition formation has been introduced on the basis of this spatial information. By means of cluster analysis the party distances have been utilised to establish all potential combinations of forming a coalition government (hierarchically and non-hierarchically). In this way it has been possible to describe the variation in coalition-formation over time within and across nations in Western Europe.

Finally, and this is a weakness of the research design, country-specific constraints and influences (exogenous and endogenous) were entered into the 'model'. However realistic this may be, it distorts to some extent the elegant combination of a priori theoretical argument with an empirically sophisticated approach. Moreover in some of the country-specific chapters it tends to dominate the interpretation of the results (e.g., particular 'rules of the game' and/or the specific position of a party in a system, for instance in Belgium, France, Norway or Israel).

The results of the comparative country-based analysis of the policy driven model of coalition formation are mixed: on the one hand, it can be concluded that the policy dimension does indeed matter, it predicts in most cases the final outcome of government formation better than a random procedure would do. On the other, it is not an overwhelmingly strong predictor and it seems that the office seeking and the policy pursuing motivations of parties go hand in hand. Second, the impact of undimensionality and multidimensionality as spatial representations of party and government policy differs from country to country. It apparently (and not surprisingly, as the editors indicate themselves) co-varies with the type and working of the extant party system. Third, it appears that the sequence of the bargaining process is an important intermediating factor in explaining the outcomes of coalition formation, which in turn is – of course – influenced by parties holding the median legislator and the policy distances within a party system.

All in all, the editors conclude that there remains quite a lot of unexplained variance in the policy driven models. Yet, at the same time it can be concluded that policy seeking motives do indeed matter, although the pay-offs are often less, or at least more mixed, than expected.

In sum: notwithstanding the mixed results of the policy-driven model of coalition government, (or perhaps due to this!) this is a very important contribution to the literature of the politics of coalition government. It is a well-structured account in which an important feature of coalition-theory is empirically tested on the basis of cross-national and inter-temporal evidence. Furthermore the editors and contributors did a remarkable job in finding a balance between the general argument and the case-based analysis. Too often comparative work tends to turn into fragmented chapters and more or less disengaged introductions and conclusions by the editors. In this sense it is a truly comparative book and a 'must' for every student of coalition theory as well as of politics in Western Europe.

HANS KEMAN
Vrije Universiteit Amsterdam

Party Organizations: A Data Handbook on Party Organizations in Western Democracies, 1960–90. Edited by RICHARD S. KATZ and PETER MAIR. London: Sage Publications, 1992. Pp. 973, 2 tables. £75. ISBN 0–8039–8783–8.

'Parties still matter'. With this opening (and understated) assertion Katz and Mair introduce the first of a series of three collective volumes which focus on the organisational dimension of parties. This dimension is now one of the very few remaining lacunae in cross-national party research, and for this reason alone it merits substantial inquiry. However, there are also other reasons, the principal among which are the questions that have been raised by the literature that contends that there is now a 'crisis of party', and that parties are under threat. While the supposed symptoms of the crisis of party – that is, the ideological, electoral, and competitive change in parties and party systems – have been subject to wide-ranging empirical inquiry, the parties' own reaction to this challenge, a core element of which necessarily involves organisational change, remains unresearched.

The Katz and Mair volume cultivates old, and breaks new, ground in several respects. One new departure is the focus on three faces of party organisation, asking how their organisational characteristics differ, and how these differences may be expected to effect the goals and incentives of their leaders. The three faces are: the party as a voluntary membership; the party as a governing body; and the party as a bureaucracy. The overall approach is guided by a single general hypothesis: that the balance among the three faces of party organisation has been changing, so that the membership is becoming less significant and the governing and bureaucratic faces more so.

There is little doubt that the main aim of this venture – to chart and to explain such developments – is being met. The editors assembled an impressive array of contributors who are among the leading scholars of political parties in their countries. The design of the volume is both clear and standardised. Data for the 79 parties (Austria, Belgium, Denmark, Finland, Germany, Ireland, Italy, The Netherlands, Norway, Sweden, UK, USA) are provided in separate country chapters with an additional chapter for the three transnational party federations. The data – presented in a series of tables – fall into five major groups. The first is primarily contextual, detailing for each party its national election results as well as its governing status, both nationally and sub-nationally. The second group of data deals with the size and structure of the party as a membership organisation. The third group concerns the party staff – the number of paid employees as the prime indicator. The fourth group addresses party rules regarding the locus of decision making as well as candidate selection and the rules about women representation. The final group concerns party finance.

A major limitation of the volume is the absence of data on the French parties as well as the Spanish and Portuguese ones. Nonetheless, the strengths of this work easily outweigh this limitation. The volume is consciously targeted toward the practitioner and as such the book deserves a wide audience among empirically-oriented political scientists. Although it is packed with information, the richness of the data and the standardised format according to which it is presented make it an easy task to digest. The aim for scholars in political parties will be to attempt to analyse the data and examine the authors' hypothesis.

MOSHE MAOR
European Institute, London School of Economics

Crisis and Choice in European Social Democracy, Ithaca and London: Cornell University Press, 1991. By FRITZ W. SCHARPF. Engl. trans. of *Sozialdemocratische Krisenpolitik in Europa*, Frankfurt: Campus, 1987. Pp.303, 21 figs., 58 tables, biblio, index, £12.95. ISBN 0–8014–2221–3.

Scholars from different disciplines have attempted to identify the economic causes and consequences underlying the worldwide recession in the 1970s. Fritz Scharpf instead sets out to explain how those consequences could have been avoided or mitigated by governments' policies.

More precisely, the central question of the book is why countries governed by social democratic parties committed to the achievement and maintenance of full employment, such as Austria, Great Britain, Sweden and West Germany, differed in their policy choices and policy effects. Scharpf detects a fundamental asymmetry of economic interests between the social partners on one side, and governmental policy-makers on the other. Therefore, the explanation of varying levels of unemployment hinges on the identification of political and institutional incentives facilitating or discouraging strategic agreement.

The book is divided in three parts. Part I outlines the main empirical questions and describes the macroeconomic policy options. In Part II the author systematically examines – by means of interviews and historical evidence – the potential scope for, and effects of, economic policy choices during the crisis period in each country. The successful experiences of Austria and Sweden clearly demonstrate that widespread unemployment in West Europe was unavoidable during the crisis.

In Part III the logic governing the strategies of political actors is reconstructed using game-theoretic models. Scharpf shows that if governments undertake to ensure unions' primary interest in job security through expansionary policies, full employment will increase unions' bargaining power. Hence, the strategy of voluntary wage restraint becomes precarious and unions will be tempted to defect and pursue their short-term interests. It follows that sociol-democratic Keynesian co-ordination has a chance of success only if it relies on institutional mechanisms that replace unions' short-term interests. Similarly, the rise in unemployment in West Germany is also explained pointing to the conflicts of interests between the Bundesbank's stabilisation policy and the governments' full-employment policy. In the German case, however, co-operation is hindered by constitutional constraints, such as the defence of price stability and the federal fiscal constitution.

In my view, the third part of the book is the most innovative and stimulating part of the work. Fritz Scharpf displays a rare ability to integrate rational choice models with historical and institutional analysis. Also, in line with a longstanding tradition in European comparative politics, Scharpf is not interested in proposing universal, quasi-scientific laws. Theories of limited application are deemed more fruitful when interpreting concrete historical experiences.

Although it is puzzling that we should wait until Chapter 9 for a theoretical explanation, Scharpf's book is well worth reading. Its interdisciplinary nature offers stimulating pages for students of comparative politics, political sociology, public policy and political economy.

ROSA MULÉ
London School of Economics

Electoral Strategies and Political Marketing. Edited by SHAUN BOWLER and DAVID M. FARRELL. London: Macmillan, 1992. Pp. x + 245, index. £42.50. ISBN 0–333–55894–4.

The decline of party loyalties has meant that many more voters now engage in a process of decision-making. Whilst a wide range of variables which influence their choice have been examined in some detail, one, as the editors of this volume point out, has been neglected: the campaign activities and strategies of the parties themselves. Hence the commendable objective of this book – which is fully realised – is to undertake a 'pre-theoretical enterprise' in which the contributors, specialists from a wide range of countries, examine 'the basic patterns of campaigning'. All follow a common analytical frame of reference which divides the campaign process into three parts, preparation and planning; organisation and control; campaign themes and images. The framework is helpful in that it encourages contributors to organise their material in a clear and systematic fashion.

Aside from providing much useful material about the institutional context of electioneering (covering constitutional forms, electoral systems, laws governing campaign finance and media systems), election strategies and campaign methods, the study identifies common trends which can be encapsulated as a shift from labour intensive to capital intensive campaign practices. These include the centralisation of campaign management, the increasing reliance upon opinion research, polling agencies and outside specialists, the intensifying use of commercial techniques and the standardisation of messages. The framework (rightly) assumes that the concept of 'image' is a vital one in modern electioneering. However, it would have been illuminating if the authors had pursued this by analysing how party strategies set about constructing images, the process by which images are formed within mass publics and the relationship between images and 'reality'.

Lawson and Ysmal in their chapter on the French presidential election of 1988 also raise some wider issues about the impact upon the political system of these new campaign practices. They note that all the main candidates used a similar type of communication discourse, comprising vague or meaningless concepts (such as *rassemblement* and *ouverture*) coupled with a concentration on matters of style, demeanour and personality, for which they adduce two main reasons. First, the narrowing of partisan differences has compelled the candidates to seek grounds other than policy and ideology to establish distinct identities; and, second, the logic of modern campaigning methods itself tends to devalue persuasive argument in favour of style and gimmickry. This, the authors suggest, raises important questions about the nature of democracy. Rather than providing a dialogue between government and citizens and a forum for reasoned debate over rival programmes, elections are now increasingly dominated by 'a pyrotechnic display of technological gadgetry and showmanship'. It would have been interesting if other authors had addressed these questions, but perhaps this would be a suitable topic for a successor study.

ERIC SHAW
University of Stirling

Developments in German Politics. Edited by G. SMITH, W.E. PATERSON, P.H. MERKL and S. PADGETT. London: Macmillan, 1992. Pp.xx + 390, 2 maps, 4 figures, 24 tables, biblio, index. £40 (hardback); £12.99 (paperback). ISBN 0–333–56756–0 and 56757–9.

This book landed on the reviewer's desk no less than four times. The fourth copy arrived via the German Embassy in London and was accompanied by a letter stating: 'We think this is an excellent book about recent developments in unified Germany. Everyone who wishes to be informed about present-day Germany would read this book.' Would one? Does this compilation of articles live up to the Ambassadorial hype and investment? Yes and no.

Given the growing interest in German politics, it is, of course, to be welcomed that longstanding observers of the Federal Republic's and the former GDR's political system engage in the task of providing us with an analysis 'of the dynamics of unification, and its implications for political institutions and the party system'. The explicit objective is to give an account of the key issues of the new political agenda -- economic reconstruction, social integration, environmental policy, immigration – and to assess the identity of the new Germany, its role in Europe and the wider international system. Aiming at the undergraduate reader and those not too familiar with basic characteristics of the German political system, the authors no doubt succeed in providing valuable information. Although one could question the logic of the volume's structure which misses crucial issues, and faces the unavoidable mixture of well-balanced and knowledgeable contributions here and disappointingly 'soft' pieces there, the reader benefits from the experience of most of the authors.

A more sceptical observer will, however, ask for more. Why is it, he would argue, that attempts at analysis are to be found in only a few articles? Is it still good enough to describe recent developments in German politics without trying to put those in, let us say, at least a historical or comparative perspective? Is it not high time to overcome the ubiquitous broad overviews by engaging in a better informed and more focused analysis of the roots, the special characteristics and the potential developments of the German political system?

Compared with the interest in other European countries and polities, Germany is for many political scientists and commentators still somewhat of a *terra incognita*. This ought to change, not least due to the country's history, its growing weight as a political actor and the challenges brought about by the impact of both unification and Europeanisation. Given this background, the volume under review serves as a useful stepping-stone. No more, but no less either.

JOACHIM JENS HESSE
Nuffield College, Oxford

Parteien in der Bundesrepublik Deutschland. Edited by A. MINTZEL and H. OBERREUTER. Opladen: Leske + Budrich, 1992. Pp.700, figures, tables, biblio, index. DM 48 (paperback). ISBN 3–8100–1052–9.

The basic law of the Federal Republic of Germany assigned political parties a central role in the process of decision making and in the expression of the general will. The reunification of the two German states has done nothing to alter this situation. Indeed, even after reunification, the basic problems, characteristic of a modern party state, remain. This general background is tackled in the introductory chapters of the first section of the compilation under review which provide a synoptic illustration of the position and functions accorded to the parties by the Constitution, their historical developments since the middle of the last century and the relationship between parties and society.

In the second section the parties represented in the Bundestag are subjected to a more detailed analysis by way of individual portraits. The smaller non-established parties, including those of the political far right, are given similar treatment. The central themes of these studies are the party histories, their ideological and programmatic profile and also their organisation, membership and electorate structures. This is enlarged upon by references to particularly relevant aspects pertaining to the individual parties themselves. Thus the chapter on the CDU, along with the following chapter on its Bavarian sister party, the CSU, deals with the special relationship between these two parties. One chapter is also devoted to the party system of the former GDR and the establishment of a plural and competitive party system in the five new *Länder* (states) following reunification. Each chapter is complemented by numerous tables and figures. The book is rounded off by reflections on the future prospects of the party system in Germany.

The appendix contains a compilation of texts dealing with the legal groundwork, party financing and trends in membership numbers. There is also a documentation of election results for federal, *Land* and European elections as well as an extensive bibliography and index. The successful, co-ordinated organisation of the book is underlined by the fact that the individual analyses of each party themselves are very similar in structure,so that even in terms of specific aspects, comparisons between parties can be drawn. This would have been all the easier if each chapter had been given its own table of contents. The over extensive use of footnotes does, however, detract from the clarity of some chapters. Furthermore, the page numbers of the bibliography given in the table of contents for the appendix do not correspond with the actual page numbers in the book.

In light of the electoral successes of parties on the far right and in particular of the Republikaner, a detailed analysis of just these parties in terms of their platforms, organisational and membership structures and also in terms of their electorates would have been very desirable. The developments resulting from reunification have rendered the chapter on the Greens obsolete, as the party has in the meantime been fused with the East German Bündnis 90/Die Grüne to form an all-German party, which is reflected in the new name of the party.

All the same, the book offers an extensive survey of the development and present state of political parties in unified Germany. Practically all of the relevant aspects of the present party landscape and the internal structures of the individual parties are dealt with, and indeed in such an easily digestible manner that it will undoubtedly remain a helpful reference guide to this subject for many years to come.

THOMAS EMMERT
Forschungsgruppe Wahlen e. V., Mannheim, Germany

Eliten, Macht und Konflikt. By URSULA HOFFMANN-LANGE. Opladen: Leske + Budrich, 1992. Pp.438 + 50 questionnaire, biblio, DM 60 (paperback). ISBN 3–8100–0962–8.

An important part of the answer to the question, how democratic is Germany?, can be found in the results of studies on German elites. Still, there is surprisingly little public and scientific debate on the role elites should play in a democratic Germany although the general mistrust of the social stratum now called the 'political class' (which includes 'non-political' social actors such as managers in industry and union bosses) has been growing rapidly since unification. This study is restricted to the pre-unification period. Its major data base is a 1981 survey. Compared to today's political turbulences it describes a still rather cosy period of German politics.

For that period it is certainly the best study on the topic of political elites. Not only does it have no serious competitors with regard to the available data, it is also outstanding because it provides a very well written and well informed overview of earlier empirical studies, the history of the role of elites in German politics (since the German Empire of 1871), and of theoretical attempts to come to grips with the phenomenon of elites in democratic societies. The author does not venture into new dimensions of theorising, but sticks to one basic thought. In every democratic society a balance has to be found between representation through elites and the cohesion of elites. The greater the latter, the more endangered their representativeness may become.

For the pre-unification Federal Republic she finds a bias of representation in favour of capital, with elite conflicts regarding socio-economic questions, and no longer regarding moral issues. The party system worked successfully as a procedural device to manage conflict, and there was a general consensus among elites in favour of tolerance and democracy. The network of elites was well developed with overlapping memberships excluding only to some extent the military and cultural elites. Central to elite cohesion was the sphere of politics and next in importance were economic interests. Defensive immobilism of the German postwar elites had been transformed by the early 1980s into self-confident incrementalism. All this added up to a picture of stability and legitimate power structures, of which German elites today can only dream.

ROLAND STURM
University of Tübingen

Political Mobilization and Social Change: The Dutch Case in Comparative Perspective. By HANSPETER KRIESI. Aldershot, Hants: Avebury, 1993. Pp.xviii + 292, 86 figures, 39 tables, biblio. £19.95 (paperback). ISBN 1–85628–518–9.

In the early 1980s several hundred thousand Dutch crowded the streets of Amsterdam and The Hague to protest against the deployment of cruise missiles. Others had been involved in the anti-nuclear, ecological, women's and solidaristic movements. Hanspeter Kriesi's book uses 1986 survey data to examine the apparent proclivity of the Dutch to support or join new social movements (NSMs), political parties, and trade unions.

Kriesi's findings are of interest not only to students of Dutch politics or new social movements, but also of participation, value change, and parties. Support for NSMs and left-libertarian parties is often associated with a shift from material to post-material values among members of the new middle classes. However, Kriesi finds Inglehart's scheme too undifferentiated and distinguishes not only among different parts of the middle classes but also among three different value dimensions: social democratic/bourgeois, authoritarian/anti-authoritarian (i.e., traditional authority vs. individual autonomy), and emancipatory/anti-emancipatory (reflecting a search for new values and life styles). Religion and class continue to structure party choice, but both these dimensions and the parties which represent them have changed. There are now two lefts (workers and social-cultural professionals) and an old and a new middle-class right. However, Kriesi also finds that partisanship is more closely related to value orientations: people with anti-authoritarian, social democratic and emancipatory values (the latter two are closely related) are more likely to support the left.

Kriesi finds that support for NSMs is more strongly related to value orientation than demographic characteristics. However, older generations are motivated by social democratic or anti-authoritarian values, younger generations by emancipatory orientations. Yet NSMs are not the exclusive terrain of the intelligentsia. Although the latter are disproportionately involved, some leaders and many followers come from the working class. The mobilisation potential of NSMs varies, and some are organisationally weak. However, Kriesi speculates that this may be a strength rather than a weakness. Younger generations, hesitant to become too directly involved, allow themselves to be mobilised by loosely organised NSMs run by professional activists.

This is a well-written book with numerous charts and tables and a good deal to say. My principal complaint is that the shading on many of the charts is difficult to distinguish. It would also be useful to know more about the numbers on which the graphs are based. And finally, there is the question of whether mobilisation potential, reported in self-administered questionnaires, will translate into actual participation.

STEVEN B. WOLINETZ
Memorial University of Newfoundland

Policy Networks: Empirical Evidence and Theoretical Considerations. Edited by BERND MARIN and RENATE MAYNTZ. Boulder, Colorado: Westview Press, 1991. Pp.330, biblio, index. $49. ISBN 0–8133–1458–5.

In recent years there has been increasing recognition of policy analysts and political scientists (among others) that policy-making in contemporary Western societies has become more complex in many ways. Moving beyond the truistic nature of such a view has led to the development of a large body of literature and theory which in one way or another concerns the notion of policy networks and network analysis. Until lately however, the term 'policy networks' has remained somewhat enigmatic: a fact which should be at least partly remedied by the appearance of this volume.

Produced largely as a result of a 1989 Conference entitled 'Policy Networks: Structural Analysis of Public Policy Making', and written by specialists drawn from the German-speaking world and the USA (from where the vast majority of policy networks literature originated), this volume provides a range of essays rich in empirical evidence and theoretical considerations – as the subtitle of the book suggests. The first two chapters making up Part I deal most explicitly with the theoretical aspect. Chapter 1 provides a good outline and discussion of what studying policy networks involves as well as what can be meant by the term within the normative context of existing theory and literature, and the perceived changes in the nature of governance and society. The second develops a very fruitful discussion and development of the link between Policy Network Analysis and Policy Analysis, and in doing so gives us a more extensive overview of both the relevant existing literature and the methodological implications. Both together provide a timely, lucid and fairly extensive account of the rationale behind, and implications of, studying policy networks.

Part II of the volume deals more specifically with policy networks in national policy domains and is the most empirical section of the book. Three chapters deal respectively with the analysis of how interest organisations are represented in US national policy-making; the development of policy networks within the German Telecommunications domain over a one hundred year period; and the importance of change in policy networks in the case of superconductors. All three are of interest not least because of the careful discussion of the methodology and sampling design used, but there are also certain weaknesses. The chapter by Ed Laumann *et al.* has much in common with the previous work by Laumann and Knoke in 1987 on *The Organisational State*, for example in its methodology and concern with 'decision making events'. Its main strength lies in providing a cross-sectoral analysis of four policy domains: agriculture, energy, health and labour, yet it is a major question as to whether the *way* it focuses on the role of organisations in political action represents anything more than a pluralist study under a new name. Government institutions for example are treated in a rather passive manner, which seems inappropriate to the very concept of networks. The chapter by Dorothea Jansen provides a highly quantitative analysis of the High Temperature Superconductors network in Germany, and emphasises the variables of 'opportunities', 'actors' intentions' and 'resources' to explain change in policy networks. Yet whilst dense with empirical evidence regarding this policy subsector, it offers little in the way of theoretical consideration. The strongest chapter in this section is that by Schneider and Werle, not only because of the variables used (influence reputation, co-operation and information exchange) and the clarity of the data that is presented, but also because of the conceptual questions it raises. One may however feel that the extent of its diachronic comparison (a period of 100 years) is over ambitious.

Part III of the volume contains four chapters dealing with the theme of cross-national variations in policy networks. The first by Pappi and Knoke analyses political exchange in the German and American labour policy sector. Viewed substantially within the area of game theory and again offering a mine of empirical evidence, the use of statistics is potentially off putting. Two further chapters by Coleman (who justifiably questions the tendency of studies on sectoral policy to 'fence off' policy areas, by looking at central banks networks in Canada and the USA) and by Kenis (who develops a three-country study of industrial restructuring in the chemical fibre industry in West Germany, Italy and Britain), also implicitly offer wider theoretical considerations by discussing some of the determining factors underpinning policy networks. However, the strongest chapter theoretically is Marian Dohler's which focuses on opportunity structures and policy networks within the context of neo-conservative reform strategies in British, US and German health policy. Apart from the very interesting nature of the topic itself, the author's attempt to combine policy networks analysis with neo-institutional analysis is impressive both because of its clarity and because it departs from the tendency of some network analysis to emphasise horizontal co-ordination in an overly sectoral way.

Despite the weaknesses, which are partly due to the gap between the high hopes of the research and the space available, we have here a volume which bears fruit because it brings together the main themes and aspects of policy networks analysis in a normative way. Very importantly, it also offers an extremely useful bibliographical source. In saying this, the question arises as to whom the book is addressed: specialists in the case studies examined, or more general theorists? In many ways the latter may find it more useful. A safer bet is that it will prove to be most useful to students and researchers at postgraduate level especially if they are concerned with organisational theory, policy analysis and methodology, as well as the sectoral areas focused upon in the book. Finally, it seems fair to say that while providing a very useful addition to the literature on policy networks and network analysis, some of the book's rather dense methodology and data presentation make it a work not for the faint-hearted.

ROBERT WRIGHT
European University Institute, Florence

Local Government in Liberal Democracies: An Introductory Survey. Edited by J. A. CHANDLER. London and New York: Routledge, 1992. Pp.viii + 209, 7 tables, 4 figures, biblio, index. £12.99 (paperback). ISBN 0–415–08875–5.

This book has been written for an audience of undergraduate and 'A' level students who 'require an easily accessible analysis of local government' (p.i.). It presents an overview of local government and of its position within the national political system for eight Western countries. The countries (UK, Ireland, France, Italy, Germany, Sweden, USA and Canada) have been chosen to present 'studies of systems of local government that demonstrate differences between political systems' (p.2).

Local government is defined as 'political institutions that are subjected to directly elected policy makers' (p.3). Each country chapter presents information on the structure and function of local government according to a similar format, with paragraphs on: (1) structure of central government, (2) development of the system, (3) structure and functions of the system, (4) finance, (5) internal structures, (6) personnel, recruitment and training, (7) intergovernmental relations, (8) parties and pressure groups, (9) electorate.

The book is comprehensive and readable, and its synoptic structure makes it easy for readers to grasp similarities and differences between countries. It provides a general review of the existing Anglo-Saxon literature on the selected countries, and this is the collection's strength and its weakness. The authors are prisoners of their sources. Thus some parts of the book give an impression of vagueness and approximation, which could only be avoided if the authors had based their presentations on firsthand research contributions. Second, the sources used are mostly old. Thus core issues of the 1990s, such as the loss of legitimacy of elected officials, the acute social and political problems of the cities, the impact of the EC on territorial policies, are hardly mentioned. Third, the presence of numerous mistakes in detail, not surprising in a comparative work, ranging from misspellings of names of authors and of institutions (e.g., *arrondisement* instead of *arrondissement*, p.56; *Casa per il Mezzogiorno* instead of *Cassa*, p.78; Aitkin instead of Aiken, p.87) to errors in dates, e.g. for cohabitation in France, p.54; the election in Sweden, p.131). Fourth, some points sound strange to the native reader. *Comprensori* have never been introduced in Italy, even if there was long discussion of their potential role in territorial and economic planning, p.83; the relevance of neutrality in Sweden as an explanation of the prominence local government has not been properly referenced, p.130; the discussion on personnel in France is restricted to territorial state administrations with no mention of the local and regional public sector, which account for some 1,300,000 employees, p.66; aspects of the structure of German *Länder*, pp.107–8. Fifth, the introductory and concluding chapters are comprehensive but short. A few additional pages might have helped to place local government in their urban and political contexts. The presence of some synoptic tables might have helped the reader (such as the ones in the chapter by M. Goldsmith in *Managing Cities in Austerity: Urban Fiscal Stress in Ten Western Countries*, edited by P. E. Mourtizen, Sage, 1992).

In conclusion, the strength of the book is greater than its weakness. It simultaneously provides a textbook introducing students to basics; a review for professionals of how local governments work in several countries; and an introductory survey of reference materials on the structure and function of local government in eight countries.

ENRICO ERCOLE
Fiscal Austerity and Urban Innovation (FAUI) Project
Istituto Superiore di Sociologia Milano

Politics, Society, and Democracy: The Case of Spain. Edited by RICHARD GUNTHER, Oxford: Westview Press, 1993. Pp.xvi + 272, 2 maps, 46 tables, 2 figures. £31.50 (hardback). ISBN 0–8133–8545–8.

This is the first of a promising four-volume series of essays in honour of Juan Linz. It is divided into two parts: the first embraces three chapters (Amando de Miguel's 'The Lynx and the Stork', 'Spain: A Recurrent Theme for Juan Linz' by Gómez Reino, Orizo and Vila Carro, and Jerez Mir's 'Juan Linz's Contribution to Political Science in Spain') revolving around the figure of Linz and his contribution to the study of contemporary Spain; the second consists of 11 chapters by different scholars dealing with a variety of social, economic and political issues relevant to the understanding of twentieth century Spain.

Part II opens with Malefaki's 'A Comparative Analysis of Worker's Movements in Spain and Italy', a brief but illuminating essay on the similarities between the Spanish and Italian labour movements in the last quarter of the nineteenth century and the first decades of the twentieth. It is followed by Cazorla's 'The Theory and Reality of the Authoritarian Regime, Thirty Years Later', which, taking as its starting point Linz's defining characteristics of Francoism, traces the survival of some of the regime's features among the Spanish population, institutions and politicians after the dictator's death. Podolny's 'The Role of Juan Carlos I in the Consolidation of the Parliamentary Monarchy' offers a lucid account of the role played by the monarch in the transition to democracy. In 'The Business Sector and Political Change in Spain: "Apertura", "Reforma", and Democratic Consolidation', Robert E. Martínez examines the attitudes of Spanish business elites towards the transition to democracy and their contribution to the consolidation of the new regime. 'Legitimacy and the meanings of democracy' is the topic dealt with by José Ramón Montero in Chapter 8. Llera's 'Conflicto en Euskadi Revisited' is the result of his 1989 survey of the Basque Country as compared with the one carried out by Linz and some of his collaborators in 1979 and offers a valuable insight into the Basque question.

In 'Divergent Paths: Labor Politics in Madrid and Barcelona', Fishman explores 'the disparity in working-class politics between the two metropolitan areas during the first twelve years of the new democratic system'. Beltrán's 'The Seventeen Spains' is a comparative analysis of the Spanish autonomous communities leading to the conclusion that in the recent past 'the territorial inequality of income' has been perceptibly reduced. Carlota Solé's 'The Integration of Immigrants in an Industrialized Society' is a series of reflections on the issue of immigration to Catalonia (why is it that the Spanish 'Cataluña' is always preferred to the English 'Catalonia' or the genuine article 'Catalunya'?), and in 'The Politics of Health Policy Reform in Spain' Jesús de Miguel and Josep A. Rodríguez analyse the impact that Socialist policies have had on the Spanish National Health System in the last ten years. Finally, 'Socioeconomic Issues and the Catholic Church in Spain' by González Blasco and González-Anleo is a survey of how the public and the clerics perceive the attitudes of the Church itself towards wealth and poverty, its ability to influence socio-economic reality, its approach to economic groups, ownership and management of business and the question of worker-priests.

The volume covers a considerable array of topics (though predictably not always with the same depth) and should be a useful tool for the specialist in contemporary Spain.

JORDI LARIOS
University of Wales, College of Cardiff

Modern Political Ideologies. By ANDREW VINCENT. Oxford: Blackwell Publishers, 1993. Pp.x + 310, biblio, index. £40 (hardback); £11.95 (paperback). ISBN 0–631–16451–0 and 16452–9.

Contemporary Political Ideologies. Edited by ROGER EATWELL and ANTHONY WRIGHT. London: Pinter Publishers, 1993. Pp.xii + 244, 10 biblios, 2 indices. £35 (hardback); £11.95 (paperback). ISBN 0–861–87096–4 and 87099–9.

These books make a strong case for continuing to view political thought through the prism of 'ideology'. The extent of their agreement on this case is remarkable. Both Vincent and Eatwell, in introductory chapters, differentiate their usage of the term to signify reasonably coherent 'bodies of thought' (Vincent, p.21) from the Marxist idea of false consciousness and defend it against claims of 'the end of ideology'. Titles apart, both books are concerned with 'modern' rather than merely 'contemporary' thought. Both examine, in the same order, 'liberalism', 'conservatism', socialism, 'anarchism', 'fascism', 'feminism' and, most seminally, 'ecologism',

There are only two differences between their rankings. First, 'socialism' is tackled by Vincent in a single chapter, whereas in the edited volume 'social democracy and democratic socialism' and 'Marxism and communism' are approached separately by, respectively, Wright and Joseph V. Femia. However, Wright, at least, would evidently concur that 'Marxism is a species within the genus of socialism' (Vincent, p.90). Marxism might instead be viewed as the paradigm case of an ideology were it not for the fact that all other genera, with their more diffuse intellectual sources, would then appear incoherent. Second, the edited volume again apparently differentiates in successive chapters, by Roger Griffin and Eatwell, between 'nationalism' and 'fascism'. However, Griffin's 'definition of nationalism' dichotomises it into a diffuse ' "liberal nationalism" ' and a substantive ' "illiberal nationalism" ' (Eatwell, pp.149–50). One might well infer that veritably ideological nationalism is synonymous with fascism, given that a shared sense of identity is insufficient to constitute an ideology.

Vincent is, in certain respects, more analytical and less essentialist than most of the other authors, affording more consideration to the problematic issues fragmenting traditional ideologies. For example, whereas Jeremy Jennings stipulates that ' "anarcho-capitalists" ' be excluded from anarchism (Eatwell, pp.142–3), Vincent is prepared to consider their ideas on their terms. In contrast, Vincent's approach makes feminism appear more cohesive than does that of Valerie Bryson who, conventionally, analyses species of feminism in mutual isolation, differentiated by adjectives derived mostly from other genera. Feminism is able to achieve coherence in so far as it derives from a common sense of purpose informed by a shared sense of identity, and the same is true of other bodies of thought.

What else differentiates these books? The edited volume is more authoritative than Vincent's as most of its authors, such as Richard Bellamy on liberalism, Noël O'Sullivan on conservatism and Andrew Dobson on ecologism, are also authors of well regarded textbooks on their subjects. It is also more concisely written and tidily organised, including useful guides to further reading. However, Vincent's work has the converse virtues of being the product of a single mind and, moreover, one that is singularly expansive and provocative. Both are undoubtedly fine books, and their different styles might be considered complementary for any undergraduate course on ideologies.

That said, it might be asked whether ideology is still the best prism through which to view the diversity of political thought. For example, Bellamy 'is currently working on a book on Pluralism' (Eatwell, p.vi) which is an important, and frequently under appreciated, body of modern political thought, yet 'pluralist ideology' would now be considered an oxymoron. Whilst both books discuss 'postmodern feminism' the 'postmodern' problem of relativism that is likely to pervade, and disrupt, any undergraduate course on ideologies is disregarded by Eatwell *et al.* and regarded too hastily, in an epilogue, by Vincent. Both cite

Habermas in their introductions, yet neither can accommodate him elsewhere. MacIntyre is cited in nailing their primary ideology (Vincent, pp.12–13), although he now denies liberalism the more significant status of a 'tradition'. It may, therefore, be time for another prism.

KELVIN KNIGHT
University of North London

British Aid and International Trade, Aid Policy Making: 1979–89. By OLIVER MORRISSEY, BRIAN SMITH and EDWARD HORESH, Buckingham: Open University Press, 1992. Pp.192. £40. ISBN 0–335–15652–5.

In recent months the Pergau dam affair has given rise to wide public debate over the extent to which commercial and political considerations should drive the British aid programme. This concise and well-researched study tackles the question head on. Interestingly, however, Morrissey *et al.* argue that, while purporting to 'commercialise' the aid budget, the Thatcher governments (1979–90) actually did little to achieve either the commercial or the developmental objectives of the aid programme.

The first four chapters set British aid in its historical and international context and consider the inputs into the aid policy-making process. They examine the structure, interaction and relative influence of government departments involved in the aid process and highlight areas where greater accountability may be required. They conclude that civil servants and ministers make aid policy with some input from insiders seeking specific concessions but only marginal input from the business and development lobbies as a whole.

The next four chapters deal with policy outputs and infer from shifts in the orientation of the aid budget the relative influence of competing aid lobbies. Impact analysis is then used to evaluate and compare the commercial importance of the main forms of aid to the British economy.

Interesting conclusions emerge from this analysis. The authors find, for example, that multilateral aid is of greater commercial benefit to the UK economy than tied bilateral aid. They also challenge the commonly held view that tied aid and mixed credits are net employment- or net trade-creating.

Arguably Morrissey *et al.* might have done more to substantiate their claim that a more developmentally-oriented aid strategy which created growth in developing countries would confer net economic gains on the UK and world economy. They might also have attached more weight to the Prime Minister's input into aid policy: Mrs Thatcher's role in linking together foreign, trade and aid policies has of course been dramatically illustrated in the Pergau dam affair but it could also be argued that it was her emergence as a world leader which ensured that foreign policy and, with it, the aid budget remained important.

Overall, this is an important contribution to an area of public policy where much research is needed: aid policy and its implications for trade, foreign relations and international redistribution. It will provide valuable insights for policy-makers, economists and academics alike.

GORDON CUMMING
University of Wales, Cardiff

Notes on Contributors

Wolfgang C. Müller is a Reader in Political Science at the University of Vienna, Institut für Staats- und Politikwissenschaft, Sozial- und Wirtschaftswissenschaftliche Fakultät. He has published widely on Austrian politics and comparative politics. His books include the co-edited *Sozialpartnerschaft in der Krise. Möglichkeiten und Grenzen des Neokorporatismus in Österreich* (Vienna: Böhlau, 1985), *Handbuch des politischen Systems Österreichs* (Vienna: Manz, 1991) and *Politics in Austria: Still a Case of Consociationalism?* (London: Frank Cass, 1992).

Vincent Wright is Fellow of Nuffield College, Oxford. He is the author and editor of several books and numerous articles on European, and more especially French government and politics. With Gordon Smith, he has edited *West European Politics* since its launch in 1978.

Herbert Döring is Professor of Political Science at the University of Potsdam and a fellow of the Mannheim Centre for European Social Research, where he is directing the project 'Parliaments in Western Europe: Majority Rule and Minority Rights'. Among his recent publications are 'Parlament und Regierung', in Oskar W. Gabriel (ed.), *Die EG-Staaten im Vergleich* (1992) and 'Higher Education and Confidence in Institutions. A Secondary Analysis of the "European Values Survey" ', in *West European Politics* 15/2 (April 1992).

Emmerich Tálos is Professor of Political Science at the University of Vienna. His research interests are social policy and welfare state, corporatism and fascism. Book publications among others: *Staatliche Sozialpolitik in Österreich* (Vienna 1981); *Materielle Grundsicherung. Popper-Lynkeus' Programm 'Die allgemeine Nährpflicht als Lösung der sozialen Frage'* (ed.) (Vienna 1989); *Der geforderte Wohlfahrtsstaat* ed. (Vienna 1992); *Sozialpartnerschaft. Kontinuität und Wandel eines Modells* (ed.) (Vienna 1993).

Gerda Falkner is Lecturer at the Institut für Staats- und Politikwissenschaft, University of Vienna. Recent publications concern the Maastricht Social Policy Protocol (Die Sozialpolitik im Maastrichter Vertragsgebäude der Europäischen Gemeinschaft, in *SWS-Rundschau* 1/1993), the EC's democratic deficit (Das Demokratiedefizit der EG und die Beschlüsse von Maastricht 1992, in *Österreichische Zeitschrift* *für Politikwissenschaft* Nr. 3/1992; together with Michael Nentwich) and social security aspects of European Integration (Soziale Sicherung und Europäische Integration, in Emmerich Tálos (ed.), *Der geforderte Wohlfahrtsstaat*, Löcker Verlag, Vienna 1992).

Giandomenico Majone is Professor of Public Policy at the European University Institute in Florence. He has also taught at the universities of Rome, Yale and Harvard. Among his recent publications are: *Evidence, Argument and Persuasion in the Policy Process* (Yale University Press, 1989), and *Deregulation or Re-Regulation?* (London: Francis Pinter, 1990). He is currently working on issues of international regulation.

Edgar Grande is a research fellow at the Max-Planck-Institut für Gesellschaftsforschung in Cologne, Germany. His research focuses on comparative public policies in advanced industrial democracies, especially within the fields of research, technology, and telecommunications. His publications include *Vom Monopol zum Wettbewerb? Die neokonservative Reform der Telekommunikation in Grossbritannien und der Bundesrepublik Deutschland* (Wiesbaden, 1989).

Michael Moran is Professor of Government at the University of Manchester, UK. He is the author of *The Politics of Banking* (1986), *The Politics of the Financial Services Revolution* (1991) and co-author with Bruce Wood of *States, Regulation and the Medical Profession* (1993).

Jeremy Richardson is Professor of European Integration and Director of the European Public Policy Institute, University of Warwick. He is the author of several works on the British policy process, including *Governing under Pressure* (1979), with A. G. Jordan and *British Politics and the Policy Process* (1987) also with A. G. Jordan. He edited *Policy Styles in Western Europe* (1982), *Lobbying in the European Community* (1993) with Sonia Mazey, and *Pressure Groups* (1993). He is currently engaged in research on the EU-policy process and is co-editor of *The Journal of European Public Policy*.

To place a subscription order for this journal, please fill in and return to us the order form below (photocopying it if preferred)

SUBSCRIPTION ORDER FORM

Please enter my subscription to
WEST EUROPEAN POLITICS
Volume 17 1994
Quarterly: January, April, July, October

UK/OVERSEAS	£38 (individuals)	£125 (institutions)
USA	$60 (individuals)	$195 (institutions)

I enclose a cheque for £/US$ ___________
(US orders should be made payable to ISBS)

Please charge my
- ❑ VISA
- ❑ MASTERCARD/ACCESS
- ❑ AMERICAN EXPRESS

Card Number ______________________________

Expiry date ________ Signature ____________________

Name ______________________________________

Address ____________________________________

____

UK/OVERSEAS ORDERS to: *Frank Cass, Newbury House, 890-900 Eastern Avenue, Newbury Park, Ilford, Essex IG2 7HH, UK. Tel: 081 599 8866 Fax: 081 599 0984*
US ORDERS to: *Frank Cass, c/o ISBS, 5804 N E Hassalo Street, Portland, OR 97213-3644, USA. Tel: (503) 287-3093, (800) 944-6190 Fax: (503) 280-8832*